# Franco-British defence co-operation

# Franco-British defence co-operation

## A new entente cordiale?

edited by
YVES BOYER,
PIERRE LELLOUCHE, AND
JOHN ROPER

ROUTLEDGE
for
THE ROYAL INSTITUTE OF
INTERNATIONAL AFFAIRS
London
and
L'INSTITUT FRANÇAIS DES
RELATIONS INTERNATIONALES
Paris

First published 1989
by Routledge
11 New Fetter Lane, London EC4P 4EE
29 West 35th Street, New York, NY 10001



Printed in Great Britain by
Billing & Sons Ltd, Worcester



*British Library Cataloguing in Publication Data*

Franco-British defence co-operation : a new
entente cordiale?
1. Defence. Co-operation between Great
Britain and France.
I. Boyer, Yves II. Lellouche, Pierre
III. Roper, John IV. Royal
Institute of International Affairs
V. Institut français des relations
internationales
355

ISBN 0-415-03112-5

*Library of Congress Cataloging-in-Publication Data*

Franco-British defence co-operation : a new entente cordale? / edited
by Yves Boyer, Pierre Lellouche, and John Roper. — English language
ed.
p. cm.
Includes index.
ISBN 0-415-03112-5
1. France–Military relations–Great Britain. 2. Great Britain–
Military relations–France. I. Boyer, Yves. II. Lellouche,
Pierre. III. Roper, John. IV. Royal Institute of
International Affairs. V. Institut français des relations
internationales.
UA700.F744 1988
355'.03304–dc19 88-26447
CIP

# Contents

Tables and Figures vii
Contributors ix
Preface xi

**Part One — Nuclear policies and possibilities for co-operation**

1 **Nuclear policies: different approaches to similar objectives**
John Roper 3

2 **Franco-British nuclear co-operation: the legacy of history finally overcome?**
Yves Boyer 17

3 **The difficulties of nuclear co-operation**
Peter Nailor 28

4 **The future of British and French nuclear policies**
Lawrence Freedman 34

**Part Two — Co-operation on conventional forces and armaments production**

5 **Co-operation between conventional forces in Europe: a British view**
Hugh Beach 47

6 **Co-operation between conventional forces in Europe: a French view**
François Valentin 58

7 **The prospects for military co-operation outside Europe: a French view**
Marcel Duval 67

8 **The prospects for military co-operation outside Europe: a British view**
Jonathan Alford 84

9 **Defence costs and budgeting in France**
Jacques Fontanel 95

10 **Defence costs and budgeting in Great Britain**
Ron Smith 116

11 **Co-operation in arms procurement: a British view**
Farooq Hussain 128

12 **Co-operation in arms procurement: a French view**
Pierre Menanteau 140

**Part Three — Towards a new entente cordiale?**

13 **A new step in Franco-British co-operation**
Ian Davidson 149

14 **The prospects for Franco-British co-operation**
Jean Chabaud 155

15 **European security: bilateral steps to multilateral co-operation**
William Wallace 171

16 **Conclusion**
Yves Boyer and John Roper 181

Index 189

# Tables and Figures

## Tables

5.1 UK collaboration in armaments procurement 56

9.1 France's defence expenditure (including pensions) in thousand million francs 105

9.2 Estimates of France's military expenditure (including pensions) in millions of constant dollars (1980 value) 106

9.3 Comparisons between French and British military expenditure in 1982 in millions of francs 106

9.4 France's initial military budgets compared with GDP and the state budget 107

9.5 France's military budgets since 1958 in 1970 constant francs ('000 million) 108

9.6 Capital expenditure devoted to nuclear forces in millions of current francs 109

9.7 Expenditure on the various forces as a percentage of total military expenditure 110

9.8 Capital expenditure by major category in thousand million constant francs (1981 value) 111

9.9 Military expenditure by cost categories in thousand million constant francs 111

12.1 Defence spending in Britain and France 141

## Figures

10.1 Defence expenditure as a percentage of market price GDP, UK and France 1949–84 120

10.2 Defence expenditure in cost and real terms, 1983/4 prices, 1974/5 to 1987/8 122

10.3 Functional division of the budget 123

# Contributors

The late **Colonel Jonathan Alford** was Deputy Director of the International Institute for Strategic Studies in London from 1978 until his death in 1986. Before this he served in the British Army in Germany, the Pacific, and the UK.

**Sir Hugh Beach** is a retired general of the British army, and in his last job was responsible for the procurement of all army equipment. He is now the Director of the Council for Arms Control and a member of the Council for Christian Approaches to Defence and Disarmament.

**Yves Boyer** is a Maître de Recherches at the Institut Français des Relations Internationales, where he specializes in defence questions. He also serves as Professor at the Ecole Spéciale Militaire de St Cyr.

**Jean Chabaud** retired in 1987 from the Secrétariat Général de Défense Nationale with the rank of Vice Admiral. He is now a member of the board of the Ecole Nationale d'Administration.

**Ian Davidson** has been a journalist for *The Financial Times* since 1960, in the field of international affairs, with special interest in European integration and east–west relations. During the 1960s he was posted to Paris and Brussels; he then became foreign editor, and, after writing a weekly column on foreign affairs from 1979 to 1987, he has returned to Paris.

**Marcel Duval** has been editor of the journal *Défense Nationale* following a long career in the French navy, from which he retired with the rank of Admiral.

**Jacques Fontanel** is Director of the Faculté des Sciences Economiques at the University of Grenoble and Deputy Director of the Centre d'Etude de Défense et Sécurité Internationale (CEDSI) there.

**Lawrence Freedman** is Professor of War Studies at King's College London, in the University of London. He was formerly Head of Policy Studies at the Royal Institute of International Affairs. His most recent book is *The Price of Peace: Living with the Nuclear Dilemma*.

**Farooq Hussain** is a freelance defence consultant. A former Research Associate of the International Institute for Strategic Studies and Fellow of the Centre for International Security and Arms Control, Stanford University, he has been a member of the scientific staff of SHAPE (Supreme Headquarters, Allied Powers, Europe) (1980–4), and Director of Studies at the Royal United Services Institute (1984–6).

**Pierre Menanteau** is now the Adviser to Thomson-CSF after a career in the French air force, which he left in 1984 with the rank of Brigadier-General. He is Deputy Commander of the Air Force Academies.

**Peter Nailor** is Professor of History at the Royal Naval College, Greenwich. He served in the Admiralty and the Ministry of Defence before becoming Professor of Politics at Lancaster University in 1969. He is chairman of the Research Committee of the Royal Institute of International Affairs.

**John Roper** is the Director of the International Security Programme at the Royal Institute of International Affairs, and is also editor of the journal *International Affairs*. Previously he was a lecturer at Manchester University and a Member of Parliament.

**Ron Smith** is Professor of Applied Economics at Birkbeck College, the University of London. He has published extensively on defence topics, and has recently completed a collaborative Economic and Social Research Council–Centre National de Recherche Scientifique project on the defence efforts in France and the UK conducted jointly with the University of Grenoble.

**François Valentin** retired from the French army in 1974, where he commanded the First Army, with the rank of General. He had previously served in AFCENT and has been the military adviser to Aerospatiale.

**William Wallace** is Deputy Director and Director of Studies at the Royal Institute of International Affairs. He previously taught at Cornell and Manchester Universities. He has written extensively on British foreign policy, on French and German foreign policy, and on West European co-operation in foreign policy and defence.

# Preface

If relations between two countries can be described as special, it would certainly be appropriate so to describe the relations between France and Great Britain. In fact, London and Paris continue to feign a cordial lack of interest in each other and, if anything, to cultivate their disagreements. However, they have never been foreigners to one another, and since the beginning of this century their traditional rivalry has been fundamentally modified by the mutual sacrifice of the trenches of the First World War and the difficult, but none the less valued, co-operation during the Second World War.

This common effort, this alliance between two countries at the worst moments of their history, seems not to have left much trace. The two countries remain at worst strangers, at best amused by each other. Between them nothing comparable exists to that which has brought Frenchmen and Germans together over the past twenty-five years. The old tradition of rivalry continues to haunt them. The English commemorate the battle of Blenheim, the French that of Fontenoy.

The study and definition of the prospects now opening up in Franco-British co-operation in the field of security cannot be undertaken without considering these psychological phenomena, which continue to disrupt relations between the two countries. The first task of this book was therefore to carry out some psychotherapy in bringing together, under the auspices of the Institut Français des Relations Internationales (IFRI) and the Royal Institute of International Affairs (RIIA), British and French authors to consider the contemporary problems of defence. Everybody expected that this would lead to the revelation of profound differences. This book has shown that in fact the reverse is the case. Even if the ways in which problems were approached did not always coincide, the solutions proposed were often similar. As a result, in future it will be more speedily recognized that in fact Paris and London think along very similar lines on both the nature and the development of contemporary strategy.

The second task of this work was to open up paths for the future.

How can Paris and London translate these common patterns of thought into a process of political and military rapprochement that will lead not only to increased mutual co-operation but also to increased co-operation with their European partners? In this respect, each of the authors in this book has made his own contribution in suggesting ways and means of augmenting Franco-British co-operation.

Both Institutes are grateful to the Ford Foundation, without whose assistance it would not have been possible to have carried out this work. They are also grateful to many others on both sides of the Channel who have played essential roles in bringing it to fruition.

*October 1988* *Y.B.*
*J.R.*
*P.L.*

Part one

# Nuclear policies and possibilities for co-operation

Chapter one

# Nuclear policies: different approaches to similar objectives

John Roper

In examining the development of British nuclear policies over the post-war period and comparing them with those of France, it is important at the outset to note two factors which have affected the expression of policies in Britain. The first is that, as British nuclear forces have been seen since their first deployment as part of NATO forces, British nuclear policy has always had two aspects: the nuclear strategy of the Alliance and the rationale for British national possession of nuclear weapons. These two aspects have had different relative importance at different times, but their twin existence has on occasion provided a certain ambivalence in British declaratory policy.

The second is that while successive governments in France, and indeed successive oppositions, have had no hestitation in their support for French national nuclear forces, the same has not been true in the United Kingdom. Although the Labour Party in government in 1947–51, 1964–70, and 1974–9 both initiated and continued the development of strategic nuclear programmes, those governments hesitated to publicise their activities, in large measure because of concern over the internal party strife that public discussion of such issues would provoke — the only partial exception to this reticence being Denis Healey in the late 1960s. Labour in opposition, and in particular in the period 1960–64 and from 1980, has at best been sceptical about British nuclear policy and has opposed the successive decisions to procure the Skybolt stand-off weapon in 1962, the Polaris missile in 1962, and the Trident missile in 1980. This lack of consensus on national nuclear weapons policy has extended to attitudes to nuclear weapons within NATO. In the period 1961–4, Labour in opposition was much closer to the views on nuclear strategy being put forward by the Kennedy administration than were the incumbent Conservative governments of Harold Macmillan and Sir Alec Douglas-Home. After James Callaghan gave up the leadership of the Labour Party in 1980, the party moved to a very critical attitude to the decision by NATO to deploy cruise and Pershing II missiles in Europe and since 1983 it has questioned the maintenance of any nuclear weapons,

British or American, in Great Britain. Scepticism over an independent British nuclear deterrent has not been confined to the Labour Party. Both in the 1960s and in the 1980s, when the decision to acquire new generations of nuclear weapons has arisen, a wide range of political and defence opinion has asked whether this is the best use of Britain's limited resources. It has been argued that Britain could make a better contribution to the collective defence of the west by strengthening her conventional resources rather than by replicating forces already provided for NATO by the United States.

There have therefore been some inhibitions in Britain in developing official declaratory policy on nuclear weapons, on the one hand because of possible contradictions between NATO nuclear strategy and national forces, and second, certainly during periods of Labour government, because of fears of stimulating internal party strife.

In examining the development of British nuclear policy, the framework set out by Raymond Aron in 1963 to analyse the case for the French nuclear force seems equally relevant.

> l'analyse en termes exclusifs de sécurité fausserait les données exactes de la délibération. Il y faut joindre au moins trois autres dimensions: *l'influence sur l'allié* ou *l'autonomie à l'intérieur de l'alliance*, le *prestige sur la scène mondiale* et enfin l'action exercée par le programme choisi sur le *développement de l'économie* et, en particulier, le *progrès de la science*.[1]

These various factors recur in discussions of British nuclear weapons from the very first post-war discussions to the present day, although their relative importance has varied in the debate over the years. That debate must also be seen against the background of Britain's changing position from a world power in 1945 to a European power.

I intend to look first at the origins of British nuclear weapons policy, and then at the critical debates in the 1960s when the relationship with the United States developed under successive governments, as they to a large measure established current British nuclear policy. The similarities in British and French policies can perhaps be best seen in the earliest period, the differences in the second.

## The origins of British nuclear weapons policy, 1945–60

The historical development of British nuclear weapons has been very well described by Margaret Gowing in her official history.[2] The decision by the post-war Labour government to go ahead with the production of nuclear weapons was made by restricted Cabinet committees with the most cursory of reports to the House of Commons, the only reference in Hansard being in a 'planted' question in May 1948.[3] As Gowing points out, this was the only information given to the public in four years that Britain was on her way to becoming a nuclear military power[4] and it was only divulged for the strange reason that the press members of the 'D' notice committee would not permit a D-notice restricting further press comment on British development of nuclear weapons to be issued unless the existence of such a programme had been reported to Parliament. There was no parliamentary debate in the whole of this period and no reference to the expenditure in the estimates.[5] There is no doubt that the US Congress and particularly its Joint Committee on Atomic Energy were much better informed than the British Parliament on the development of British nuclear policy.

The British Chiefs of Staff had made clear within months of the Hiroshima explosion that 'the best means of defence against the new weapons was the deterrent effect that the possession of the means of retaliation would have on a potential aggressor'.[6] Churchill in opposition in a debate on foreign policy in November 1945 had said, 'This I take it is already agreed, we should make atomic bombs'.[7] This evoked no ministerial response. In fact the decision was not made by a small group of ministers until January 1947 and by then it was clear that Britain would have to carry out the research and development on her own as the American commitment to post-war nuclear co-operation set out in the Quebec Agreement and Hyde Park aide-memoire died with Roosevelt. That was to have its effect on British attitudes for a considerable period; as Andrew Pierre has put it, 'The great sense of betrayal which grew after the breakdown of nuclear co-operation fostered a distrust of the United States which strongly influenced British politicians and civil servants during the quest for an independent deterrent'.[8] It is perhaps only fair to say that the US failure to continue co-operation in nuclear matters with Britain was only matched by Britain's failure to continue the pattern of co-operation with France, which has been very fully discussed by Goldschmidt.[9]

As Margaret Gowing makes clear,

> The British decision to make an atomic bomb had 'emerged' from a body of general assumptions. It had not been a response to an immediate military threat but rather something fundamentalist and almost instinctive — a feeling that Britain must possess so climacteric a weapon in order to deter an atomically armed enemy, a feeling that Britain as a great power must acquire all major new weapons, a feeling that atomic weapons were a manifestation of the scientific and technological superiority on which Britain's strength, so deficient if measured in sheer numbers of men, must depend.

> The decision was also a symbol of independence. . . there was at this time — in 1946 and 1947 — no United States military commitments to come to Britain's help in war. If Britain wanted to be sure of being covered by an atomic deterrent, she had no option but to make it herself.[10]

This assessment of Britain's reasons for the 1947 decisions is particularly interesting because many of them precisely parallel the arguments subsequently deployed for French nuclear weapons.

Nearly three years after the British decision to build their own weapons, negotiations in Washington suggested that a *modus vivendi* might be established between Britain and the United States whereby nuclear co-operation could be re-established with weapons being produced for Britain in the United States. This was after Anglo-American defence co-operation had been restored with the basing of Strategic Air Command bombers in East Anglia and the North Atlantic Treaty agreed. Ernest Bevin as foreign secretary was however very sceptical about such a dependence on the United States for nuclear weapons and, as Gowing reports, was

> especially unhappy at the idea of any agreement which would place British capacity for atomic energy production entirely in the hands of the Americans. If war should break out, it might be a matter of life and death for the British to use atomic weapons, but their supply might be denied by American delays or disapproval of British policy. Moreover Western [European] Union defence was based very largely on the supposition that when the time came Britain should have all the latest weapons (including atomic bombs) at her disposal.[11]

This was one of a number of reasons why agreement was not reached, but it is the first reference I have discovered to Britain holding nuclear weapons as part of her contribution to the defence of Western Europe.

Britain continued her own development independently and early in 1952, after the change of government, Churchill was able to report to the House of Commons that Britain had developed her own nuclear weapons. In the debate that followed on 5 March 1952, Attlee as Leader of the Opposition made one of his very few statements on the rationale for the development of nuclear weapons: 'I do not believe it is right that this country should be utterly dependent on the United States of America, that is one very good reason for going ahead with our own work on the atomic bomb.'[12]

In 1952 the military basis for British nuclear defence policy was developed and set down in the Chiefs of Staff *Global Strategy Paper* of that year. This challenged the need for the level of conventional forces — 96 divisions — that NATO had put forward at Lisbon in February 1952 and provided a strategic argument similar to that put forward the following year in Eisenhower's 'New Look' defence policy whereby nuclear weapons were advocated as a means of achieving economies in defence budgets. The deterrent effect of the threat of massive nuclear retaliation meant that initially Churchill could cut the defence budgets he had inherited from Labour, and the same argument carried to its logical conclusion would enable Sandys in the 1957 Defence White Paper to announce the end of conscription. At the same time, in a world in which nuclear weapons were seen as playing an increasingly important role, the case for independence was also stressed by the Chiefs of Staff.

> We feel that to have no share in what is recognised as the main deterrent in the cold war and the only Allied offensive weapon in a world war would seriously weaken British influence on United States policy and planning in the cold war and in war would mean that the United Kingdom would have no claim to any share in the policy or planning of the offensive.[13]

The argument regarding influence on the United States was linked to concerns that American targeting plans would not include the Soviet air bases from which attacks on the United Kingdom would be launched. The Swinton Committee reported to the Cabinet in 1954:

> These bases will doubtless figure among the targets to be attacked by the American Strategic Air Force. But we cannot be sure what priority the Americans will accord them in relation to other targets on their list of bombing objectives. . . Since the very survival of Britain would depend upon the promptness and thoroughness of the counterattack against these Russian airbases, it is essential that we should ourselves possess and control a bomber force capable of performing this vital task.[14]

At this stage British nuclear weapons were required for a counter-force role as American aircraft might be giving priority to counter-value targets — urban and industrial areas.

The views of the Chiefs of Staff on the centrality of nuclear weapons were confirmed by the testing of America's first thermonuclear weapons in February 1954. Foreign Secretary Eden noted in his memoirs: 'One consequence of the evolution from the atomic to the hydrogen bomb was to diminish the advantage of physically larger countries. All became equally vulnerable'.[15] This was an argument that became very familiar in the French debate. The argument of great power vulnerability was also seen by the Chiefs of Staff as a restriction on the value of alliances, another argument to be subsequently heard in the French debate. In a report of a sub-committee of July 1954 we read,

> Retaliation does not provide a global defence, it can only defend those places that are completely integrated politically. When New York is vulnerable to attack the United States will not use her nuclear weapons in defence of London. The United Kingdom must, therefore, have its own retaliatory defence. Similarly, however, we will not be prepared to sacrifice the United Kingdom in the defence of Darwin [Australia], and eventually each political unit must have its own means of retaliation.[16]

Extended deterrence seems to have been challenged in 1954 in an unambiguous way.

These documents were of course not public at the time but their argument could be found in the speeches and writings of Sir John Slessor (Chief of the Air Staff, 1950–52) and in successive Defence White Papers, of which that of 1957 is best known.[17] Apart from announcing the end of conscription and considerable cuts in forces outside Europe, there were proposals for reductions of the British army in Germany from 77,000 to 64,000 (to be followed by a reduction to 55,000 in 1958/9) and a halving of the size of the RAF in Germany. These were to be compensated by the deployment of nuclear artillery to BAOR and atomic weapons to RAF Germany. This was an implementation of the changes presaged in the Chiefs of Staff document of 1952.

Nuclear weapons were not only seen in their military role. Macmillan indicated in a prime ministerial television broadcast in February 1952 that there was also a political rationale:

> The independent contribution . . . gives us a better position in the world, it gives us a better position with respect to the United States. It puts us where we ought to be, in the position of a Great Power. The fact we have it makes the United States pay a greater regard to our point of view, and that is of great importance.[18]

Although, as we shall see, the cancellation of the British Blue Streak missile in 1960 and the agreement to buy the Skybolt stand-off weapon from the United States meant that independence became tinged with interdependence, General Gallois could write an article in June 1962 entitled 'Deux budgets militaires, une politique de sécurité'.[19] This quotes approvingly from the 1962 Defence White Paper and argues that 'plus que jamais, la sécurité des Iles britanniques etait fondée sur une arme nucléaire de dissuasion nationale'. He goes on to contrast the British doctrine, which he considers still to be based on 'représailles massives', with the new American strategy for Europe of flexible response. Gallois finds, on what some might consider to be a somewhat selective reading of the British White Paper, all the concepts that were subsequently to play a central part in French strategic thinking, 'sanctuaire nationale, repli sur le territoire nationale, effectivs réduits, forces limitées, integrité nationale protégée, risque totale',[20] and is able to conclude that 'Ainsi, dans les faits, le gouvernement de Londres pratique la seule politique de défense qui ait aujourd'hui quelque signification'.[21] Perhaps this article marks a high point of Franco-British convergence in nuclear thinking.

## The 1960s — decade of divergence?

Even before General Gallois had written his article, the seeds of the divergence that was to mark British and French nuclear policy had been sown. As has been said, the British plan to develop their own ballistic missile launcher (based in part on the US Atlas missile) had been deemed unsuccessful and cancelled in the spring of 1960. President Eisenhower then offered Macmillan the possibility of buying the as yet undeveloped American Skybolt missile. This was to be the turning point for the Labour Party, which had until then maintained bipartisan support for Britain's nuclear policy. The fact that Britain could not develop launchers for her own nuclear weapons indicated to them that effective nuclear weapons were outside the scope of a country of Britain's size. They were therefore receptive to the arguments introduced in 1961 by the incoming Kennedy administration, which was very sceptical of 3rd and 4th nuclear powers. Within four months of his inauguration Kennedy had received a review[22] from Dean Acheson on North Atlantic problems for the future and had adopted a 'Policy Directive Regarding NATO and the Atlantic Nations'[23] which provided the basis for the 'flexible response' approach. The policy directive included a very clear indication that the United States did not want to encourage national nuclear forces in Europe and stated specifically,

> Over the long run, it would be desirable if the British decided to phase out of the nuclear deterrent business. If the development of Skybolt is not warranted for U.S. purposes alone, the U.S. should not prolong the life of the V-bomber by this or other means.
>
> The U.S. should not assist the French to attain a nuclear weapons capability, but should seek to respond to the French interest in nuclear matters in the other ways indicated above.

The ways suggested had been the commitment of five Polaris submarines to NATO, with the deployment and targeting to be worked out by the NATO commands and the US.

This initial attitude of the Kennedy administration was made known to the Allies in McNamara's Athens speech to the North Atlantic Council in May 1962 and became public in a declassified version in his Ann Arbor speech a month later. His views on European nuclear forces were clear — they were described as being 'dangerous, expensive, prone to obsolescence and lacking in credibility'. Such rhetoric was immediately taken up by the Labour opposition in Britain and caused fury to Conservative ministers. Macmillan described it in his memoirs as 'an ill-disguised attack upon the determination both of Britain and of France to maintain their separate independent nuclear forces'.[24] The minister of defence, Harold Watkinson, complained and McNamara issued a 'clarifying statement' in which he stressed that his remarks referred to nuclear forces 'operating independently', thus excluding British forces. There was a good deal of scepticism in the British government about the general thrust of the new strategic doctrine and in early December, in a speech to the WEU Assembly in Paris, the new British minister of defence, Peter Thorneycroft, spoke of Europe as a potential world power which must be equipped with commensurate military capability.[25] It is suggested that during this period Thorneycroft and Amery, then minister of aviation, had constructive discussions in Paris on the development of an 'entente nucléaire'.

This situation was transformed by the announcement of the cancellation of the American Skybolt project and Macmillan's meeting with Kennedy at Nassau leading to the Polaris Sales Agreement. In the light of the strong opposition to national nuclear forces that had been indicated, it is in many ways surprising that Macmillan persuaded Kennedy to provide Britain with submarine-launched missiles. The apparent concession to the American position was that, in the words of the Nassau agreement, 'it created an opportunity for the development of new and closer arrangements for the organisation and control of strategic Western defence and that such arrangements in turn could make a major contribution to political cohesion among the nations of the Alliance'.[26] Britain was to get the missiles but they were to be part of a NATO multilateral force (MLF) except where 'supreme national interests are at stake'. The agreement was a compromise, possibly a contradiction; Henry Kissinger described it as an attempt 'to reconcile integration with independence, the American belief in the need for an indivisible nuclear strategy with the British desire for autonomy'.[27]

Macmillan's achievement at Nassau was not universally welcomed in Britain. Labour renewed their opposition to the maintenance of British nuclear weapons and some Conservatives were worried that the independence of British nuclear forces had been prejudiced. The government continued to make clear that there was a case for the independent British deterrent within the defence of the Western Alliance. The 1964 Defence White Paper, the last before the Conservatives lost office, made explicit the contribution of British nuclear forces to the defence of the west.

> Even a small number of Polaris submarines would possess immense destructive capacity. To suggest that the independent deterrent might be abandoned in the interests of non-dissemination overlooks the fact that if there were no power in Europe capable of inflicting unacceptable damage on a potential enemy he might be tempted — if not now then perhaps at some time in the future — to attack in the mistaken belief that the United States would not act unless America herself were attacked. The V-bombers by themselves are, and the Polaris submarines will be, capable of inflicting greater damage than any potential aggressor would consider acceptable. For this reason the British nuclear forces make a unique contribution to the main deterrent.[28]

This statement of the case for British nuclear weapons is now over twenty years old, but it has remained the primary case deployed by governments. It suggests that there could be doubts about 'extended deterrence' in the future that would justify British nuclear weapons but as a loyal ally that doubt is attributed to the potential enemy. This 'second centre of decision' case, as it has become known, squares the circle of maintaining confidence in the American nuclear guarantee while keeping British weapons as an insurance policy. While this formulation of the case for a national nuclear force does not explicitly challenge the reliability of the United States, the idea of a second centre of decision-making was of course totally opposed to the Kennedy administration's view that there should be a unified central control of all nuclear weapons within the Alliance. The Americans were very concerned about the prospect of national nuclear forces triggering more general nuclear war.

Another strand in this statement, which is very close to an element of French nuclear policy, is that of 'proportionate deterrence' or deterrence 'du faible à fort'. It is made clear that British nuclear forces would deter because although small they could inflict unacceptable damage on any potential aggressor. The third interesting aspect of this statement is the reference to Europe. It may be drawing too much from the formulation to argue that it implies that British nuclear weapons provide a 'sanctuaire élargie' for Europe but it is noteworthy that the case is made on a European rather than a purely British basis.

The next paragraph of the 1964 Defence White Paper asserts the independence of the British Polaris force:

> The Polaris submarines will be built in British yards and, although the delivery system is American, the nuclear warheads will be British and free from all control by any other power. At Nassau the Government of the U.S.A. agreed to make Polaris missiles available 'on a continuing basis'.[29]

This assertion of both strategic and technical independence for British nuclear forces was later blurred by the positions of the Labour government (there was virtually no substantive discussion of British nuclear policy in any of the annual defence White Papers between 1964 and 1970) but it remains a statement of continuing British nuclear policy which in practice has not been significantly varied by subsequent British governments.

The Conservative government after Nassau was committed to some form of multilateral nuclear force and to 'increasing the effectiveness of their conventional forces'.[30] It continued however to be very unhappy about the full implications of the American proposals for flexible response'. Having abolished conscription and significantly reduced British forces in Germany between 1957 and 1962, it could not look with enthusiasm at proposals to make major increases in conventional forces. Although it was France that withdrew in November 1963 from the work of the Military Committee that was intended to develop a force structure that would permit a move away from a 'trip-wire' strategy towards 'flexible response', the American officials concerned believed at the end of 1963 that,

> French, UK and German views on strategy are closer together than to the US view. Each has a common strong 'trip-wire' flavor, depreciates the value of non-nuclear forces, the value of air superiority and the importance of the contingency of limited conflicts affecting NATO. There is a good chance that an explicit UK, French and German consensus on strategy, very different from our own view, will emerge in the coming months.[31]

The December 1963 NATO ministerial meeting therefore decided to continue the force planning work on the basis of a range of strategic views within the Alliance, thus obviating the need for confrontation of the divisive strategic issues.

By the time that the issues were next considered within NATO, there had been a change of government in Britain. One can only speculate on whether a Conservative government in Britain in 1965 and 1966 would have continued to resist the adoption of the new strategy, and the implications that this might have had for French attitudes. In opposition, Healey and Gordon Walker, the Labour defence and foreign ministers, had keenly supported a more restrictive role for nuclear weapons and thus the American approach.[32] In his first Defence White Paper in February 1965 Healey argued that 'at present all NATO forces in Germany, including our own, are deployed in accordance with a strategic concept which in our view now requires revision'.[33] Healey therefore willed the ends of the American objective of reducing the reliance on nuclear weapons. He was not, however, prepared to will the means if that meant greater defence budgets or the reintroduction of conscription. This was revealed by the statement in the 1967 Defence White Paper that 'Ever since October 1964, the British Government has argued inside N.A.T.O. that allied strategy must be designed to fit the forces which the national governments are prepared to make available. It has been apparent for many years that none of the N.A.T.O. governments is willing to pay for the forces which SACEUR would need to carry out his mission as hitherto defined.'[34] The agreement on NATO's new strategy, MC 14/3, which had been the major reason for France leaving the integrated military, was therefore rather more symbolic than substantial.

The other area in which the British Labour government played a major role was in the development of the Nuclear Planning Group (NPG). On taking office in 1964, the Labour government had rapidly decided, in spite of its electoral rhetoric, to proceed with the development of the Polaris programme although, rather surprisingly, Harold Wilson after two months as Prime Minister still assured the House of Commons that 'the fact is that there is no independent deterrent because we are dependent on the Americans for the fissile materials for the warheads'.[35] The original plan was 'to internationalise our nuclear strategic forces' by transferring them to an Alliance Nuclear Force (ANF) for 'as long as the Alliance lasts'. It was not immediately clear whether there was any significant difference between this formulation and the Nassau agreement, but Wilson and Healey had to be able to persuade their own party that they had fulfilled their election pledge to renounce the independence of British nuclear weapons if not the weapons themselves.

The ANF was no more negotiable than the earlier American proposals for an MLF but Healey believed that there was a need for more effective nuclear consultation in the Alliance and that this was particularly important in view of the prohibition on Germany becoming a nuclear power. He therefore worked with McNamara on the establishment of the NPG in 1967 and, once it had been established, with successive German defence ministers (Schröder and Schmidt) on the development of 'Provisional political guidelines for the initial defensive tactical use of nuclear weapons' in Europe. These were adopted by the NATO Council in December 1969,[36] and, as with the earlier Athens guidelines of 1962, applied to British theatre nuclear weapons as well as to American ones.

It is not clear what was the precise value of the rather general formulas that were adopted. Some would argue that they merely rolled on the ambiguities and compromises inherent in the decision on flexible response. They did give Europeans a sense of participation in the consideration of Alliance nuclear policy and did expose the Americans to European concerns and sensitivities, and it has therefore been argued that the process of mutual education was of greater value than any particular outcome.[37] It was however a process which in the absence of France appeared to widen the gap between France and Britain on nuclear policy. The guidelines have not been made public. According to one analyst, the proposal was that

> Nuclear weapons would be used 'as late as possible, but as early as necessary'. In short, NATO was not committed to the automatic use of nuclear weapons; at the same time, nuclear weapons would not necessarily be used only after conventional forces were on the verge of collapse.[38]

If this is an accurate summary, there are certainly some parallels with the argument put forward at the same time by General Fourquet for the use of tactical nuclear weapons.[39]

It is easy to criticize the NPG and its inadequacies — the nuclear weapons states continue to make the decisions on nuclear weapons — but there is some evidence that over its nearly twenty years it has facilitated nuclear consultation within the Alliance and reduced the opportunities for intra-alliance friction on nuclear matters.

## Conclusions

It may seem at first sight surprising that a discussion of the development of British nuclear policy should stop at the end of 1960s. In fact, there has been a remarkable continuity in policy since then, both in the national nuclear policy as put forward in 1964 by the Conservative government and in NATO's nuclear policy as developed with active British participation in the later 1960s. There have of course been subsequent developments in the implementation of both policies — in the case of the national nuclear forces, by the development of Chevaline by successive Conservative and Labour governments in the 1970s to ensure the credibility of the Polaris missile against Soviet ballistic missile defences, the decision by the Labour government to build a national tritium plant in 1976 to guarantee a continuity of supply of nuclear materials in the light of possible changes in US policy,[40] and the decision to buy the C-4 Trident missile from the United States in July 1980 and the decision to switch to the D-5 in March 1982. None of these have however reflected any change in the underlying policy. In the same way within NATO, the decision on the deployment of Intermediate Nuclear Forces (INF) in 1979 and the Montebello decision in 1984 to reduce the number of battlefield nuclear weapons do not represent a change in the policy of flexible response which was hammered out in the late 1960s.

The most significant challenge to both British and NATO policy came in President Reagan's Strategic Defence Initiative of 23 March 1983. The debate on the effects of this on British nuclear policy will continue but the issues have been very clearly set out by Sir Geoffrey Howe, the current British foreign secretary.[41]

## Notes

1. Raymond Aron, *Le grand débat* (Paris: Calmann-Levy, 1963), p. 119.
2. Margaret Gowing, *Independence and Deterrence, Britain and Atomic Energy 1945–1952* (2 vols) (London: Macmillan, 1974).
3. Vol. 450, *House of Commons Debates* [HC Deb], col. 2117 (12 May 1948).
4. Gowing, *Independence and Deterrence*, Vol. 1, pp. 212–13 and passim.
5. Andrew J. Pierre, *Nuclear Politics: the British experience with an independent strategic force 1939–1970* (London: Oxford University Press, 1972), p. 84 reports that Nigel Birch told the House of Commons in 1962 that the expenditure on nuclear weapons development had been concealed in the Civil Contingencies Fund under the sub-head, 'Public Buildings in Great Britain'.
6. Gowing, op. cit., Vol. 1, p. 164.
7. Vol. 415, HC Deb, col. 1300 (7 November 1945).
8. Pierre, op. cit., p. 120.
9. Bertrand Goldschmidt, *Les Rivalités atomiques 1939–1966* (Paris: Fayard, 1967).
10. Gowing, op. cit., Vol. 1, p. 184–5.
11. Gowing, op. cit., Vol. 1, p. 297.
12. Vol. 497, HC Deb, col. 537 (5 March 1952).
13. Quoted in Gowing, op. cit., Vol. 1, p. 441.
14. CAB 129/71, C(54) 329: *Defence policy: report of the Swinton Committee*. I am grateful to N.J. Wheeler for this reference and for ref. 15. A fuller discussion of these issues appears in his article 'British nuclear weapons and Anglo-American relations 1945–54' *International Affairs*, Winter, 1985–6.
15. Anthony Eden, *Full Circle* (London: Cassell, 1960), p. 368.
16. Defe 8/47, COS Air Defence Sub-Committee, Air Defence Working Party, 2 (54)16, 14 July 1954.
17. Cmnd 124, *Defence: Outline of Future Policy*, 1957.

18. Pierre, op. cit., p. 178.
19. Pierre-Marie Gallois, 'Deux budgets militaires, une politique de sécurité', *Revue de défense nationale*, June 1962, pp. 937–53.
20. Lothar Ruehl, *La Politique militaire de la cinquième république* (Paris: Presses de la fondation nationale des sciences politiques, 1976), p. 170 discusses the Gallois article as one of the sources of French strategic thinking.
21. Gallois, op. cit., p. 948.
22. *A Review of North Atlantic Problems for the Future*, March 1961, National Security File, Box 220, NATO Acheson report, 3/61 John F. Kennedy Library. (I am grateful to Jane Stromseth for this reference and for references 23 and 31; a fuller discussion of these issues will be found in her book *The Origins of Flexible Responses: A study of the debate over NATO strategy in the 1960s* (London: Macmillan, 1988.)
23. *National Security Memorandum No. 40*, to members of the National Security Council from McGeorge Bundy, 24 April 1961 with attachment, Vice Presidential Security File, Box 4, NSC-1961, Lyndon B. Johnson Library.
24. Harold Macmillan, *At the End of the Day* (London: Macmillan, 1973), p. 341.
25. Pierre, op. cit., p. 224.
26. *Statement on Nuclear Defence Systems — 21 December 1962*, The Nassau Agreement, para. 5.
27. Henry Kissinger, *The Troubled Partnership* (New York: McGraw-Hill, 1965), p. 83.,
28. Cmnd 2270, *Statement on Defence: 1964*, para. 7.
29. Cmnd 2270, para. 8.
30. Nassau Agreement, para. 10.
31. *NATO Force Planning*, p. 1, National Security File, International Meetings and Travel File, Box 30–34 NATO Defense Policy Conference, 12/2/63, Lyndon B. Johnson Library.
32. Denis Healey, *The Race against the H-bomb* (London: Fabian Society, 1960).
33. Cmnd 2592, *Statement on Defence Estimates 1965*, para. 18.
34. Cmnd 3203, *Statement on Defence Estimates 1967*, para. 7.
35. Vol. 704, HC Deb, col. 702 (17 December 1964).
36. Paul Buteux, *The Politics of Nuclear Consultation in NATO 1965–1980* (Cambridge: Cambridge University Press, 1983), pp. 90–105.
37. Stromseth, *The Origins of Flexible Response*, op. cit., Chapter 8, passim.
38. Stromseth, op. cit., Chapter 8.
39. General Fourquet, 'French strategic concepts', *Survival*, July 1961.
40. John Simpson, *The Independent Nuclear State: The United States, Britain and the military atom* (London: Macmillan, 1983), p. 196.
41. Geoffrey Howe, 'Defence and security in the nuclear age', *RUSI Journal*, June 1985.

Chapter two

# Franco-British nuclear co-operation: the legacy of history finally overcome?

Yves Boyer

Several years ago, in 1984, a Gallup poll showed that only 13 per cent of British people considered the French to be reliable allies. For their part, fewer than 30 per cent of French people considered that Great Britain was still an important nation.[1] These figures sum up the state of co-operative Franco-British defence relations: almost non-existent and hindered by mental reservations inherited from a tumultuous common history.

At a time when the Atlantic Alliance is showing signs of weakening and when the political situation in Central Europe is showing signs of change, suspicion, doubt, and even incomprehension are becoming luxuries that neither London nor Paris can much longer allow themselves in their relationship. Fortunately, there are many signs that Franco-British defence co-operation is no longer a utopian ideal. The European orientation of Whitehall diplomacy, which Sir Nicholas Henderson's 1979 final ambassadorial despatch from Paris recommended, is being confirmed. On the French side, military co-operation with London appears to be a very desirable option for Paris, as noted for the first time in an explicit way through the Preamble to the law setting out the 1987–91 military programme.

A new alliance between the two capitals presupposes that the numerous mental reservations that have too often cast a shadow over defence co-operation have been erased. Each of the two countries has its own particular position within the Atlantic Alliance. Both are already pursuing similar objectives with different strategies.

London's role in the integrated military structure of the Atlantic Alliance goes hand in hand with its particular position arising out of the place of nuclear weapons in British strategy. Whitehall can thus play a major role within NATO while at the same time having the means for a national nuclear strategy concealed behind particularly carefully worded declaratory policy.

By contrast, the military policy of France's Fifth Republic is formulated in a highly visible manner. It is characterized by a framework of strategic thinking that incorporates within the same concept the principle of autonomy of decision-making as regards the use of nuclear weapons and the affirmation of very firm solidarity with the Allies. It is not surprising then that, following the British example, the role of the French forces is to combine a strategy of deterrence based on a nuclear arsenal and a strategy of action to organize the French contribution to the defence of Western Europe.

France's particular role outside the military structure of NATO therefore parallels the British role played within NATO. For London, this particular role explains as much as it justifies the central place Washington occupies in the determination of British military policy. This exclusive place occupied by the United States continues to weigh very heavily on Whitehall's European options. Up to now it has given the British considerable additional value on the strategic chessboard, just as it has indicated the limits set on British co-operation with France.

## The poor start for Franco-British nuclear co-operation

Nuclear military co-operation between France and the United Kingdom got off to a poor start and this has not yet been put right. The first phase of this attempted co-operation was marked by an imbalance between the two partners, Britain's capabilities and resources then greatly exceeding those of France. It was 1962 before Great Britain recognized France as a nuclear power. But then was it not already too late to consider co-operation?

In May 1946 Frédéric Joliot-Curie, one of the two people responsible for the newly created French Atomic Energy Commission, visited Great Britain to discuss officially the problems of patents connected with the inventions of French atomic scientists who had contributed to the allied effort between 1940 and 1945. These discussions were in actual fact used to sound out the British position on the possible development of nuclear co-operation between the two countries. The British Atomic Energy Commission gave a negative answer. In the background was the American partner with whom London had concluded a series of agreements which did not allow the contracting parties to communicate information relating to nuclear matters to third parties without mutual consent.

For Paris, any planned co-operation with London became futile for a long time after September 1947 when France's request for a sample of graphite to be tested at the Harwell nuclear power plant was turned down. In 1954, a new attempt at co-operation between the French and British Atomic Energy Commissions concerning the construction in France of an experimental gaseous diffusion nuclear power plant was to be quickly doomed to failure. Once again the privileged relationship between the United States and Great Britain was at the root of the British refusal.[2]

The build-up of the French nuclear effort and the gradual construction of French nuclear weapons were to open up a second period in attempts at co-operation on military nuclear matters between London and Paris.

In 1962, two members of the Macmillan Cabinet, Peter Thorneycroft, the defence minister, and Julian Amery, the aviation minister, indicated during private and official visits to France that they were in favour of a 'nuclear understanding' between the two countries. However, Thorneycroft and Amery were in a minority position within the British Cabinet. When, shortly before the Nassau conference between the President of the United States and the British Prime Minister, General de Gaulle suggested to Macmillan the possibility of nuclear co-operation between the two countries, his suggestion was not taken up by the British. The indirect repercussion of this episode was France's refusal in January 1963 to allow Great Britain to join the Common Market.

One of the underlying reasons for this failure was the extremely important role Great Britain allowed the United States to play in her defence policy. The special relationship between London and Washington acquired a military dimension with the Second World War. There was no guarantee that this relationship would last and nuclear weapons were rapidly to become for the British both the essential tool for maintaining major power status for their country and the means of sealing a unique and original alliance with Washington. As Alastair Buchan reminded us, one of the reasons why the Attlee government started the atom bomb project was to strengthen the British position in Washington rather than in Moscow.[3]

According to Ernest Bevin, the decision to produce an atomic bomb had been taken because London could not accept the American monopoly intended by the MacMahon Law approved by the US Congress in 1946. This British national effort showed London's independence from the United States in a crucial area. It also backed up a diplomatic effort to re-create the level of intimacy that had existed during the Second World War between London and Washington.

This effort was beginning to produce results: in January 1948, a *modus vivendi* had been outlined between the two capitals in the area of nuclear co-operation. Whitehall abandoned its right of veto — the outcome of the Quebec agreement of 1943 — on the use of atomic weapons by the United States in exchange for which the latter would agree to exemptions for the sharing with London of secrets relating to civil nuclear technology.

Several months after the agreement on the *modus vivendi*, in the middle of the Berlin crisis, American B-29 strategic bombers arrived in Great

Britain. The arrangements for their use for nuclear bombing missions and the requirements for the agreement of the British authorities were not clear. This problem was settled when Churchill visited the United States in 1952. It was decided that the use of American nuclear weapons from British soil would be the subject of a joint decision. This secret agreement is still in force. It would now apply to the use for nuclear missions of the American F-111s currently based at Upper Heyford and Lakenheath, as well as to the cruise missiles based at Greenham Common until they are removed.

There was thus some rapprochement between the British and the Americans on strategic choices. Indeed, at the very moment in 1952 when Churchill was deciding to go ahead with the testing of a nuclear warhead, he was asking the Defence Ministry to consider the strategic implications of a British deterrent. The Chiefs of Staff were required to give their opinion. Their conclusions are contained in the *Global Strategy Paper*,[4] which emphasizes the crucial, revolutionary role of atomic weapons. Nuclear weapons involved such changes in the conduct of operations that the structure of the armed forces had to be rethought so as to maximize the deterrent effect of British nuclear weapons. This new approach to military problems was first implemented a few years later with the reduction in the manpower of the British army made by Duncan Sandys, as minister of defence.[5] Before that, however, the conclusions of the *Global Strategy Paper* were to contribute towards the shaping of the defence policy of the new Eisenhower administration during the 'New Look' period. The reflections of the Chiefs of Staff were in fact passed on to the American Joint Chiefs of Staff Committee, where they had a considerable impact and left their mark on the Joint Chiefs of Staff's analyses of the role and function of nuclear weapons in American strategy.

This strategic convergence between the United States and Great Britain led to the resumption of close co-operation on atomic weapons. In 1954, Great Britain drew the first dividends from this co-operation — she was given preferential treatment when the MacMahon law was amended as part of the 'Atoms for Peace' programme. In 1955, the RAF's Bomber Command and the US Air Force's Strategic Air Command opened discussions concerning nuclear strike plans.

After the Bermuda agreement of March 1957 on the deployment of Thor rockets in Great Britain, Eisenhower announced his support for the lifting of 'artificial barriers to the sharing of knowledge between close allies'.[6] This opening up by the Americans was given concrete form in the US/UK agreements of 3 July 1958, which still govern relations between the two countries as far as nuclear weapons are concerned.

A skilful policy thus helped the British to regain the level of intimacy with the Americans they had lost in 1945. The Nassau Conference in

1962 was the ultimate result of this policy, whose outcome owed nothing to any form of European co-operation.

The influential role that London derives from its nuclear co-operation with Washington goes beyond the strict limits of the special ties between the two capitals since it also affects Great Britain's role and place in Europe. John Nott emphasized in 1981, when he was defence secretary, that he would have 'more than a feeling of *discomfort* if France, with its policy of non-engagement in Alliance strategy, were the only nuclear power in Western Europe'.[7]

Current nuclear co-operation between Great Britain and the United States involves, with Trident D-5, an extremely sophisticated weapons system whose capabilities go beyond British requirements. The financial cost of Trident, even if it is not exorbitant, disrupts a fragile budgetary balance constructed in such a way as to maintain military capability across the missions assigned to the British armed forces. Is there a European, i.e. basically French, alternative that would enable Great Britain to remain in the nuclear club more cheaply?

As far as strategic weapons are concerned, recent decisions in Great Britain do not seem to indicate that such an approach is now possible in the short term. This is what emerges from all the official analyses justifying the purchase of the Trident D-5, which show it to be more attractive than any equivalent French system (the M-4 or M-5 missile). The American path is indeed preferred for a whole range of reasons. Apart from helping to maintain the special relationship between London and Washington, it gives the British the means of keeping until 2020–30 a strategic system that enables them to face up to any Soviet anti-ballistic missile developments.[8]

Recent British experience in this area with the Chevaline programme, involving multiple re-entry vehicles and decoys, has proved excessively complex (particularly as regards miniaturization) and expensive. The costs of the Chevaline project, estimated at £175 million in 1972, had become £1,000 million by 1980. Finding a successor to it on a purely national basis seems financially prohibitive for Britain, with her defence budget showing no increase in real terms. By choosing the Trident D-5, the British have easy access, thanks to their privileged co-operation with the United States, to the advances made in systems to penetrate enemy defences.

With a French strategic missile, the question of the definition and adaptation of the British nuclear warheads would have arisen. Moreover, the British had no guarantee that the French would be capable of quickly obtaining penetration capabilities similar to those the Americans already have.

In spite of the repeated failures at strategic nuclear co-operation between Paris and London, the idea of such a rapprochement is revived from time to time by a number of French and British politicians. In March 1970, the Bow Group, a Conservative discussion group, published a defence paper in which it expressed its support for a 'nuclear understanding' between the two countries: 'It is essential to look for ways of bringing the British and French strategic nuclear forces closer together.'

On the French side, in January 1980 Michel Poniatowski, who was a minister during Giscard d'Estaing's presidency, suggested the pooling of the strategic forces of the two countries to act on behalf of Europe. Also in 1980, on the occasion of the annual meeting of the Franco-British Council, Mrs Thatcher called for the development 'of closer and fuller defence co-operation' with France. For his part, the British ambassador to France at the time, Sir Reginald Hibbert, pinned a lot of hope on co-operation between the two countries while recognizing that it was a matter of 'slow, difficult, gradual' change over several decades.

In the mid-1980s, prospects for Franco-British nuclear co-operation remained what they had always been: very limited, although Paris and London are still confronted with identical problems of renewing or improving the quality of their strategic forces. In the long term the option of co-operation still exists, but each of the two countries has made choices that commit them far beyond the first few years of the next millennium.

However, not all the areas for co-operation on nuclear systems are closed to Franco-British collaboration. The renewal of the RAF's tactical nuclear component could have been the opportunity for rapprochement between Paris and London. In the spring of 1987 there were persistent rumours in both capitals that the RAF might equip its Tornados with the existing French medium-range air-to-ground missiles. Such a transaction now seems doubtful. If it were to materialize, it would have considerable repercussions and would be of symbolic value.

If there is to be rapprochement between the two countries for the purpose of strengthening European defence, the question of the role of their nuclear forces will be posed. As General Lacaze, the former Chief of Staff of the French forces, emphasized, the nuclear weapons which London and Paris have 'pose a fundamental problem to the construction of European defence'.[9] The respective positions of the two countries are relatively close as far as the role and the missions they give to their strategic forces are concerned.

The rationale for the British nuclear effort is extremely close to that adopted by the French. The fundamental idea is that of a 'second centre' of decision-making. It is essential for there to be in Western Europe itself a power capable of taking the place of the United States for the employment of nuclear weapons. In other words, the decision to use nuclear weapons in the event of a Soviet attack in Europe must not depend exclusively on Washington. This is what Francis Pym, then defence secretary, reaffirmed in the Commons in January 1980 when he said 'the decision to use nuclear weapons . . . would be taken by a power separate and independent from the United States, by a power whose survival in freedom would be far more directly and clearly threatened by a war in Europe than the United States would'.

Similarly, in the area of arms control, an objective interest brings Paris and London closer together and could lead them to harmonize their position as they did after the Reykjavik summit between the Americans and the Russians. Finally, in the face of the challenge posed by President Reagan's Strategic Defense Initiative, both countries share similar interests which can only encourage them to find a way to co-operation in the strategic area.

## Preserving the nuclear deterrent

The questioning of nuclear deterrence through the SDI has in fact very quickly become a major preoccupation for the French and British leaders. In Paris they were very quick to seize on the dangers of a destabilization of the strategic situation that would result from the introduction of anti-missile defences. Since March 1983 the French leaders have continually repeated their attachment to nuclear deterrence. It is the foundation of the French strategy that nuclear weapons enable the weak to deter the strong, the cardinal principle of which is the equalizing power of the atom summarized as follows by General de Gaulle: 'Beyond a certain nuclear capability and as far as each country's direct defence is concerned, the proportion of the respective resources no longer has any absolute value.'[10] Paris has also emphasized the benefit Europe draws from the stability made possible by the atomic bomb. In the spring of 1984 Defence Minister Charles Hernu stated that 'an anti-missile systems race would make the situation in Europe even more unstable, in so far as it would increase the value of having conventional superiority'.[11]

Thanks to the national consensus on nuclear defence in France, Paris's attachment to nuclear deterrence did not cease with the change of majority following the parliamentary elections of March 1986. The defence minister in the Chirac government stated a few weeks after taking up his post: 'anti-missile defence cannot replace nuclear deterrence. It could only be a means of complementing and strengthening it.'[12] During the 'cohabitation' period between 1986 and 1987, President Mitterrand and Prime Minister Chirac, despite the fact that they belong to different political parties, used a similar argument to reject the incorporation of the French forces in an overall anti-missile defence system under the control of the United States. Jacques Chirac, for example, made it clear that France 'will not incorporate in advance its resources in a system over which it could not, when the time comes, exercise its sovereign decision'.[13]

These are statements that the British leaders, for their part, could not repudiate. For them, as for the French, returning to a pre-nuclear age would amount to allowing the Soviet Union the possibility of pursuing a strategy that would no longer have to face the awesome problem of nuclear weapons. One of the points in the communiqué released in December 1984 following the Camp David meeting between Mrs Thatcher and President Reagan runs along these lines since both leaders recognize that the aim of the SDI research programme 'is to enhance, not undercut deterrence'. Of course, President Reagan does not perhaps have the same conception of deterrence as Mrs Thatcher, but for the British there is no doubt that deterrence means nuclear deterrence. Moreover, a few months later, during a speech to the Royal United Services Institute for Defence Studies, Sir Geoffrey Howe recalled the attachment of the British authorities to the maintenance of mutual vulnerability resulting from nuclear deterrence: 'this Government, in exactly the same way as its predecessors, is not committed to destruction. It is committed to preserving peace, by ensuring that potential aggressors are deterred from threatening it. We are confident that this will continue to be effective, so long as would-be aggressors are faced with the credible prospect of unacceptable damage in return.' In March 1987, Sir Geoffrey also emphasized the absolute necessity of not 'denuclearizing' Europe. With this in mind, he called for increasing partnership in the nuclear field between Paris and London.

The French and British positions are therefore both characterized by great scepticism towards the Strategic Defense Initiative, which is primarily part of an internal American debate, the strategic justification for which is inconsistent and the technical concept of which remains extremely uncertain. From now on, it will be as if American declaratory nuclear policy has changed because the instruments on which the strategy depends have also changed. One of the most eminent French strategists, General L. Poirier, who was largely responsible for the creation of France's strategic doctrine, has best described this factor as follows: 'now we have military strategies based on make-believe . . . it is as though a dominant player could achieve certain current political ends, while being spared the effort of providing proof of his power with real forces.'[14]

This will hasten the development of French and British attitudes in opposition to SDI. Paris and London will react along the same lines but in different ways. In Paris a detailed analysis of the American stance will lead to its being shown to be incomplete as regards strategic reasoning, whether it is a question of the function of the project in the Soviet–American strategic equation or the nature of the objective to be achieved. On the British side, the response to the new American declaratory policy has taken other forms, which can be explained by the special nature of relations between Whitehall and the White House. First of all the British apparently wanted to make sure that they had a minimum reassurance

— a reminder of their attachment to nuclear deterrence — before committing themselves to participation in research as part of the SDI programme. This is the four-point agreement concluded in December 1984 at Camp David between the leaders of the two countries. Also, after the difficult period over the deployment of the Euromissiles, so as not to arouse the reactions of a public opinion particularly divided on defence matters, they avoided (unlike the situation in France) discussion of the strategic rationality of the American project. Moreover the British political–military establishment was for its part not really ready to launch into the battle because it remained sceptical towards, or even opposed to, SDI. This hostility was of course marked within the Labour Party, whose National Executive Committee condemned the SDI in a resolution in July 1985, just as the Liberal–SDP Alliance did. But even within the Conservative Party there were dissenting voices with regard to the SDI project, which former prime minister Mr Edward Heath described as 'decoupling, destabilising and a diversion of resources'.[15]

It is clear then that, regarding contemporary strategic issues, the positions of London and Paris are close on many essential points. Unfortunately the burden of history and structural inflexibility have up to now prevented close nuclear co-operation. This inflexibility also affects co-operation to the same degree on conventional weapons.

The underlying trends of French and British defence policies have so far been only marginally affected by European co-operation. Nevertheless, one should not minimize the possible impact in the very long term of the growing political and economic forces in London and Paris in favour of a rapprochement between European partners in security matters, particularly between the French and the British. The game they are playing is, however, far from being won. As Ian Davidson stressed in the *Financial Times* of 8 October 1984, 'the British, who have already on numerous occasions in the past mismanaged their strategic relationships with Europe, seem once again determined to remain on the fringe and are navigating between a sort of third-rate Gaullism and a traditional rigidity orientated towards NATO'.

This was a harsh diagnosis. That is why the European orientation of these British political forces with regard to security issues must get all the support it deserves from Britain's continental partners. In this respect France can play a leading role, although up to now co-operation between Paris and London has been practically non-existent.

'The age-old rivalry is not dead and buried', one reads in the *Financial Times* of 22 October 1984. 'The most serious psychological problem the British have when they deal with the French stems from the fact that, while they have never sought to be the leaders of the new Europe nor considered what they could do with this leadership if it fell into their hands, they take offence and oppose the fact that if this leadership belongs naturally to any State, it belongs to France.'[16]

For forty years, depending on the circumstances of the time, suspicion or appeasement has prevailed between the two countries. On the British side, there is suspicion about the relation between the strategic doctrine endorsed by Paris and that of NATO, or about France's assertions of her independence while firmly supporting NATO, which in the eyes of some British people creates a situation in which the French remain 'a bloody nuisance'.[17] On the French side, one could mention the difficulties in understanding how a state can have an independent nuclear force but appear to leave decisions about its use to an integrated military command. One should also mention the fact that certain British actions are perceived as being motivated more by Washington's attitude than by what happens in Europe. In his time, did not Edward Heath denounce 'the instinctive tendency of some British officials to wonder first of all what Washington will think and how it will act'?[18]

It is in the light of this special psychological climate that any joint effort to develop security co-operation between Paris and London must go through a stage where differences are clarified and acknowledged.

French willingness to have a security dialogue does not mean — at least in the foreseeable future — the abandonment of the concept of deterrence as it is publicly presented by Paris and which differs at least in terms of presentation from that adopted by London. Conversely, France should not expect the British to relinquish their attachment to NATO.

As far as conventional forces are concerned, it is certain that the French point of view differs in certain aspects from that of NATO. This is particularly true as regards the use of conventional forces, the prolonged engagement of which is repudiated by Paris. The role of the French field forces is to to check any advance at France's borders or to provide the Alliance with a support echelon. Though the operational use of the French 1st Army may therefore seem to be different from the role allotted by NATO to the conventional forces, it is not certain either that the BAOR's role is identical in all possible situations with what the Commander in Chief Central Euorpe (CINCENT) wishes.

In spite of all these differences, common security approaches to defence questions are still possible between the French and the British, for example on out-of-area action and also, and this is worth recalling, in Central Europe. Indeed, Paris, concerned about defence problems in Europe, particularly in the Federal Republic of Germany, is working on additional possibilities for the engagement of French forces thanks to new instruments such as the Force d'Action Rapide and the Hades tactical nuclear missiles. These new options may signal the beginnings of military co-operation between Europeans, particularly between Paris and London.

London must still first improve its definition of the role it intends to play in Europe and there must be better communication between the French and the British in order to avoid the perpetuation of misunderstandings on the long-term objectives that each sets the other in possible defence co-operation.

## Notes

1. *L'Express*, 21 January 1984.
2. Bertrand Goldschmidt, *Les Rivalités atomiques, 1939–1966* (Paris: Fayard, 1967).
3. Alastair Buchan, 'Britain and the bomb', *The Reporter*, 19 March 1959.
4. On this period, see John Baylis, *Anglo-American Defence Relations, 1939–1984*, 2nd edition (London: Macmillan, 1984); Andrew Pierre, *Nuclear Politics: the British Experience with an independent strategic force — 1939–1970* (London: Oxford University Press, 1972).
5. Cmnd 124, *Defence: Outline of Future Policy*, 1957.
6. State of the Union Speech, January 1958.
7. John Nott, quoted by Lawrence Freedman, *Britain and Nuclear Weapons* (London: Macmillan, for the RIIA, 1980).
8. John Roper, 'The British nuclear deterrent and new developments in ballistic missile defence', *The World Today*, May 1985.
9. General Lacaze, 'Concept de défense et sécurité en Europe', *Défense Nationale*, July 1984.
10. Press conference, 23 July 1964.
11. Charles Hernu in the French Senate on 27 April 1984.
12. Statement by the French defence minister during a visit to the ONERA on 17 June 1986.
13. General policy declaration by the French prime minister in the Assemblée Nationale on 9 April 1986.
14. Lucien Poirier, *Les Voix de la stratégie* (Paris: Fayard, 1985), p. 488.
15. Quotation taken from Trevor Taylor, 'Britain's response to the Strategic Defense Initiative', *International Affairs*, 62, (2), Spring 1986.
16. 'France at the fulcrum', *Financial Times* 22 October 1984.
17. Air Chief Marshall Sir Alastair Steedman, 'NATO's future: a view', in RUSI and Brassey's *Defence Yearbook 1983*.
18. Edward Heath, quoted in *Le Monde*, 20 May 1971.

Chapter three

# The difficulties of nuclear co-operation

Peter Nailor

This is not only a British view, but a personal view, which reflects nothing of what might be implied by my Chatham House and Ministry of Defence connections. Neither of these institutions can be held responsible in any way for my opinions.

## I

The military fact that France and the United Kingdom both possess national nuclear weapon capabilities periodically attracts a special type of political or academic interest; and the possibility that there might be advantage in some form of co-operation between the two states is mooted. The phenomenon is sufficiently well established for a pattern to have become discernible. A proposition is floated, usually in very general terms and often in a very tentative way. Sometimes there is a flurry of public interest, sometimes the response is muted; perhaps the files are dusted off and consulted. Always, nothing happens.

But the phenomenon recurs. It seems that the advantage that may be gained is a sufficiently persistent thought to prevail intellectually, even when it seems that it cannot be harvested practically. But 'advantage' and 'co-operation' are very general terms, and it may be necessary to look at them a little more closely in order to see what it is that these recurring suggestions are meant to signify.

If we take *co-operation* first, it could refer to quite a wide range of possibilities. It could, for example, mean very close co-operation — the sharing of ideas, resources, and facilities, to joint benefit, in a co-ordinated and positively managed or directed fashion. Or it could merely mean a looser and more episodic exchange of information. These different levels of intensity might apply in the scientific, industrial, or military areas of activity, which are all involved in nuclear force activities; and all of these possibilities have been scouted on the occasions since the late 1950s when Anglo-French nuclear relationships have been raised as an issue for public discussion. Co-operation might in theory range from a fairly straightforward intellectual dialogue, through the optimum mutual disposition of operational assets, to collaborative research or development or production.[1] But, in fact, the *advantages* that might accrue would be of an equally wide range of possibilities.

However, they break down into two broad groupings. The economic advantage, of saving money or some other scarce resource by pooling national efforts, clearly has an attraction. The history of those international collaborative efforts that have lasted long enough to bear some sort of harvest offers us a range of lessons: one particularly relevant one might be that, while the amounts of money saved by substituting collaborative effort for a purely national programme are not always as great as might be hoped, collaboration often enables a state to procure something jointly which it cannot easily afford — financially, industrially — on its own.

The political advantage of successful co-operation may be less precise than any economic benefit, but it may none the less be highly prized; especially if it occurs in an area of policy to which the state itself has already attributed significance. National nuclear forces are clearly such an area, both in France and in Great Britain, and if one can for the moment put on one side the difference that, in the matter of delivery systems, the French style has been resolutely national and the British resolutely co-operative with the United States since 1960, there is clearly an interesting question to be explored: what the political advantage to be gained from Franco-British co-operation — of whatever sort — would be likely to be.

## II

The separate ways in which the French and British nuclear forces have been planned and brought into service reflect, in a very distinctive way, differences between the two states' security perspectives that are now of more than thirty years' standing. While there is, fundamentally, a good deal of agreement about the major factors which comprise the European security framework, there have been substantial differences between France and Great Britain about emphasis and interpretation. The upshot is that the nuclear forces, as conceived, provided with resources, and equipped, embody these differences in a way no other single manifestation of the state's security purpose can represent. Their intrinsic power is only a part of their significance, and we cannot ignore the political truth that they have represented, for both states if in rather different ways, a determination to retain a distinctive attribute of sovereign power.

If then, this power is now to be qualified in some way that brings 'advantage', we must take into account the symbolic inferences about what change would imply, even though we might be able to point to some economic or operational benefit. What would co-operation mean in that sense? It is clear that, for the British, it would mean something about the American connection. It would mean something too for the French conception of independent development. These considerations, of course, derive from past experience, past politics, and past expectations about the functions that national deterrent forces can serve. These all exert very powerful constraints upon the present; they tell us not only about the shape of present policy, but about the way in which present policy is viewed. These same constraints may even define the limit of what future possibilities might be and, in that sense, will be inhibitions that will persist — unless the external environment, the international system within which European security and the security predicaments of the two states themselves are set, itself undergoes major change. If that were to be the case — that major change is forcing re-evaluation — then continuity loses some of its preservative effect; and the risk that is associated with change, and must be calculated carefully as an element in expected advantage, assumes a different proportion. It would be true, then, that major change would sweep up more — perhaps much more — than the nuclear forces; but the nuclear forces would then not be isolated as a symbol of change.

So long as they are isolated, any matter of saving money or scientists' time — welcome though that might be for other reasons — is hardly a sufficient political cause for change, though it may be an advantage that governments desire to obtain. Both the French and the British, in the ways in which their policies have developed, have found themselves on economic procrustean beds, to be stretched or lopped, and it presents them with practical budgetary problems. But the two states are in separate houses of faith; and in the current pantheon of deterrence doctrine there are not many alternative mansions in which they could easily cohabit. Co-operation, if it is to have serious political content, means some change of current doctrine, in at least two respects. First of all there is the question whether 'extended deterrence' is an acceptable assumption in relation to dependence upon a superpower. Second, there is the question whether a combination of small national forces can themselves create 'extended deterrence' for their regional partners. The particular difficulty at the nuclear level is that so much credit has been pledged, in maintaining the current faiths, that the prize to be won by conversion — or recantation — has to be very clear, and distinctly beneficial.

## III

From that perspective, one has to ask if the recurrent suggestions about co-operation are themselves symbolic: enquiries about whether one or either party senses the time has come for change, and that the perspective in which they should be viewed is one of future opportunity rather than of current budgetary or technical pressure. So, for example, both Pompidou in 1969 and Heath slightly later were possibly sketching out their first ideas of what a novel Europe might eventually want to comprehend, and a number of the later suggestions up to the present are of a similar, rather tentative, nature. Here one has to say that we confront a familiar theoretical difficulty; if there is to be a system transformation of some sort, is defence a manageable issue with which to begin the change, or is it the sort of issue that is set in place at the end: is it a foundation, or a keystone, to a new edifice? And even in this case, should nuclear forces be regarded as the highest form of defence activity, or an integral part of the political arrangements that describe and define how power is exercised? How would the new management replace or transform the power of the single state? It all sounds rather removed from practical policy-making; but it has significant practical force.

To be entirely speculative, one may wonder whether, at some time and in some circumstance, the attributed significance, as well as the real military power, of nuclear weapons will change. For the last forty years, they have had great importance and embody, as well as symbolize, high values at both the political and military level. However, it is true that, in historical terms, they are still novel; and the world of states, and even a world separated in a significant way by alliances, is still learning about them. It is not inconceivable that the current interpretation of their significance and utility may change: the Strategic Defense Initiative, or an advance in arms limitation — or a breakdown of the non-proliferaiton regime — could make a re-evaluation of current orthodoxies necessary, though whether apprehension will go up, or diminish, is still very uncertain. It seems quite likely that France and the United Kingdom might, in those circumstances, share some common viewpoints, both about what a desirable outcome might be for them, or about what a manageable alternative could be. It is true, of course, that if we try to extrapolate from current policies how these new perspectives would emerge, one outcome is that the reactions of the two states could diverge, rather than converge; so that even in this novel security environment, co-operation would not be a foregone or easy outcome.

If we take a pessimistic view of future developments, there are extreme alternatives. At one extreme, a new security environment might cut away the requirement for national deterrents. This might, in the end, be a more hopeful prospect for the world, in so far as we might have the threat of nuclear weapons removed in some way. It might well require heavier burdens of conventional defence and, in some ways, a less secure balance between east and west, at the military level; but if it did, it seems much more likely that co-operation, for future benefit and advantage, would occur at this conventional level than over how to play the nuclear card.

At the alternative end of the pessimistic spectrum, imagine a world more intensely insecure. Is this an environment for co-operation? It might be, if the insecurity was pervasive and corrosive of existing connections and frameworks. If it led to panic, to the sense of the impending doom that began to colour European attitudes in 1938 for example, some of the existing technical models for future co-operation would be inappropriately long term. But they might nevertheless help to continue to deter the eventuality of war.

What all of this implies is that Franco-British co-operation at the nuclear level attracts so much in the way of historical clutter that it cannot be dealt with simply as an exercise in defence economics. It is, of course, the case that exercises in the collaborative defence procurement of conventional equipment are not simple cases of economic planning either; but the hopes and fancies that accompany them are not as central to the security purposes of the state, nor are they so closely linked to the psychological level of deterrent credibility, as those that sustain nuclear weapon deployments. From this perspective, Franco-British nuclear co-operation would be open to the construction that current national postures and policies were no longer adequate; and that co-operation was an enabling device, *faute de mieux*, to find a level of activity between the two states which, by the standards of all that has gone before, exemplifies compromise. To bring advantage out of compromise is not an unknown political skill; but it requires considerable gifts of persuasion, and some determination.

## IV

There remains one other consideration, which ought to be touched upon. To the extent that this phenomenon — the recurrence of these suggestions for some sort of advantageous co-operation — is persistent, it is clearly a resilient idea even though, because nothing happens, it remains a conceptual ornament. What does it say about relationships between France and Great Britain? It says, it can be argued, that there is a persistent, resilient, and largely instinctive feeling that the two states ought to be more closely aligned, in security matters, than recent history has led them to be. The tentative feelings express themselves in a way that describes what ought perhaps to be, rather than what is. If this is in any way true, it bears some witness to the essential nature of the relationship between the two states: they are linked as only neighbours and allies can be, they do have many common experiences and many common problems. But . . . the one word, by itself, also expresses a great deal about Franco-British relationships.

There is an interpretation to be put upon these recurrent wisps of thought about nuclear co-operation that may sound cynical, or dismissive;

but in truth is really rather sympathetic. We talk about these things to each other when we cannot think what else to say: not so much in the expectation that anything will immediately happen, but to remind ourselves that — at this symbolically difficult level of affairs as well as in many other ways — one day we really must start to try and see how we can make a better fist of the future. Now if you think that foreign offices and ministries of defence would have little to do with such romantic gobbledegook, and that, even if they would, the nuclear puzzle would be the worst place to start, you would, of course, have logic on your side. But politics is not only concerned with logic; and perhaps an instinct to go to the heart of the problem is not a bad way of reminding ourselves how big the problem is.

## Note

1. There is an interesting and up-to-date discussion of these issues in an article by Stephen Pullinger, '*The resurrection of the Euro-bomb*', in *ADIU report*, 8 (6), November 1986 (University of Sussex).

Chapter four

# The future of British and French nuclear policies

Lawrence Freedman

## I

In the 1950s and early 1960s there was controversy as to whether nuclear weapons offered a means by which powers now slipping into the second class could regain their great power status, or whether this effort was doomed to failure in that small nuclear forces could never meet the exacting standards being set by the superpowers.

In the event it has proved possible for Britain and France to stay in the nuclear business, but the investment has not provided them with the political muscle that they might have anticipated. There may be occasions in the future when these forces may become critical should it become necessary to put together a new framework for European security without the backing of the United States.

The concern in this paper is with the capacity of the British and French to continue to maintain credible nuclear deterrents, with regard in particular to technical and diplomatic factors. In a way the experience of the last twenty years has contradicted Robert McNamara's claim that small nuclear forces were 'prone to obsolescence'. Can this be assumed to be the case in the future?

## II

In 1962, when Robert McNamara made his claim, it seemed to have had some point. The British government had achieved an impressive capability with regard to nuclear warheads but its experience with delivery systems had been less satisfactory. Three different aircraft types had been ordered to deliver the first British nuclear bombs, but as they were coming into service it was recognized that the age of the missile was going to pose enormous problems. A national attempt to develop ballistic missiles was abandoned and Britain looked to the United States for assistance. This came first with the air-launched Skybolt; when McNamara cancelled this in late 1962 he appeared to be confirming his own warnings on the fate of small nuclear forces. In the ensuing crisis Britain secured Polaris submarine-launched missiles (SLBMs). This has served better than anyone envisaged at the time in permitting Britain to stay in the nuclear business. The system has remained credible as a second-strike force, and will be in service now until the mid 1990s — almost thirty years. It was built and has been maintained at a modest cost. The real cost was political rather than financial because it meant that Britain was now dependent on the United States for the missiles necessary if she was to maintain a credible nuclear capability.

France avoided this dependence by building her own systems, though she has on occasion still drawn on US technology. In addition France did not decide to concentrate on the most secure system — SLBMs — but opted to build a triad of bombers, land-based, and sea-based systems. In the late 1970s she even toyed with building her own cruise missiles. Over time, however, France has come like Britain to concentrate on SLBMs. France's independence has been expensive — a regular 20 per cent of the defence budget. Britain's expenditure has been a few per cent of a comparable budget. Yet France's independence has gained a domestic consensus behind the national nuclear force that has not been obtained in Britain.

## III

There are two consequences of the differential dependence. The first concerns the possibilities for future co-operation between the two countries. Britain has now put the most Atlanticist construction possible on her nuclear rationale, which jars somewhat with a Gaullist rationale (however much that might be supported in private) and would make the break quite dramatic if suddenly replaced with a European rationale. The British forces reflect in all ways the close co-operation with the United States — which involves targeting and supply of spare parts as well as the purchase of the actual missiles. Furthermore, the terms of the agreements on which the co-operation with the US is based — the 1958 one covering technology transfer and the 1963 one on Polaris sales — make it extremely difficult for Britain to share information with a third party (i.e. France) and give it any role other than a NATO role.

The second, and more immediately relevant consequence, is that Britain's nuclear capability is vulnerable to domestic politics in a way that is simply not the case with France. This peculiar British matter is compounded by the fact that the Polaris fleet is suffering group obsolescence and therefore the decision to replace it is a once and for all decision, at a substantial cost and at a time of pressure on defence expenditure. Although Polaris is already to be kept going beyond its originally allotted life-span, there is no longer any other cost-effective alternative available to the Trident missile. At the time the decision was taken (initially July 1980 and amended in March 1982 to move from the C-4 to the D-5 version) there may have been alternatives. As we now move into the period of high expenditure on Trident a combination of past investment and contractual obligations would make any alternative excessively expensive. In 1987 these were not high enough to preclude abandonment of Trident. The current government has no intention of abandoning Trident and there is no reason to expect that this view will change, even though the defence budget is coming under increasing pressure.

It is now even possible that Trident would survive a future government in which the Conservative Party was not part. Although it will not yet be in service by the time of the next general election, few resources could be saved through its cancellation. The rest of this discussion assumes that the Trident programme will go ahead.

## IV

If this is the case then there are two important questions to be faced. The first concerns the viability of small nuclear forces based on SLBMs in the face of technical developments in either anti-submarine warfare (ASW) or ballistic missile defence. The second issue is whether, with a revival of arms control, Britain and France will be obliged to accept restrictions on their nuclear forces.

Up to now SLBMs have gained their reputation for invulnerability on the basis of two technical judgements. The first is that anti-submarine techniques are developing incrementally and have not yet reached the point where a serious challenge can be mounted to a modern nuclear submarine missile (SSBN) force, patrolling sensibly and quietly (and that the West is at any rate ahead in this development). The second is that existing means of ballistic missile defence, and any means consistent with the 1972 Anti-Ballistic Missile (ABM) Treaty, allow for a serious deterrent threat to be posed to the Soviet Union.

The second of these issues is the most controversial at the moment though it is arguable that over the long term the first may be more serious. However, at the moment there seems no reason to question the orthodox view that ASW techniques are not yet sufficient to force the SSBN out of business. Counters are available in the form of larger patrol areas and keeping noise down, and these are being exploited. It is still likely that in the future an SSBN will be caught only by the enemy's good luck rather than good management. Certainly, so long as the Soviet Union has to consider a large American SSBN force as well as the British and French SSBNs, then it is unlikely that either of the small deterrents will be shot out of the seas. Whether it would be so easy for either to stand alone against a concerted Soviet ASW campaign is a different matter, but it is still likely that London and Paris could enjoy reasonable confidence in the level of invulnerability of the SSBNs.

The question of strategic defence currently dominates the debate. It is widely believed that the British and French governments' clear reservations about the Strategic Defense Initiative (SDI) are based wholly on the threat of an 'ABM race' to their national nuclear deterrents. It should be noted that, at least in the British case, care has been taken to separate reservations about SDI from the fate of the national nuclear force. The main concern over SDI has been the challenge it poses to extended deterrence and to arms control. It has been felt that if the threat to the national deterrent was seen as the main objection this would turn the whole thing into an exercise in special pleading and would seem somewhat parochial given the enormity of what is being proposed — at least in the form of President Reagan's 'vision'.

That being said, it is still assumed that British and French concern over the viability of their nuclear forces does inform their overall perspective on SDI. Furthermore, both governments have made it clear that they are certainly considering the implications of SDI in considering the future development of their forces.

The concern is with a Soviet attempt to match the SDI rather than the SDI itself (including, if one insists on taking these things at face value, the possibility of an American transfer of the relevant technology to the Soviet Union). For the moment the Soviet Union has said it will not attempt to do this, but will instead counter SDI by offensive countermeasures, including an expansion of warhead numbers. There is no reason to doubt this: many independent observers have already outlined this as the most prudent response for Moscow.

However, Moscow distinguishes between space-based systems and the ground-based defences that are extensions of its current Galosh system around Moscow, which is already in the process of being upgraded. While it is unlikely that it will do more than continue to explore (and perhaps occasionally step over) the limits of the ABM Treaty in respect to ground-based systems, as illustrated by the phased-array radar at Krasnayorsk and the testing of the SA-10, the position may be that the Soviet Union will not feel that there is any great advantage in abrogating the treaty for the moment itself — as this would certainly give the green light to the US SDI. Nevertheless, should the US reach the point where it either (a) had decided to abrogate the treaty or (b) had moved from a 'restrictive' to a 'permissive' interpretation of treaty constraints, the Soviet Union might feel itself no longer under any obligation and build up its defences on the basis of available technology.

For the moment the United States insists that it will do neither of these things, and British and French policy will no doubt be directed to ensuring that this remains the case. Even with growing confidence in the potential of the new defensive technologies, it will be difficult for the US to abandon the treaty before it is almost certain that the project will be successful, and the point of departure will simply come too early to be sure.

The formal review conferences will be watched with close attention but it would be surprising if anything dramatic happened there. More likely is that there will already have been an attempt to clarify these issues at the Geneva talks or in the Standing Consultative Commission. Apart from anything else, abrogation or amendment can occur at any time: there is no need to wait for the review conference. Meanwhile, the treaty is of indefinite duration. No decision is necessary at the review conference for it to continue.

Should the treaty fall, the major danger is of build-up of more mundane forms of missile defence rather than the exotic types currently being explored by the US. Although politically (especially in Britain) this would raise question marks against the viability of the French and British forces, there is no reason in principle why this should prevent them posing a credible nuclear threat. Both have already undertaken modernization programmes that increase their ability to penetrate Soviet defences — Britain with Chevaline; France with M-4. With Trident Britain will substantially increase her numbers of warheads. Because neither side needs to threaten the complete Soviet target set, it has the option of concentrating its forces on one particular target — or a few targets. They should therefore be able to saturate the defences protecting any given target (as Britain already hopes is the case with Chevaline's capacity against the Moscow defences). Because of the flexibility of choice available to both, it is unlikely that the Soviet Union could build up nationwide defences of such a density to deny the Europeans all significant targets. It is of note that the optimism that the United Kingdom expresses on this score — that four SSBNs with 64 missiles can constitute an effective deterrent until 2010–20 — hardly supports the US view of a Soviet potential for a great surge in its ballistic missile defence capabilities.

All this of course simply reaffirms the advantages that the offence still enjoys and will continue to enjoy for the foreseeable future, and indicates why the Soviet Union will probably not attempt to build up nationwide defences on the basis of known technologies. Whether exotic technologies will yield much more is another matter. My own view is that in the end SDI will be defeated by its own weight. The technological ambition is matched only by the confusion of the rationale, and this does not augur well in a battle to convince a reluctant Congress to release the relevant funds at a time of tight budget. Even the optimists who retain some grasp of reality still acknowledge that the sort of strategic defences that they envisage are unlikely to be operational until well into the next century. The problem then, if there is one, will be for the next generation of European nuclear forces. The balance of probability is still that this problem will not emerge at all, despite the current American enthusiasm.

## V

The final factor that is important to mention is that of the potential role of British and French forces in future arms control negotiations. The Soviet Union has sought to draw these forces into the negotiations from the start, though not with the same conviction that it has chased the American forward-based systems. Indeed the relative priorities are indicated by the use of the former in recent years to make a case for the exclusion of the latter.

In May 1972, following the signing of SALT I, the Soviet Union argued that it should be allowed to increase the number of SSBNs in its fleet if the combined British and French totals exceeded nine. This implied a credit in the SALT totals for existing and planned European SSBNs. However, the Soviet statement was rejected by the United States and was never really followed through.

The role of the British and French forces was raised on occasion by Soviet negotiators thereafter (via, for example, its concept of 'equal security'). The Soviet difficulty was that emphasizing this issue compromised its basic position that the strategic arms relationship was essentially a superpower relationship and not one between two alliances, which meant that *all* US systems that could hit the USSR had to be included but Soviet systems, admittedly of comparable range, were irrelevant so long as they could not hit the US. Drawing in the British and French forces inevitably led to drawing in Soviet forces threatening those two countries. Surprisingly, in 1980, even when Brezhnev agreed to talk about Soviet medium-range missiles in the context of his efforts to head off the cruise and Pershing deployments, Britain and France received little mention.

It was nevertheless inevitable that any discussion of the European balance would soon get locked on to the British and French question. In any attempt to demonstrate a pre-existing 'Euro-strategic balance' which NATO's proposed deployments must not be allowed to disrupt, the European forces were essential to make up the NATO numbers. In 1982 Andropov made these forces the centrepoint of the Soviet position by seeking to establish a direct link between the numbers of British and French missiles and SS-20s.

Such a link was a historical nonsense. Neither side planned its forces with such a relationship in mind. There were around 700 SS-4s and SS-5s facing Britain and France before those two countries had any long-range missiles of their own. When these missiles did arrive they were expected to deter the totality of the Soviet capability and not just one component.

It was also clear that the Soviet objective was not to seek reductions in British and French forces, though it has acknowledged that should these forces be reduced the Soviet Union would follow suit — missile by missile! The real objective was to use these forces to make a case for excluding American forces from the Continent. The Soviet draft treaty of 1982 made this explicit.

Despite these points, there has always been some sympathy in the west with the Soviet position. Americans have noted the structural problems that might be created if superpower arsenals went down while British and French warhead numbers went up. The extra warheads with Trident (on average eight per missile) and the M-4 (six) are said to put these two powers into a different league. The Soviet Union once even insisted that Chevaline was already doing this for Polaris, by assuming that this put six warheads on each missile (the actual figure was two and so actually involved a slight reduction). Italians have expressed sympathy with the thought that it is not unreasonable for the Soviet Union to express a concern with missiles pointing at them ('they are not on the moon' — Signor Craxi).

A combination of higher warhead numbers and Soviet publicity ensure that these weapons loom larger on the strategic landscape. This does not necessarily mean that they will become the 'victims' of arms control.

Although the two sets of forces are normally considered together, there are important differences that lead to more pressure on London than on Paris. British governments have always been much more positive about arms control and have justified nuclear status in part because of the influence it is presumed to bring when such matters are being discussed internationally ('ticket to the top table'). In addition, the domestic controversy surrounding the nuclear force is unlikely to be eased if it is identified as a barrier to arms control. The Labour Party debate at the time of the 1983 election was whether Polaris should be scrapped through arms control — and therefore supposedly Soviet concessions — or just scrapped. Labour and the SLDP still look to arms control as a more popular alternative to unilateralism. Britain uses American missiles and, while Polaris is no longer in the US inventory, in the 1990s both will share Trident. Lastly, Britain has assigned its forces to NATO and they are targeted with US forces at Omaha (though there are separate target lists).

France's national consensus supporting the *Force de Frappe* and her clear scepticism when it comes to arms control, which has historically been viewed (not without reason) as a means of undermining French nuclear aspirations, leave less room for equivocation. It is moreover easier for France to distinguish herself from the US. Her missiles are her own and she is not part of NATO's integrated military command.

The British government, in its effort to head off pressure, made a number of points: that it did not accept the Soviet premise of the link with SS-20 numbers; that, while the number of warheads will go up when Trident enters service, the Soviet Union has hardly been dragging its feet when it comes to adding extra warheads, so that the ratio of British to Soviet warheads with Trident will be similar to that when Polaris entered service. In the end the INF Treaty did not depend on British concessions. But European SSBNs always fitted more into the Strategic Arms Reduction Talks (START) than INF. START is also a bilateral negotiation and the US cannot be expected to negotiate on behalf of other sovereign powers. Nor could the US be expected to reduce its forces to make way for the British let alone the French. Remember the Jackson amendment! Indeed, if it came to the crunch, US expectations of parity with the Soviet Union would constitute the major barrier to acceptance of the Soviet position.

Despite these objections, London has not ruled out some involvement in arms control (we 'never say never' — Geoffrey Howe). Two conditions would have to be satisfied: first there would have to be a substantial reduction in the offensive inventories of both the superpowers; and second, no improvement in Soviet defensive capabilities. This second condition puts the government in line with the Soviet government in arguing the unreality of expecting limitations on offensive arms when there are long-term doubts over the defensive position. This condition emphasizes Britain's stake in the persistence of the ABM Treaty.

The link with superpower reductions in offensive forces is more surprising for it suggests that Britain could make proportionate reductions to match those of the superpowers. But Britain could not reduce her four SSBNs to two to match a 50 per cent superpower cut because that would mean long periods when no boat was on station (because of the pattern of patrol times and the long refits). Four SSBNs really constitute a minimum deterrent, although with the longer periods between long refits with Trident, three boats might just be feasible. In practice, Britain lacks a flexible negotiating position.

The hope in London and Paris is that the Soviet Union has no great expectations with regard to the two European forces and is only pointing to them for bargaining purposes. In the end the most important matter is the US-Soviet relationship. There are plenty of indications that, when it comes to the crunch, the pressure will be relaxed if that is necessary to obtain the primary objectives with regard to US forces. This hope depends on United States continuing to recognize that it is against its interests to include these forces, which will be the case so long as they are being used to take up the American allowance.

should arms control prosper in the coming months. Some 'fix' may be required. If the two superpowers want to take British and French forces into 'account' then there is nothing that either European country can do about that except make it clear that they are not bound themselves by any such understandings with regard to future force levels. Nor can the two countries pretend that they have no interest in the outcome of the Geneva talks. Both are anxious for improved east-west relations and for the maintenance of the ABM Treaty. Britain has more special concerns. For example, one of the key Soviet objectives is to stop the Trident D-5 programme. If this succeeded Britain would be in an awkward position. She would have to return to the C-4 version with which she was always perfectly happy until the dictates of 'commonality' forced her to follow the US line of development into the D-5.

While both Britain and France quickly rejected Gorbachev's October 1985 offer of separate talks (and Britain was relieved that the offer was made in Paris and not in London), discussions of some sort have not been ruled out. If Britain, for example, were to agree to bilateral talks with the Soviet Union, she could not accept the terms in which Gorbachev's offer was couched. All that could be done would be to offer a straight freeze on numbers of SSBNs or launch tubes. There might be some possibility of an agreement to come into force with a wider US-Soviet agreement, involving a ceiling on warhead numbers (say six — which is what Chevaline was once credited with by Moscow) or a slight reduction in launch tubes (easier to verify). For the Soviet Union all this would achieve would be an acceptance of the principle that when Soviet forces are constrained those of all its potential adversaries should also be constrained. There would be little other change and indeed some legitimacy would have been accorded the British force. Nor could they be sure that Paris would follow. However, both London and Paris have signed separate 'hot-line' agreements with Moscow, so there are precedents.

As a footnote it might be noted that Gorbachev's January 1986 proposals appear to envisage substantial reductions in UK or French capabilities only after the completion of the first-phase reductions of 50 per cent in 1993. These reductions would then be part of general and complete nuclear disarmament. The British and French governments are unlikely to feel that the success of this scheme will depend entirely on their compliance.

## VI

From this it can be seen that there are no irresistible external or technical pressures that might force either country out of the nuclear business. In that sense they are no longer 'prone to obsolescence'. The costs of staying in this business are high but not prohibitive. Both can afford nuclear status if they wish to do so. Britain is dependent on American assistance and so would be vulnerable to an American decision to squeeze her out of her nuclear status. The US would presumably only do this as part of a much more general reconsideration of its commitments to Europe, which would possibly encourage Britain to find another way of remaining 'nuclear'. Once the Trident force is completed, its main vulnerability will be to a loss of the spare parts relationship. With Polaris this would give Britain some eighteen months to take drastic action. The longer time between long refits with the Trident SSBNs would mean that there was some three years' grace. (In a sudden crisis it would be extremely difficult for Washington to prevent London from operating its nuclear capabilities independently.) The other main challenge to Britain's nuclear status is neither technology nor diplomacy but domestic political change; this, however, seems a more distant threat after the 1987 general election.

Part two

# Co-operation on conventional forces and armaments production

Chapter five

# Co-operation between conventional forces in Europe: a British view

Hugh Beach

Ask any Englishman to describe a typical foreigner and his answer (probably unconsciously) will depict a Frenchman! This reflects the dismal fact that France and Britain, designed by geography to complement each other, seem doomed by history and temperament to compete and often to find themselves at odds. In matters of defence these two countries have far more in common with each other than either has with any other country. Both, for example, have equipped themselves with and are bent on retaining an independent strategic nuclear capability; yet it is by no means uncommon to find even senior French officers who firmly believe that France is the only European country which has this capability. Both countries retain substantial commitments in colonial and ex-colonial territories: the French some 24,000 in Lebanon, Djibouti, New Caledonia, Réunion, Chad, Gabon, the Central African Republic, Ivory Coast, Senegal, Guyana, and Polynesia, with small fleets in the Indian and Pacific Oceans; the British some 24,000 in Antarctica, Ascension, Belize, Brunei, Canada, Cyprus, Egypt, the Falklands, Gibraltar, Hong Kong, with an intermittent naval presence in the Indian Ocean. Yet in all these activities the two countries go their own way — with no co-ordination and a minimum of mutual understanding. Not since the reoccupation of Suez in 1956 has a joint operation of any magnitude taken place. In recent years both countries formed part of the Multinational Force in Beirut but there was no multinational force command and the only real co-operation took place during the withdrawal when French forces staged in the sovereign bases on Cyprus. Both countries took part in the mine-clearing operation in the Red Sea, but again there was no multinational command and the forces operated in different areas.

It is possible to explain, if not to excuse, this lack of co-operation and mutual understanding: in the case of strategic nuclear policy by the principle — explicitly stated in the French case and fudged in the British — that national freedom cannot be diluted into any international alliance system. In the case of overseas commitments outside the NATO area, old colonial rivalries left over from the days of empire-building die hard.

But both these areas of policy are the subject of other papers in this book and are mentioned here only to provide a global setting for the remarks which now follow on the topic of conventional forces and policies within the North Atlantic Treaty area. For here again the same paradox is immediately apparent. On the one hand France and Britain, as founder members of the Western European Union (WEU) and original signatories of the North Atlantic Treaty, share the clear understanding that the security of Western Europe depends primarily upon the cohesion of the Atlantic Alliance. To this end both countries have stationed substantial forces (around 50,000 men) in West Germany in peace-time and equipped them accordingly. Both countries devote substantial naval and air forces to the defence of the Atlantic and its seaboard, and between them constitute the key areas for the staging of US reinforcements in any time transition to war. Both countries provide a garrison (around 3,000 men) in Berlin.

And yet, if we exclude certain collaborative equipment projects (also the subject of a separate paper), any concept of *joint* planning, training, and formulation of doctrine for the defence of north-west Europe and the eastern Atlantic is relatively low-key, and has been ever since France withdrew from the integrated military structure of the Alliance in the mid-1960s. The aim of this paper is to take stock, from a British viewpoint, of the role and task of conventional forces in the common defence, to review developments, and to suggest ways in which co-operation might be enhanced in future.

Although France toyed for a while with the concept of defence 'à tous azimuts' it is now common ground that the threat to be defended against is that which called the Alliance system into existence in the first place: namely the spectre of uncontrolled Soviet imperialism. The key factor here is the *horror vacui*: the fear that any uncommitted country upon one's boundaries (the *limes* of the Roman Empire) will fall to one's enemies and be converted into a threat to oneself. Thus Britain went into Egypt to protect the route to India from the French, and ended up going into Uganda to protect the Nile from the Germans. The Russians themselves, in their saner moments, concede that when one becomes 'too big' one falls a prey to fears. Moscow's invasion of Afghanistan at Christmas 1979 seems to have been due far less to any master-plan than to the bungling of local Afghan communists, which seemed likely to lead to a military anti-communist Islamic regime in Kabul, allied to China or to the USA, or to both, and setting the worst possible example to the Soviet Muslim republics in Central Asia. It is in response to precisely this *horror vacui* in north-west Europe, and to mark off clearly in advance the respective spheres of interest in east and west, that the Western Alliances were founded and have been maintained. Since imperial systems rise and wane over the time-scale of many decades, if not centuries, the west will have to keep up its guard for a very long time.

The essential contest between east and west lies in the economic, social, and political arenas and the west holds most of the cards. But if these contests are to be settled on their merits the military must hold the ring, and it is precisely in the military field that the Russians come closest to being able to call the tune. This is for two reasons. First, the military precondition is simply that there be no option open to the Russians, to which the west has literally no effective counter. Second, while the west has effective parity at the strategic level, at the level of conventional forces there is a long-standing and unresolved disparity in favour of the Soviet Union. General Leopold Chalupa, the German Commander-in-Chief of Allied Forces in Central Europe, has recently offered the following assessment of the situation on the Central Front.[1]

> The Warsaw Pact could deploy within a few days more than 40 active manoeuvre divisions, mostly Soviet, and all stationed in . . . the German Democratic Republic, Czechoslovakia and Poland. That number could be almost doubled within a couple of weeks by reinforcements from the Western Military Districts of the USSR and after some weeks could be built-up by further strategic reserves to almost 100 divisions, which would include several airborne formations . . . The greatest threat to us therefore would be their echelonment in depth . . . Over 3,000 aircraft assessed to be initially available in the forward area would be quickly reinforced from the western USSR to over 4,500.

Turning then to NATO he writes:

> Our in-place land forces, expressed in division equivalents, would comprise about 22 divisions which could be reinforced only slowly to over 30 divisions. Our in-place air forces would have available about 1,300 combat aircraft which could be reinforced to over 2,000 aircraft in a shorter time frame. By way of comparison, considering all our reinforcements and even the commitment of French forces, the ratio of land forces would quickly increase from about 2 : 1 to over 3 : 1 in favour of the Warsaw Pact, and for air forces he (sic) would enjoy an advantage of about 2.5 to 1 from the outset.

Admiral Wesley L. McDonald, when Supreme Allied Commander, Atlantic, came to the conclusion that across the board SACLANT is currently about 50 per cent short of requirements. The worst shortages are in modern destroyers, frigates, nuclear and diesel attack submarines, maritime patrol aircraft and assets used in mine warfare.

Small wonder then that NATO ministers, in their Defence Planning session in Brussels on 22 May 1985 showed concern at the current disparity between NATO's conventional forces and those of the Warsaw Pact and gave the highest priority in the Resource Guidance to the need to narrow the gap. The reason they gave was that the current imbalance 'risks an undue reliance on the early use of nuclear weapons. This would be an unacceptable situation which we are determined to avoid.'

This clause brings us to the heart of the current argument about conventional forces, since it calls into question a central tenet of the policy known as 'flexible response'. This is a NATO concept, never explicitly endorsed by the French, although a similar concept is *implied* by the existence of the French Tactical Nuclear Arms (two squadrons of Mirage 111E, three squadrons of Jaguars, five Pluton regiments, and a flotilla of carrier-based Super-Etendard 11F). This concept relies upon conventional forces to counter any Soviet non-nuclear attack as far forward as possible and to allow time for reinforcements to arrive. In the NATO view, the function of theatre nuclear forces is to provide a link between conventional and strategic nuclear forces, providing options short of a strategic exchange and deterring the use of theatre nuclear forces by the other side. In the French view this doctrine could lead to the 'acceptance' of war in western Europe — presumably on the grounds that it purports to provide a concept of operations in the event that deterrence should fail. But in the French formulation recourse to tactical nuclear weapons would indicate the ultimate warning, before the use of the strategic nuclear riposte, should the enemy continue his operations. It is stated categorically that the link between strategic and tactical nuclear forces 'excludes all possibility of a nuclear battle'; but if this is true, how is the ultimate warning to be given any time at all to take effect?

The fact is that, while any concept for the 'first use' of nuclear weapons by the west, if there were no other way of stopping the Warsaw Pact or persuading them to desist, has much to commend it as a declaratory doctrine for the purposes of deterrence, and as such is a great money-saver, nevertheless as an operational doctrine if deterrence should fail it is fundamentally incoherent. The reason is that no one can possibly predict what the consequence of such 'first use' would be. It may be that it would so horrify the Russian leadership, by bringing home to them NATO's determination to resist at all costs and the consequent perils to their own people, that they would back away and stop the war. If so, well and good. But it is at least possible that Russians would take their own doctrine seriously and respond to any first use of nuclear weapons by the west in like measure — or even more extensively. Clearly one of the reasons the Russians say that they would do this is to counter

NATO strategy at the declaratory level. But it would be grossly irresponsible for the west not to take seriously the possibility that in the event the Russians would do exactly what they say they would. The consequence would then become wholly indeterminate, not the least likely outcome being the destruction of precisely those 'western values' which it is the whole aim of strategy to defend.

This huge factor of uncertainty regarding the outcome of any 'first use' of nuclear weapons imparts a large element of irrationality into the whole concept of deliberate escalation. This is first because, as innumerable war games and studies have revealed, if the west used nuclear weapons and the Russians did no more than retaliate like for like, though the Russians might be held up for a time, their advance could soon be resumed more effectively even than before. The reason is that attrition would increase, and that favours the side with the 'big battalions'. Second, with the very survival of peoples at stake, it is impossible to exaggerate the difficulty of obtaining political agreement to the use of nuclear weapons. It may be that NATO, with its many nations involved, would have the greater problem. In France, the decision would lie in the hands of one man only. But he too would need to be assured that a conventional defence alone was no longer viable. And for France to act first, and on her own, would be to invite a unique retribution. A French President might well prefer to wait, on the grounds that the security and vital interests of France would be ill served by calling down upon herself alone the nuclear might of the Soviet Union. Third, there is a moral incoherence in any doctrine that relies upon the threat of escalation for its deterrent effect, but recognizes that to carry out that threat would be to run a finite risk of destroying the very civilization that the policy exists to defend.

There is good reason, therefore, for NATO ministers to seek to de-emphasize the part to be played by nuclear weapons on the battlefield by making a 'special and coherent effort' to improve conventional capabilities. There have always been those who see more danger than profit in this suggestion because of its dilution of the concept of deterrence. West Germany, in particular, has always hankered for a quasi-automatic link between any incursion across the inner-German border and the release of nuclear weapons — for easily intelligible reasons. Any conventional war would be fought on German soil, at dreadful cost, and with no guarantee that any lost territory could ever be regained. But this is to cry for the moon. Since the Soviet Union has attained parity with the west in both strategic and tactical nuclear capability, the concept of a nuclear tripwire lacks credibility of any kind. It follows that the west has no option, in confronting a purely conventional attack, other than to deal with it initially at least by conventional means. The greater the chance that this conventional defence will succeed on its own terms, the less its attraction to any Soviet leadership, and the greater the likelihood of dissuading any recourse to war. General W. Rogers, Supreme Allied Commander Europe, made it clear that by establishing the credible prospect that an Allied Command Europe conventional response might succeed, our deterrent posture will be enhanced and the nuclear threshold raised.[2] NATO, as we have seen, has recognized this imperative explicitly and the French, as we shall see, by implication.

The decisive step, so far as NATO is concerned, was taken as long ago as May 1977 when the Defence Planning Committee, in Ministerial Session, called upon member countries to develop a long-term programme for the 1980s and the corresponding resource guidance set as a target an annual increase in real terms of defence budgets in the region of 3 per cent. This commitment was endorsed in subsequent years, most recently in May 1985, and has provided an invaluable stimulus to member countries. Over the period 1975–83 the United States and Luxembourg averaged 6 per cent a year real growth in defence budgets, and only West Germany, Denmark, and Belgium slipped below 2 per cent. Britain averaged 2.9 per cent a year real growth over these years, but this includes expenditure on the Falklands; if that element is excluded the figure comes down to 2.2 per cent. France, though naturally not party to the Defence Planning Committee of NATO and its decision, nevertheless achieved an average growth rate of 2.3 per cent in real terms over the same period. This steady growth in the resources available for defence, over a sustained period, has enabled real progress to be made in the introduction of modernized tanks, guns, armoured personnel carriers, rocket launchers and guided missiles, tactical aircraft, anti-submarine forces of all kinds, and the tools of command, control, and communication. War stocks, infrastructure, aircraft shelters, and a variety of other logistic preparations have also been set in hand, not least those relating to the staging and reception of reinforcements from the United States. However, as the recent ministerial guidance indicates, there is still much to be done, and there can be no guarantee that additional resources will be made available in future on the scale necessary to cope with what is needed.

In the British case, this arises from the fact that the commitment to 3 per cent growth was abandoned in the financial year 1985/86, after which the allocation of resources to defence, in real terms, is assumed to be static. The implications of this for the British defence programme were spelled out in evidence given by the Chief of Defence Staff, Field Marshal Sir Edwin Bramall, to the Defence Committee of the House of Commons on 6 February 1985. The Field Marshal explained that a regime of level funding in real terms on paper would tend in practice to represent a decrease in budget volume by as much as 4 per cent a year, owing to such factors as the increasing cost of successive generations of equipment, insufficient allowance for inflation in setting cash limits, the need to absorb pay settlements in excess of an unrealistic norm, fiscal changes, the fluctuating dollar exchange rate (at this moment a positive factor), and not least Trident, which, however necessary, will take up a large share of the budget in the 1990s. The government's aim is to mitigate the effects of level funding by means of greater reliance upon competitive tendering in equipment procurement, more stress upon international collaboration, the contracting-out of support functions, further switches of manpower and resources from 'tail' to 'teeth', and more devolution of financial responsibility. In the opinion of the Defence Committee these measures are unlikely to go more than part of the way towards bridging the financial gap. To the extent that this comes true the consequences are likely to include: taking elements out of the programme (for example the amphibious capability to deliver the UK–Netherlands Amphibious Force to the Northern Flank); slipping of in-service dates; cutting down on equipment specifications; failing to close capability gaps (for example on mine counter-measure vessels, ammunition and fuel stocks, and equipment purchases to make good accidental losses); and forgoing the more expensive forms of training. This remarkably frank exposé by the Chief of Defence Staff sits rather ill with the British government's endorsement of the NATO aims of achieving real increases in defence spending in the region of 3 per cent a year, let alone of narrowing the gap between NATO's conventional defence capabilities and those of the Warsaw Pact, so reducing dependence upon the early recourse to nuclear weapons.

Nor is the French case much more encouraging. France had a five-year defence plan for the period 1983–8 totalling 830,000 million francs, but this implies no more than 2 per cent real annual growth and almost a quarter of this funding is allocated to the nuclear programme. The defence budget for 1986 was 4 million francs less than mandated by the five-year plan. The army in particular, though twice the size numerically of the British army, contains over 60 per cent of conscripts, the basic period of compulsory service being only twelve months. It seeks as one of its major aims to contribute to the development of the spirit of defence by instructing young French conscripts. It is reorganizing and reducing in size.

It is salutary for the British to recognize not only that the French maintain a corps in West Germany (2nd Corps: HQ Baden Baden) which is much the same size as the British corps (1st (BR) Corps: HQ Bielefeld) but that the role of the two other corps of 1st Army (1st Corps: HQ Metz and 3rd Corps: HQ Lille), supported by the tactical air force, is also to act in co-operation with the NATO allies in the event of aggression, albeit that none of these are front-line troops and are ready to act only as second echelon in the event of a breakthrough. However, the most striking feature of the years 1984 and 1985 was the creation of the Force d'Action Rapide, with a strength of nearly 50,000, which has now completed its experimental phase (April 1983–July 1985) and is becoming permanent. Its headquarters is at Maisons-Laffitte near Versailles. It has taken over three pre-existing formations: 27th Alpine Division (HQ Grenoble); 11 Airborne Division (HQ Toulouse); 9 Marine Infantry Division (HQ St Malo). The Alpine Division is unchanged, but the Airborne and Marine divisions have had the proportion of regular soldiers in the regiments increased at the expense of the 1st Army units. One reason for this is to make it easier for these formations to be used overseas: conscripts cannot serve overseas without a special dispensation. A new formation has been created called 6th Light Armoured Division (HQ Nîmes) based mainly on wheeled armoured vehicles. It has a high proportion of Foreign Legion units and is stationed in the south of France and along the Mediterranean seaboard, which suggests that its primary orientation is African, though it could in some measure and for a limited duration support an assault by airmobile forces. The major novelty has been the creation of 4th Airmobile Division from the previously existing 4th Armoured Division (HQ Nancy). This is the spearhead of the Force d'Action Rapide, based on helicopter regiments. Again the loser has been the 1st Army, which has been stripped of half of its helicopter assets to create this division. In the longer term France is co-operating with Germany to build a helicopter to equip this force. Its aim is to intercept, and stop or destroy, enemy armoured formations within a range of action 350 km deep. However it has no proper logistic tail to support it at present, and even when it does the duration of action in the combat zone is limited. Its effectiveness would clearly depend critically upon obtaining air cover and support from the tactical air force and one could ask if they are keen to take on this task at the expense of deep interdiction tasks in support of the NATO 4th Allied Tactical Air Force. The question of nuclear support has never been properly faced.

The Force d'Action Rapide has been heralded politically as the French answer to co-operation alongside its NATO allies. It is foolish to look a gift horse in the mouth, but some scepticism may be in order. In the first place no initiative has yet been taken to place the Force d'Action Rapide into the NATO battlefield — other than in exercises between the French and the West Germans. At no stage have the British, for example, been approached to co-operate in joint force level exercises with the French. It may be that the Alpine Division has been given a more forward defensive role covering the area along the Alps in case of an assault through Austria and Bavaria, but this is very much a backstop so far as NATO is concerned. If some parts of the Force d'Action Rapide were to be committed to the Central Front this would be helpful, and the British in particular would welcome any suggestion of possible deployment of the 4th Airmobile Division in support of a 1(BR) Corps counterattack. Meanwhile the obvious detractions of regular manpower and equipment (particularly helicopters) from 1st Army could be a negative factor in the NATO context.

Other forms of Franco-British co-operation, in the conventional NATO context, are low-key in character. Annual exercises between RMA Sandhurst and St Cyr have been re-instigated as well as a small number of company, squadron, and platoon exercises, but these have dwindled recently owing to the severe budgetary restraints placed on the French units — and as already explained this may well apply to the British in future. So far as the Franco-British mutual defence interest in the Atlantic and the Atlantic seaboard from air and sea attack is concerned, there is a French liaison cell at the Naval Headquarters at Northwood and there is a good deal of co-operation between CINCEASTLANT, a NATO command, and CINCFLEET, the British command, both based at Northwood, and CECLANT, the French command at Brest. But naval exercises, although fairly frequent and widespread, are for the most part limited in size and scope. The British would welcome increased co-operation in this area. And much the same applies to air force matters. The British and French maintain an air force liaison officer in each other's air defence command centres but there might be room for more even bilateral co-operation in the use of our early warning systems complemented by better response from the French air force to the protection and benefit of both nations. There have been limited interchanges between air force squadrons but the French have kept these on a very low key.

How then can we view the future of Franco-British co-operation in the field of conventional military strategy in the common defence? Britain remains wholly and, as it seems, irrevocably committed to the NATO context, for as long as this subsists. France, while adhering fundamentally to this alliance, treasures her autonomy of decision and gears her whole defence doctrine to the defence of *La France* (including, of course, her territories overseas). There is a strong element in French thinking of the need to be independent of all nations (not least Britain); identifiable as the non-partisan source for countries of the Third World to turn to for arms purchase and military support, untainted by influence from the USA or the USSR.

These two pathways show no particular sign of convergence in the 1990s and it is probably too much to hope that the revitalization of the WEU will produce any dramatic changes of course. Perhaps both sides must be content with modest progress at the grass roots. To the extent that Britain, having defected from the regime of 3 per cent real growth in defence allocations, tries nevertheless to contribute to the NATO aim of improved conventional capability, this may well lead to contributions

*Table 5.1* UK collaboration in armaments procurement, UK statement on Defence Estimates, 1985

| *Project* | *Participating countries* |
|---|---|
| *In service:* | |
| Naval equipment: | |
| PARIS Sonar | UK/FR/NL |
| Land equipment: | |
| FH70 Howitzer | UK/GE/IT |
| Scorpion Reconnaissance Vehicle | UK/BE |
| Aircraft: | |
| Jaguar | UK/FR |
| Tornado | UK/GE/IT |
| Lynx ) | |
| Gazelle ) | UK/FR |
| Puma ) | |
| Missiles: | |
| Martel (air-to-surface) | UK/FR |
| Milan (anti-tank) | UK/FR/GE |
| Sidewinder (air-to-air) | UK/GE/IT/NO |
| Other equipment: | |
| Midge Drone | UK/CA/GE |
| *In development or earlier study phases:* | |
| Naval equipment: | |
| NATO Frigate Replacement (NFR 90) | UK/US/NL/FR/CA/SP/GE/IT |
| Sea Gnat Decoy System | UK/DE/US |
| Land equipment: | |
| SP70 Howitzer | UK/GE/IT |
| Multiple-Launch Rocket System Phase I | UK/FR/GE/IT/US |
| Multiple-Launch Rocket System Phase III | UK/FR/GE/US |
| Aircraft: | |
| Harrier GR5 | UK/US |
| Naval ASW Helicopter (EH101) | UK/IT |
| European Fighter Aircraft | UK/FR/GE/IT/SP |
| Missiles: | |
| Short-Range Anti-Radar Missile | UK/US/BE/GE/CA/NL/IT |
| Long-Range Stand-Off Missile | UK/US/GE |
| Milan Improvements | UK/FR/GE |
| TRIGAT (anti-tank) | UK/FR/GE |
| ASRAAM (air-to-air) | UK/GE/NO |
| Other equipment: | |
| Midge Post-Design Services | UK/FR/GE |

*Note:*
BE = Belgium: CA = Canada; DE = Denmark; FR = France; GE = Federal Republic of Germany; IT = Italy; NL = Netherlands; NO = Norway; SP = Spain.

in the field of emerging technology in support of such concepts as Follow-on Force Attack. Projects in this field are expensive, demanding, and call out for a collaborative approach. It is notable that, in the list of collaborative projects published by the British government in April 1986 (Table 5.1), many of the more innovative lie in the field of emerging technology, and almost half include the French as participants. This seems to be the most promising route to a brighter future in defence co-operation in the conventional field — fortunately it is the subject of separate papers by more expert authors.

## Notes

1. Royal United Services Institute for Defence Studies, *RUSI Journal*, vol. 130, no. 1 (March 1985), p. 14.
2. 'Power and policy: doctrine, the Alliance and arms control', *Adelphi Papers*, no. 205 (London: 11SS, 1986), p. 6.

Chapter six

# Co-operation between conventional forces in Europe: a French view

François Valentin

Franco-British co-operation is not what it should be. In addition to the burdens of past quarrels which have tended to separate Paris and London, particularly outside Europe, France, when it was in the integrated military organization, had its conventional forces at the heart of the Central Army Group and the 4th Allied Tactical Air Force (ATAF), excluding them (except in Berlin) from the sort of co-operation with the British that was achieved with the Americans and the West Germans. With the French withdrawal from NATO's integrated military structure, it was precisely to show her willingness to co-operate with the Northern Army Group that in 1974, as part of the agreements extending the Ailleret–Lemnitzer arrangements to the French 1st Army, France established contacts with this group of forces and, in the joint plans drawn up between the Nato Commander for Allied Forces in Central Europe (AFCENT) and the French forces, provided for possible French intervention in its Northern sector, at least in the Southern part.

I shall examine later the conditions for the use of the French army and air force in the Central European theatre of operations, but before tackling this it would be useful to make a few remarks about the French conception of deterrence.

## I

I have two remarks to make about deterrence as far as strategic nuclear weapons are concerned, to which I will add a third which, as it relates to the theory of flexible response, concerns both tactical and strategic atomic weapons. Although the specific problems relating to these weapons are covered in other chapters, I believe that defence policy is a whole and this overall aspect of deterrence forces me to encroach on other people's territory.

General Beach is right to stress in Chapter 5 that there is great similarity between the French and British concepts of the use of strategic nuclear weapons: these ultimate weapons for the defence of the nation's vital interests are, for the country which possesses them, an asset of which it intends to be in sole control — in any circumstances as far as France is concerned, and whenever considered necessary as far as Britain is concerned. I believe that the French understand this element in British policy. In particular, when British spokesmen vigorously indicated their opposition to the inclusion of Great Britain's nuclear forces in Soviet-American negotiations, and asserted that no one outside Her Majesty's Government has a mandate to speak on Britain's behalf, one can see Britain's desire for independence. If French beliefs in this respect have sometimes been shaken, it is because both at the time of the Nassau agreements and more recently over the Trident missile the UK has seemed, at least as far as missiles are concerned, to place herself in a position of subordination with respect to the United States. Technical and financial arguments have undoubtedly been decisive. However, some British authors have themselves underlined that, at Nassau, Britain's giving up of the idea of developing her own missiles had unfortunate repercussions on the whole of British industry; James Bellini's and Geoffrey Pattie's book is significant in this respect.[1]

My second remark concerns the 'tous azimuts' strategy. These words in fact simply reflect the first justification given by General de Gaulle at the time of the creation of the French nuclear force when he asserted that since France can be attacked anywhere and at any time with weapons of such destructive power, she must be capable of launching identical weapons at any time and anywhere. There was also the ambition (which was at the root of General Ailleret's paper[2] which gave this 'tous azimuts' formula its notoriety) to produce a very long-range missile of 10,000 km range (an ambition that France subsequently abandoned), and finally a vision of a future world in which unforeseeable changes would occur. However, it should be noted that at the time he published this paper General Ailleret was signing comprehensive agreements with General Lemnitzer on co-operation between French and Alliance forces. There was no neutralist tendency in the mind of General de Gaulle or of his subordinates.

My third remark concerns French opposition to the doctrine of flexible response. This opposition did not arise from the rejection of tactical atomic weapons, nor from a desire to accept an 'all-or-nothing' policy. What de Gaulle feared was that the United States might use the concept of 'graduated' or, worse still, 'qualified' escalation as a pretext for committing itself only half-heartedly in Europe, refusing to go as far as using nuclear weapons, and leaving the Europeans, who would be fighting for their very existence, alone to throw in all their resources. This fear was perhaps exaggerated but it was understandable in the light of McNamara's writings. It has subsequently been justified to a degree by some of the declarations made by Kissinger and, more recently, by the recommendation of a stance of 'no first use' by McNamara and his followers. Moreover, this fear is not exclusive to the French. In any event, it was the real cause of France's rejection of the concept of 'flexible response' which the United States got NATO to accept. In my opinion, this rejection was not at all based on what I consider to be the specious theory according to which deterrence would be weakened by the existence of field forces with tactical nuclear weapons at their disposal. As General Beach has pointed out in Chapter 5, the decision to equip the French army with Pluton shows that the French government was convinced of the need for these weapons. Moreover, the decision in principle to produce them was taken long before production began, since it was necessary to wait until France had enough plutonium, which was not the case in 1963.

## II

I now come to the central part of this paper: the mission of the French land and air forces in the defence of Europe. In this respect it is necessary to draw a distinction between declarations of principle and actual measures. Official documents have often emphasized theoretical concepts (test function, final warning, etc.) more than the concrete aspects of the deployment of French forces. There are various reasons for this, including the French liking for abstraction and the occasionally ill-disposed tendency of elements in NATO to use France's signified wish to co-operate outside the integrated structure as a sign that she was coming 'to Canossa'. Internal politics have also played their part: after General de Gaulle's departure, everyone was afraid of appearing less Gaullist than him. Nevertheless, if one refers only to the declarations of the General's former minister for the armed forces, Pierre Messmer, to the Assemblée Nationale in 1976 and 1978, there is no ambiguity, either as to the priority danger of the Soviet threat, or as to the priority given, after that of the strategic nuclear force, to field forces in Europe, or as to the need for co-operation, prepared in detail, with the Allied armies. What was hardly mentioned publicly was the new role given to the French forces. When they were integrated in NATO, the French land forces were, in the second echelon, entrusted with a defensive mission in the south of the Central Europe sector, next to the southern border of the Swabian Jura. Then, in the eyes of General de Gaulle and of NATO's military leaders, the French policy of non-integration and the need for a large reserve for counter-attack purposes, justified French forces being placed in reserve at AFCENT level and being ready, when decided by the French government, to act *offensively* so as to force the enemy to reorganize his resources to face up to a western initiative. Owing to the application, in 1974, of the Ailleret–Lemnitzer arrangements to the 1st Army, the scope of this stance was widened: a series of operations was planned deploying the French 1st and 2nd Corps, if necessary reinforced. Envisaged principally in the Central Army Group zone (CENTAG), these operations included, as I said above, intervention in the Northern Army Group sector (NORTHAG). This would certainly be more difficult and presupposed longer execution times. However, it is essential to bear in mind that, if the enemy made a push westwards in the Centre and in the North, a large-scale counter-offensive, threatening his southern flank and even his rear, would be extremely helpful to the Allied forces attacked in the northern part of the theatre of operations. In fact, not only would one thus draw enemy divisions, one could also, by relieving the sector from which the French forces would counter-attack, release German or American units. These could be moved, at least in part, northwards.

Before tackling the delicate problem of tactical atomic weapons, I think it useful to note that, since this concept was born, considerable change has affected the conditions of the use of the French forces, if not in principle then in practice. Two structural reforms have weakened the French 1st and 2nd Corps. First, the formation of a 3rd Corps, with its headquarters in Lille, seems to be intended to face up to a threat in the North; no doubt it is also included in the 1st Army but, unless an intervention in the East or close to the Rhine in the Northern Army Group zone is envisaged and planned, I do not see what effective role the small resources of the 3rd Corps could play if the enemy had fanned out on the Belgian plains. Moreover, the tactical air force (FATAC), bearing in mind its capabilities, could not be deployed in two different directions. It would be necessary to choose between supporting the 1st and 2nd Corps and supporting the 3rd Corps if the latter were deployed separately. Second, a further change has been the setting up of the Force d'Action Rapide (FAR), or rather of the latter's two light divisions (the 4th Airmobile Division and 6th Light Armoured Division). Here again the question of air support would be crucial. I will not examine here the use of these two divisions as part of the 1st Army, which would not raise any problem. But it is another matter if one envisages their intervention, particularly of the 4th Airmobile Division, to carry out an armed helicopter mission to support an Allied corps in difficulties. Unless logistics are pre-positioned within a corps chosen in advance, support and protection units are designated beforehand, and flight plans are prepared in detail, the deployment of this force 250 km from its base would involve considerable delays. At best, a simple calculation taking into account all the liaising, movements, reconnoitring, and briefings to be carried out between the receipt of the call from the threatened army corps and the arrival of the armed helicopters shows that the minimum delay would be six hours. During this time, how far would a mobile, enterprising enemy have moved? I therefore fully share General Beach's opinion when he advocates that, if these light divisions of the Force d'Action Rapide are to intervene to help out the British corps, this should be to participate in a counter-attack. This solution would be less risky than taking defensive action against moving forces, engaging with the enemy in a sprint race which one cannot control. To my mind therefore, if the Airmobile Division should in the future remain independent of the French 1st Army, discussions between the British and the French should be turned towards its use as part of a counter-attack.

However that may be, I doubt whether splitting up the French forces is the most economical and most effective way of deploying them. I believe it would be far sounder for them to be used together, under the orders of the 1st Army, supported by the tactical air force, in a single direction.

## III

I now come to tactical atomic weapons. The French government has decided that the Hades, the replacement for the Pluton launchers, which should be operational in 1992–3, will be grouped together under a command independent of the 1st Army. I will not deal here with this future aspect of things, and will confine myself to current conditions. I will first point out that, apart from any theoretical justification, the deployment of the Pluton satisfied the following need: the other armies — the Soviet army on the one hand and the Allied armies on the other (thanks to American weapons) — had tactical nuclear weapons and so the French army, which was no longer integrated, required its own to avoid being in a position of inferiority. Comparable reasoning applied to the French strategic nuclear strike force. In this connection I will mention a personal memory. Before France had her Pluton, the Ailleret–Lemnitzer arrangement stated that, if the conflict were to become atomic, the integrated command would provide the French with nuclear weapons. France had bought the Honest John missile system, and her artillery was operating this hardware in training units; but, as a result of France's withdrawal from the integrated organization, the Americans cut the link which, in the event of a crisis, would have enabled her to receive nuclear warheads. In May 1968, leaving the post of assistant to the French Commander in Chief in Germany to take up the post of assistant to the Chief of Staff for the Armed Forces, I visited the American Commander of the Central Army Group, and suggested that we could perhaps re-establish this link in the event of an alert. It would have made it possible to use the French Honest John and to save on Allied units. He told me: 'You are right. When you are in Paris, put in the request. I will support it, but I doubt whether they will give you satisfaction in

Washington since you are no longer integrated. It is highly regrettable because, to give you this support, I will have to take Honest John units from somewhere else: I will be in a difficult position and it will take time.' France did not get satisfaction in Washington, which shows how, as soon as she was no longer integrated, it was necessary to have *national* tactical atomic weapons.

Having said that, the link made by France between strategic and tactical weapons, through the notion of 'final warning' weapons, does not mean that France would wish to resort to nuclear weapons as soon as an enemy company crossed into Western Europe. However, the French believe that, if they let the aggressor think that he could achieve his ends while keeping the fighting conventional, they encourage him. In fact:

(a) He can then safely concentrate his forces, which makes his offensive easier.
(b) His aim obviously being a fast, deep thrust towards the Atlantic, the use of atomic weapons would create obstacles far more damaging to the enemy than to the French because of their great radius of action and notwithstanding their accuracy of delivery.
(c) It is not possible to replace nuclear deterrence with 'conventional deterrence' because in a mechanized fight the aggressor can choose his lines of attack and adapt his resources to the efforts he wants to make, whereas the defender, spread over a vast geographical area, must in addition spread himself in depth. Unlike in 1914–18, the defender must therefore have forces at least equal or even superior to those of the attacker.

Even if one managed to establish a certain balance between east and west before the deployment of the Soviet second echelon or reserves — and successive Supreme Allied Commanders for Europe have reminded us that we are very far from having such a balance — it is clear that, after a few days or weeks, the balance of power would put western defence at great risk. The sophisticated resources called for by General Rogers would at most alleviate this imbalance. Moreover, they could be one of the enemy's priority targets and be partly neutralized. France must therefore retain the threat of recourse to nuclear weapons, which is the only argument the Soviets deeply fear. This need cannot spare France from efforts in conventional equipment, because conventional forces are the first line of defence and, the stronger this defence, the less likely France is to be pulled into this vacuum, rightly brought out by General Beach. The main thing is to have no illusions about this exclusively conventional defence, particularly about its duration.

Concerning tactical nuclear weapons, I will make two further remarks: The first is that the divergences of dogma between the French and the

Allies would undoubtedly not survive actual experience: NATO's plans have been developed on the basis that there would be recourse to nuclear weapons if co-ordinated conventional defence by Allied forces no longer proved possible. The enemy would have pressed us to this position and I do not see why the French should judge the situation differently. My second remark concerns, in this connection, the hypothesis envisaged by General Beach in Chapter 5 in which only the French would threaten to use or would use tactical nuclear weapons. If the threat comes off, as Sir Hugh writes, all is for the best. If not, retaliation against France could be such that one would question the validity of the French decision. One could even question its plausibility and credibility, to use current jargon. I must say that I am very hostile to this argument. First, broadly speaking, because it is the argument that all opponents of deterrence use against strategic nuclear weapons as well as against tactical nuclear weapons. People are thus trying to deter the French rather than to deter the enemy. There is no symmetry in this. France has never had any aggressive design in the west, nor has she had the appropriate conventional resources. She does not need to be deterred; she knows that, if there is open conflict, France's fate is sealed: either immense destruction, or slavery, or both. Even without atomic bombs, conventional battles of any duration would cause incalculable destruction. France has no other choice than to hold over the enemy the threat of damage that he could not sustain without himself being paralysed or mutilated for years. In addition, he would, if he occupied her ruined territory, risk having charge of an uncontrollable, wounded population whose economy and industry would for a long time be unusable for him. It is a prospect he cannot avoid. To return to tactical nuclear weapons, considering the unrealistic hypothesis in which only the French resorted to them, the enemy would be at a loss to know at what level to fix his response: either he would raise the stakes and would risk causing France to resort to strategic nuclear weapons, or he would respond in a limited way against military targets, but this would make his advance arduous. Also, it would be difficult for him to attack only French military targets, and hence the risk would increase of the Allies also resorting to atomic weapons within an unpredictable period of time.

These considerations strengthen me in the opinion that, on these nuclear issues, the French conception is well supported, even though its overdogmatic, excessively abstract presentation is questionable. To conclude, I will recall Winston Churchill's warning that atomic weapons should not be abandoned before one is sure, and more than sure, that one has other means of preserving the peace.

## IV

I now come to the last part of this paper: what recommendations to make to improve relations between our armies in the area of conventional forces? I will not deal with arms co-operation. On the other hand, I will tackle the problem of the structure of the ground forces because, though inter-operability is in the first place a matter of equipment, it is also conditioned by the similarities and differences between organizations. While in 1959 the French army adopted for its main formations a structure very similar to that of the Americans, Germans, British, and other Allies, both sides have since then annoyingly diverged. It is a setback. In the foreseeable but not immediate future, structural reforms will be justified by the changes which research and development projects, emerging from the US Strategic Defense Initiative but concerning conventional equipment, will bring. It is to be hoped that our Chiefs of Staff can seize this opportunity to harmonize their views, either bilaterally between the French and the British, or multilaterally between Europeans.

The second point I will mention applies to military doctrines, which themselves depend on developments in technology. It would be neither very expensive nor very difficult to increase exchanges at similar levels between organizations: just as trilateral technical co-operation gives good results in the study of the third generation anti-tank missile, so joint tactical research, bringing together the West Germans, the French, and the British, could be carried out, particularly on the use of formations ranging from small units to divisions, on specific matters such as the acquisition and use of intelligence, the exercise of command, ground–air forces liaison, etc. No doubt NATO groups are already addressing these questions. However, if very small teams from the three largest countries in Western Europe, directly under their high military authority, put their respective thoughts in the same melting-pot, perhaps a productive result would come out of it reflecting unity of conception between Europeans. Exchanges of officers between staff colleges on both sides of the Channel have always been valued; they would be successfully extended by the contacts suggested here. Furthermore, failing exercises with troops (sometimes prohibitively expensive because of the distance between our basing areas in the Federal Republic of Germany), headquarters exercises could be set up at regular intervals in the field or indoors.

I will end by calling for the establishment of closer links between France and Britain in terms of their European and overseas strategies and the preparation of defence policies. The barriers that have existed up to now within each country between the various categories of forces will be increasingly less impenetrable. We have entered the military space age of observation and communication satellites, battlefield monitoring equipment, and so on. All these systems use the third dimension at varying distances from the Earth: they affect not only the strategic nuclear forces, but increasingly all armies, in Europe and overseas. Frontiers between states are not barriers that extend indefinitely into space. On this general level, co-operation should be organized, not on a piecemeal, partial, and sporadic basis, but in a continuous form.

I will not give any advice here on the institutional aspect of the problem, which is for the politicians to deal with. However, it is important to state the need for co-operation, whatever the solution adopted as regards the authorities through whom the understandings would be implemented. Moreover, the achievements of British and French people in some advanced areas show what we are capable of.

## Notes

1. James Bellini and Geoffrey Pattie, *A New World Role for the Medium Power: The British Opportunity*, London: Royal United Services Institute for Defence Studies, 1977.
2. Général d'Armée Ailleret, 'Defense ''dirigée'' ou défense ''tous azimuts''?', *Revue de defense nationale*, December 1967, pp. 1923–32.

Chapter seven

# The prospects for military co-operation outside Europe: a French view

Marcel Duval

At present, Franco-British military co-operation for handling crises outside Europe is virtually non-existent. Before examining the future prospects for co-operation, and leaving aside those difficulties resulting from the historical memories of the two countries (which have more often than not been rivals overseas in the course of their glorious histories), I will concentrate on the obstacles encountered in the recent past.

First, in order to bring out convergences and divergences, I will compare the French and British points of view on the following matters: assessments of current threats outside Europe, the interests affected by these threats, and the strategies adopted on both sides to defend them. Second, I will describe the practical problems raised by possible Franco-British military co-operation, both in its principal technical aspects and then in the various geographical theatres. Third, after recalling the solutions devised to organize overseas inter-Allied co-operation in the past, I will endeavour to set out improvements which can be envisaged in the future, initially at the level of Franco-British co-operation and then at the European level, before adding a few personal conclusions.

I will attempt to present on all these matters the point of view most generally accepted by my fellow French citizens, or, where I know it, the official French point of view, while at the same time committing only myself in my interpretations and in my comments.

## Comparison of French and British views

### *Assessment of threats*

I will begin therefore by examining how, on the French and the British sides, the threats which hang over us Europeans and more generally over all those who belong to the west are perceived.

On both sides, it is not challenged that these threats come above all from the Soviet Union, since quite obviously its political plan is antagonistic and expansionist, and since it moreover has formidable aggressive capabilities. These threats affect us inevitably in the first place here in Europe, but also and increasingly throughout the world. However, for Europe an important fact must be recorded at the outset: in France, in the government, among political elites, and among the public as a whole, there is greater confidence than in Great Britain in the ability of nuclear deterrence to protect the 'national sanctuary' and more generally Western Europe. The result of this is that the risk in Europe seems to the French to lie in psychological and political blackmail rather than in purely military aggression. This leads them to attach greater importance in their plans to handling crises rather than to preparing for a generalized, prolonged war.

If we now consider the situation outside Europe, the French believe that the effectiveness of nuclear deterrence in the area in Europe surrounding the metropolitan sanctuaries contributes towards the transfer of east-west competition to the south, that is, to the Third World, where it finds numerous opportunities to operate through the many crises there. It is moreover obvious that the Soviet Union intends to intervene increasingly actively overseas and that it now has military resources suited to this end, particularly in the maritime sphere. But here again, the French believe that it is pursuing in this way a great political rather than military design, and consequently that, as in Europe, its strategy is essentially indirect.

Moreover, the French consider that it would be unrealistic to assume that the threats that hang over the interests of the west outside Europe all arise from the actions and capabilities of the Soviet Union. The Third World states have their own motivations for being disruptive and belligerent, as we can see every day, and these may threaten world peace through their regional consequences or their entangling effects elsewhere. These states, the vast majority of which are coastal and insular, are now often equipped with sophisticated military resources, particularly naval and air (which east and west generously supply). They may be tempted to use them or to threaten to use them, and they sometimes do use them against our nationals, our friends, and our sources of supply or our lines of maritime and air communications, which they are often well-placed geographically to control, in support of their grievances or their claims against those who belong to the north.

On the British side, it appears that the threats situated outside Europe are not considered negligible, particularly those resulting from the intrigues of the Soviet Union. The fact remains, however, that Her Majesty's governments, whatever the party in power and in spite of the severe warning of the Falklands affair, have unshakeably pursued the policy adopted at the time of the Defence Review of 1966, when it was decided to withdraw British military forces deployed east of Suez. This stems from the almost absolute priority given to the threat in Europe.

There is, finally, a new category of threat which is also a world-wide phenomenon, and that is terrorism. The French and British have both suffered the effects often enough to appreciate its seriousness and, I believe, to analyse its causes in a fairly similar way. Although it is probably the threat for which European co-operation is most urgently needed, and although the use of military force may sometimes be considered in order to counter it, I mention it here only as a reminder.

*Interests on both sides*

Let us now compare the French and British interests which may be affected by these threats, in what the French refer to as 'the third circle', that is, the one that takes in their overseas territories and the Third World ('out-of-area' in NATO terms). The first circle covers the national sanctuary and the second circle takes in Europe and its surrounding area (the area covered by the Atlantic Alliance).

Let us first of all consider French and British overseas possessions, since the first responsibility of a state is to guarantee the security of the people and property that make up the nation and its heritage. We see that on the British side there is no equivalent to France's 'overseas departments and territories', which give France world status. These, all insular or coastal, are inhabited by 1½ million French citizens, cover a total area of 600,000 square km, have a total of 11 million square km of 'exclusive economic zones' at sea, and finally, with the Mururoa nuclear test centre in French Polynesia and the Kourou space launch centre in French Guyana, play a crucial role for the future credibility of France's deterrent and for the future of Europe in space. As for Great Britain, she has retained overseas very few national possessions: they are Gibraltar, the Falklands, Hong Kong (until 1997), plus a few small scattered islands, which, in the case of those that are of strategic value, have been made available to the United States (Ascension and Diego Garcia). As for the French and British citizens living overseas in foreign countries, to whom we also owe help and protection, they number in both cases approximately 1½ million, half of whom live in Third World countries.

If we move on to the economic interests which are vulnerable to the threats overseas, we see that France depends totally on imports for her oil and coal needs, which is not the case for Great Britain. For the other raw materials essential to their economic and social survival, both countries are in the same situation of total dependence on imports, more often than not from the Third World. Their level of dependence on maritime trade is similar, but, on the French side, a far lower level of this trade is carried under its own flag. The British merchant fleet, while, like the

French, being in rapid decline, still remains far larger in terms of tonnage.

If, after these material interests, we examine the political and cultural interests of the two countries, we see that they have both retained great influence throughout the world, Great Britain particularly through the Commonwealth and more generally through the English-speaking community, which together comprise approximately 1.5 billion inhabitants. The French-speaking world comprises only 300 million people but the links that France maintains with her ex-colonies in Africa and the Indian Ocean are comparatively close, and in these regions they sometimes extend to ex-colonies of Belgium, Portugal, and even Britain. France has agreements with twenty-four of these countries for technical military assistance and with eight others for their defence in the event of aggression, whereas Great Britain's formal commitments concern only two Commonwealth states which have recently attained independence: Brunei and Belize.

There is one important area where France is now probably very different from Great Britain, at least at first sight. This is in the ambition for world influence, an ambition which both countries had shared until now throughout their history, and moreover more often than not as rivals. I personally believe that the British have not abandoned the wish to continue to play a world role, but that they are going to great lengths to express it quite differently from the way they have in the past, namely, through the preservation of the 'special relationship' with the United States and by strengthening the British position in Europe, through the institutions of NATO and the European Community. This is shown in the choice of strategic priorities, which I shall now examine.

### *Respective strategic priorities*

In Great Britain, at least until now, strategic priority was officially given, as in France, to nuclear deterrence. However, as I have stressed above, there is a very great difference between the two countries as regards confidence in this strategy, and also in the status of their respective deterrents — the British system is technologically and strategically integrated into the American system, even though the decision-making freedom of the British government remains total as far as use is concerned. These fundamental differences have considerable psychological and political consequences, since they condition the ways the threat is perceived and therefore the strategic choices. In effect, because of the restrictions on the resources available for defence, the major dilemma with which the two countries are faced, as middle-sized nuclear powers, is that of the relative priority to be given, after providing for deterrence, to a strategy of emphasizing the immediate defence of Europe or alternatively 'of outside deployment', to use the French term — in other words, the priority to be given to a force structure that would enable force to be deployed and, if necessary, used 'out-of-area' (in NATO terms).

Great Britain has given overriding priority to the first alternative: she devotes 95 per cent of her defence budget to NATO and almost all of her armed forces are assigned to it, as successive Statements on the Defence Estimates by the British Government again have underlined. The result in particular is that her maritime forces are planned and trained to participate in protecting the passage of American reinforcements and subsequent logistics to Europe, as well as in supporting the European theatre, particularly its Northern flank. The United Kingdom can therefore give only secondary priority to her military activity outside the NATO area, and this activity is undertaken by drawing upon the forces assigned to NATO, as was the case for the Falklands operation.

The French position is very different since, whilst being conscious of their decisive role in the immediate defence of Europe and contributing significantly to it, the French consider that their external deployment strategy is the logical extension of their deterrence strategy. Like the latter, it is basically a peace-keeping strategy; thus it is not predominantly military. On the contrary, it attaches the greatest importance, sometimes considered by its allies to be exaggerated, to the economic, social, and political aspects of north–south relations. But, whilst giving priority to the non-military aspects of the assistance to be given to the states in the south in order to avert crises, the French consider that it is proper for their external deployment strategy to have a military aspect to retain its credibility. Naturally the use of military force or its demonstration must occur in close, discreet support of diplomacy, so as always to combine determination and negotiation. I will leave aside passive military measures to prevent crises, measures such as technical military assistance and some arms transfers. However, far from all British and French arms sales are concerned with crisis prevention and, what is more, the two countries increasingly often act as rivals for arms sales in the Third World, neglecting their own strategic interests and those of their allies.

As an active measure, it is to the 'pre-positioning' of forces that the French give priority, i.e. to a military presence with all that it implies in terms of being reassuring for friends, pacifying for the unstable, and convincing for the troubled. In this respect they attach a great deal of importance to the presence of maritime forces, when this is possible, because of their legal status, their ability to remain in an area, their quality of discretion, and their flexibility of use.

Whilst giving priority to what one might call 'military diplomacy', France does not rule out the possibility of 'intervention', i.e. the actual use of force to settle a crisis, or at least to bring it to a head. Evidence of this are the twenty or so interventions which have been undertaken in Africa and in the Indian Ocean during the last ten years. However, except when it is a case of defending her overseas territories or rescuing her nationals abroad, French policy has always worked on the principle that military intervention can be envisaged only at the express request of the legitimate government concerned, or else to implement an international consensus. It is then a question of 'interposition' and not 'intervention'.

Great Britain appears to have a far more cautious strategy for external deployment, even though she was drawn, in the case of the Falklands, into a major intervention through not having taken the appropriate precautions by pre-positioning military forces to avert the crisis. At least militarily, she handled this intervention brilliantly.

## Practical problems of Franco-British military co-operation

### *Technical*

Turning to the practical problems posed by co-operation between the two countries in out-of-area deployment, I start by quickly examining the military capabilities which exist to achieve this in the two countries, and their inter-operability.

If we begin with overseas pre-positioning, since the French consider it to be the most effective way of averting crises, we see that France has put this policy of presence into practice far more widely than Great Britain. However, Britain has made an effort in this direction since the Falklands affair and since the negotiations opened with China concerning Hong Kong. She now has about 20,000 men deployed overseas, compared with fewer than 10,000 earlier, whereas France has for a long time had about 30,000. Britain has also increased the out-of-area deployment of warships and the number of overseas exercises, but she has no equivalent to France's permanent maritime forces in the Indian Ocean and the South Pacific.

As far as ground intervention capabilities are concerned, France's are far superior: five light divisions and 47,000 men in the Force d'Action Rapide, whereas on the British side there are only two brigades and approximately 10,000 men, but there is within that an embryo of a joint headquarters. French maritime and air resources which are completely available since they are not assigned to NATO, include fully capable aircraft-carriers, not to mention the additional nuclear-powered aircraft-carrier recently ordered: these have no equivalent on the British side. The Royal Navy is on the other hand better equipped than the French navy with nuclear-powered attack submarines, which can also be very useful in overseas crises as was seen in the Falklands, but France has now begun an effort along the same lines. The amphibious capabilities of the two navies are currently of the same order, with an advantage for the future on the French side where three new large landing craft transporters are planned. The same is true of mobile logistics capabilities, which can be strengthened by using civilian maritime transport resources, as Great Britain demonstrated magnificently in the Falklands war, and as the French have put into practice more modestly in Lebanon. There are, on the other hand, inadequacies on both sides, in the areas of heavy air transport and Awacs (airborne early-warning systems). One can add that there is no problem of inter-operability between the French and British maritime forces, since they use the same tactics, have common codes, and are now compatible in data communication; their inter-operability has moreover been verified in frequent joint exercises. The situation is not so satisfactory for the air and ground forces, whose incompatibility in the area of logistics is well known.

Let us examine finally the area of command, control, communications, and intelligence (C3I), since its role is of the utmost importance in out-of-area deployment. France has a world-wide military communication and command network. This is no longer the case on the British side, which poses a serious problem for co-operation, especially in the maritime field. France now has, like Great Britain, a military telecommunications satellite which covers, it seems, about the same area from the middle of the Atlantic to the middle of the Indian Ocean. Neither France nor Britain yet has a military observation satellite, but Britain appears to have access to information from the American network of satellites, both for observation and possibly for telecommunications. Finally, Great Britain has considerable intelligence resources, particularly in the field of electronic monitoring, and her talents in this area are well known, but it is probable that her 'special relationship' with the United States could hinder Anglo-French co-operation in this area.

It does not seem worthwhile to pursue further this functional analysis of the technical problems that may hinder Franco-British military co-operation outside Europe, before having examined whether there may be particular developments in the world that would make such co-operation desirable or necessary. Such co-operation can be envisaged only if the two countries have common interests to defend in a given geographical area and available military capabilities on both sides to do this.

### *Geographical*

We will therefore examine theatre by theatre where such common interests and military capabilities might lie.

For the Mediterranean, my analysis will concern only the risks of north–south crises, since for east–west crises this region is covered by commitments in the North Atlantic Treaty. France is much involved in this area: she borders on the Mediterranean, and north-west Africa is to France what Mexico is to the United States; moreover, she is historically and culturally linked with several countries in the Near East. Thus it is in the Mediterranean that she has currently concentrated most of her maritime forces, and her metropolitan air forces can intervene there at any time, as can her Force d'Action Rapide. However, for France, possibilities for military co-operation in the settlement of crises in this theatre arise essentially with United States armed forces, particularly the Sixth Fleet, and with those of the other countries bordering the Mediterranean, particularly Italy and Spain. Indeed Great Britain now has a military presence there only in Gibraltar and Cyprus. In Cyprus she is involved in the UN peace-keeping force and also has sovereign base areas agreed by treaty. Possibilities for bilateral military co-operation could however present themselves in the Near East, especially as the policies of the two countries, for a long time rival, now seem to have drawn closer together. Moreover, in peace-keeping missions in Lebanon and in the Red Sea, their forces have been present recently side by side, without formally co-operating with each other.

If we now consider the Middle East and in particular the area around the Gulf, currently the trouble spot *par excellence*, we note divergences in the policies of the two countries towards the Iran–Iraq conflict and increasingly active competition over arms sales to neighbouring countries, such as Saudi Arabia. Divergences and a confrontation of the same order also exist in respect of Pakistan and India, in the neighbouring sub-continent. With regard to all these countries, Great Britain has retained great political and even military influence, but she no longer deploys any forces there, except at sea with the patrol she now maintains in the Straits of Hormuz. France, for her part, has never ceased operating such a patrol, which relies on the permanent presence in the Indian Ocean of a significant air and sea force, which can be reinforced if need be by an aircraft-carrier, attack submarines, and minesweepers, as has happened on several occasions in the past. France also has a military presence in Djibouti, which is the closest western base of operations to the Gulf and which is moreover situated opposite Aden and next to Dahlak, where Soviet air and sea forces are based. France in effect operates an air and ground force that is itself significant on the territory of the Republic of Djibouti, in agreement with its government. Problems of co-operation in security matters in this region arise again in the final analysis with the United States, which has a permanent presence there with a very large air and sea force, and which can quickly redeploy there equally large air and ground forces, under the permanent joint command they have set up.

Further south, Great Britain no longer has a presence at all, except through the sovereignty she has retained over the British Indian Ocean Territory, where Diego Garcia has been put at the disposal of the United States to set up the rear base for its forces. It is therefore France alone that provides the west's political and military presence in the southern part of the Indian Ocean, with her department of La Réunion and her territory of Mayotte. These are situated, together with the 'Scattered Islands', in the area around the Mozambique Channel, i.e. on the route from the Gulf and more generally from Asia to the Cape. Further south again, France also has a presence in the 'Southern Islands' situated on the route from Australia to the Cape.

There are hardly any problems with Franco-British co-operation in security matters which might arise in sub-Saharan Africa, since France again has the only military presence here. In southern Africa, there is the increasingly explosive situation in South Africa and Namibia. The points of view of Britain and France on the political solutions to be applied, do not always converge as is evidenced by their respective attitudes in the matter of sanctions. These came after their differences within the 'Contact Group' and with regard to the 'Front Line' states. However, for the time being, one should note the total military absence of the West in this region, whereas the Soviet Union has a very active presence. The region is of considerable importance to the West, both because of its strategic position on the Cape route, and because it is the only region that can supply us with certain strategic raw materials essential to our high-technology industries. If problems of military co-operation ever were to arise in this area, they could only be multilateral, challenging, and under the leadership of the United States.

Moving on to the South Atlantic, we note that Great Britain is this time the only European power with a permanent military presence, first of all with her base on Ascension Island, which she shares with the United States, and now with the considerable forces, both air/ground and naval, she has installed in the Falklands. Her presence in this region could be of strategic interest in the event of the closure of the Panama Canal, but for the moment it has negative psychological and political consequences, since it is holding up inter-American military co-operation projects in the South Atlantic. Basically, the problems of co-operation in this region arise for Great Britain, and here again in relation to the United States.

If we now look at the region situated further north which is not covered by the Atlantic Pact, i.e. the Caribbean, we see that Great Britain now only possesses very small islands there. Her other former possessions have all attained independence whilst generally remaining members of the Commonwealth — like Grenada, which was the subject of the recent American intervention. Militarily, Great Britain now has a presence in this region only through the deployment of naval forces, generally effected when ships detached to the Falklands are relieved. In addition, she maintains a garrison in Belize, formerly British Honduras and now independent, which considers itself threatened by the ambitions of Guatemala.

France's military presence, on the other hand, remains considerable and her warships put in on numerous occasions to the islands of Martinique and Guadeloupe and the territory of Guyana, all three French departments. Guyana has very great European significance, as I have already noted, with the Kourou space centre. The threat for France in the region stems essentially from incipient internal agitation, which can be put down to a very small minority of the population who want independence, encouraged by neighbouring supporters of Castro. It does not appear that direct or even indirect aggression on the part of Cuba is conceivable, especially as it could not fail to lead to intervention by the United States. It is therefore with the United States, and in practice not at all with Great Britain, that issues of possible co-operation in security matters in the Caribbean region could arise for France.

Before moving on to the Pacific, I will quickly mention South-East Asia. Since her withdrawal from Indo-China, France has abandoned any military presence, if not political activity. Great Britain, on the other hand, still has a presence there, through the garrisons she maintains on the territory of Hong Kong, which will revert to China in 1997, and in the Sultanate of Brunei, formerly British Borneo, now independent, and which considers itself threatened by the ambitions of Indonesia. The problems of co-operation in security matters which arise for Great Britain in this region are therefore temporary and concern for the most part her relations with China and the United States.

France's security problems in the South Pacific do not need to be mentioned at length, since they are much discussed in the media. For the benefit of English readers, let me try nevertheless to summarize the situation as it is generally perceived in France. New Caledonia, which has 140,000 inhabitants, currently all French citizens, has considerable nickel reserves and a vast exclusive economic zone (2 million square km). It played an important strategic role for the United States during the Pacific War. Worrying internal agitation has begun on account of the aboriginal minority in its population. Moreover, its independence is requested more and more insistently, and even demanded, by the states of the South Pacific Forum, most of which are very recently created micro-states but which are led by Australia and New Zealand, two of the oldest members of the British Commonwealth.

Furthermore, the same states, again led by Australia and New Zealand, have embarked upon an increasingly virulent offensive against the underground nuclear tests carried out by France on the Mururoa atoll situated in French Polynesia, an archipelago also with 140,000 inhabitants, all of them also French citizens, whose exclusive economic zone extends over more than 5 million square km and where no internal agitation has developed to date. One can compare the anti-nuclear offensive thus undertaken against France with the more cautious offensive that has been started against the United States, which has resulted in American warships being banned from calling at New Zealand ports and in threats of similar bans by Australia. This has called into question the ANZUS military alliance concluded between the three countries.

It appears from the declarations of Australian and New Zealand leaders that these countries now want France to withdraw from the South Pacific. As France has no intention of acceding to this demand, and there is in this respect national consensus, tension can only continue. French military presence in the region already amounts to about 12,000 men and includes significant naval forces, which can be reinforced if need be, as has been done in the past. The decision has already been taken to improve significantly the capabilities of the operations base at Noumea.

As for Great Britain, she no longer has a presence in the South Pacific, except for the small island of Pitcairn, which has only fifty-four inhabitants. However, one may hope that she might use her influence, which is certainly great, with Australia and New Zealand to get them to show more reserve and objectivity. France's departure from the South Pacific would in effect leave a vacuum that these two countries are totally incapable of filling, but that the Soviet Union, increasingly active in the region, would certainly try to fill. The balance of forces in the Pacific and consequently world peace would therefore gain nothing from France's leaving, nor would regional peace and prosperity or the prosperity and freedom of the populations directly concerned.

## Possible improvements

### *Past attempts*

The need for, and even the possibility of, British co-operation in security matters currently arises only in the Near and Middle East. Everywhere else, the issues of co-operation that face the two countries are rather in their respective relations with the United States. However, there remains for France, as for all the other countries in the Free World, the need to co-ordinate their political strategy outside the area covered by the Atlantic Pact. Although the problem posed by this co-ordination lies not only at the Franco-British level, I will touch on it quickly by glancing first at the past since it helps us to understand the present.

For the threats from the East situated outside Europe, regional defence organizations, concluded (like NATO) under the Atlantic Pact under the aegis of the United States, were first devised at the beginning of the 1950s:

SEATO under the Manilla Treaty for South East Asia and CENTO (or Baghdad Pact) for South West Asia. France and Great Britain were parties to the first, and Great Britain only to the second. However, these defence organizations did not survive the immediate causes that had brought them into being, the disagreements between their members, and the development of the phenomenon of 'non-alignment'. The same was true of the treaty devised for the South Atlantic, again at the initiative of the United States, which never gained real substance, and which seems permanently compromised following the Falklands affair.

From NATO's foundation, the possibility of extending the geographical area covered by the treaty has been considered, particularly for the control and protection of merchant traffic in the South Atlantic and in the Indian Ocean. The negotiations conducted on this subject did not lead to any official conclusions, but they did result in unofficial trilateral arrangements between France, Great Britain, and the United States.

The idea of enlarging NATO's sphere geographically was revived at the end of the 1970s on the initiative of the United States. But it was again rejected by the other members of the Alliance, either through indifference towards threats outside Europe, or through fear of being drawn into conflicts that did not concern them. Moreover, some NATO members do not have appropriate forces, or they refrain from any outside intervention on grounds of principle or law, as is the case with Federal Germany. Faced with the rejection of a geographical extension of the scope of NATO's activities, the United States then recommended a geographical distribution of tasks, with a view to ensuring that the forces it would possibly be called upon to take from Europe to provide a military presence or carry out an intervention overseas, might be replaced in NATO's military forces by appropriate reinforcements supplied by its European allies. However, this suggestion met with no more success.

Another approach to the problem of the west's co-operation in security matters outside Europe was tried in 1958 by General de Gaulle in his famous proposal for a tripartite world 'directorate' of the United States, France, and Great Britain. It did not receive a positive response from the Americans or the British, and the General abandoned it completely when in 1962 Great Britain refused to co-operate with France in the area of nuclear deterrence and adopted the American Polaris missile, thus confirming the priority she gave to her 'special relationship' with the United States.

The idea of a strategic directorate of the Free World was however later revived by the United States' government, at the initiative first of all of Mr Brzezinski at the end of President Carter's mandate, and then by President Reagan himself. It took the form of institutionalizing the economic summit meetings of the seven major industrial powers of the

Free World, and allowing them to discuss security matters. Up to now it has resulted only in a declaration of principle, produced at the Williamsburg summit in 1983, recognizing that the security of the Free World is indivisible.

The same idea had been advanced in 1981, independently and in a personal capacity, by the directors of the four international relations institutes of France, the United States, Great Britain, and Federal Germany, in a joint report which created quite a stir at the time. It too recommended that the summit of the seven should systematically discuss major geopolitical and security matters, but it proposed furthermore that for regions in crisis or potentially dangerous regions a 'monitoring group' be set up made up of the 'main nations' concerned by the problem in question and 'ready to contribute directly towards solving it'. According to the authors of the report, the group should be built around a basic core consisting of the United States, France, Great Britain, West Germany, and Japan, to which any other concerned power could be added.

At the same time, specifically European solutions to the problem of co-operation in security matters were also envisaged, especially for Europe itself but also outside Europe. In 1981, the European Parliament, in a resolution, even invited the countries of the European Community to intensify and co-ordinate their maritime presence in the Indian Ocean. However, it was a pious wish since, for the time being, only the informal meeting of foreign affairs' ministers, in what is called 'European political co-operation', is competent in the areas which come within the province of consultation as regards foreign policy and security policy. The Single European Act on co-operation in foreign policy matters only institutionalizes this practice.

A more European security policy is also being sought at the moment, especially and one might say solely on the French side, in a reactivation of the Western European Union. I do not personally believe that it will succeed, because of the hostility shown towards this solution by the other partners and particularly by Great Britain. One can note, however, that it is valid legally, since the WEU treaty is the only one that formally envisages co-operation in the event of a threat to peace 'wherever it may occur'.

Before leaving these institutional aspects of the west's co-operation outside Europe, I must add that I personally consider such institutionalization pointless and even, in some respects, harmful. It is pointless because, in the final analysis, only the United States, France, and, to a lesser degree, Great Britain have military resources suited to out-of-area actions of a certain scale, and the will to use them. Foreseeable co-operation between allies out-of-area is, when all is said and done, a matter for bilateral or trilateral ad hoc agreements. But I have said that I also consider new treaties on this subject as possibly being harmful, for the reason that they would certainly be rejected by Third World states. Though the latter often wish to be able to call upon France for assistance in the event of a crisis, it is on condition that she remains discreet and that, to achieve this, she stays 'over the horizon' beforehand.

France will thus improvise, and moreover she will exploit a major asset that democracies and therefore the west have, namely diversity and pluralism. From the point of view of effectiveness, we can also note that an institutionalized alignment would deprive France of the tactical alternatives that the diversity of her diplomatic relations with the Third World states gives her, both in the event of the failure of one of her initiatives and for facilitating compromises. I therefore believe that it is far better, for co-operation in security matters outside Europe, to go no further than pragmatic solutions, a discreet but honest partnership, it being understood that the latter implies total solidarity between the partners in the event of a serious test for one of them.

### *Future prospects*

I have justified my scepticism towards institutional solutions for resolving the problem of Franco-British co-operation in security matters. But this scepticism stems especially from the absence of political will shown to date by both sides in this area.

However, to prepare the way for a possible change in the respective policies of the two countries, one can start to build on the exchanges of general staff officers, cadets in training, and even of personnel in the units specializing in out-of-area deployment. These exchanges would lead to very informative contacts. One could also organize high-level general staff consultations or seminars on these matters. One can even take advantage of these circumstances to organize exercises, which would test the inter-operability of the forces and pinpoint the real technical problems that might arise in connection with joint intervention. Finally, on the occasion of exercises or joint presence operations, when the (normally maritime) forces of the two countries are side by side, technical contacts between their commanders can be authorized, even encouraged.

If some sign of political will for possible co-operation begins to show itself on both sides, one can go further in preparing the way for co-ordination, by tackling the technical problems concerning the exchange of intelligence, making communication networks mutually available, and rendering command organizations compatible. One must stress in particular the current need for extensive co-operation, which involves the three prerequisites above, with regard to the sharing of maritime and air space, and in the longer term, perhaps, of outer space.

Another equally important area for co-operation, but which presupposes even more specific political commitment, is that of logistics facilities. Logistics resources themselves, such as heavy transport aircraft and specialized or adapted merchant ships, could even be made mutually available. Finally one can, or rather one must, tackle openly and clearly the problems of co-operation in the fight against terrorism, and in particular against terrorism at sea and in the air, to which France and Britain are very vulnerable.

When the problems of political and military co-operation are tackled at the European level, it is customary to express wishes, or even incantations, that there might be co-operation in arms production. This may seem like black humour at a time when France and Great Britain have recently had a fundamental disagreement over the future European combat aircraft. This split is particularly serious because it has shown not only the differences in strategic ideas, which I have already noted, but also the political rivalry in which the two countries are engaged in Europe.

Franco-British co-operation is however eminently desirable in space matters and in particular for military observation and telecommunications satellites, precisely the sorts of equipment essential for the judicious handling of crises and outside deployment. The same applies to Awacs aircraft.

Finally, there is an area, connected with the previous one, that I believe it important to consider in relation to the future prospects for Franco-British co-operation in security matters outside Europe; it is the area of arms sales, particularly in the Third World. I have already stressed that not only are these arms sales not generally dependent, either in France or in Great Britain, upon strategic considerations, but they increasingly give rise to fierce and ruthless competition between the two countries.

This fierce rivalry has not only commercial, industrial, and social motivations; it is also evidence of a return to the political rivalry between the two countries throughout the world, as has occurred so often and to their mutual detriment throughout their history. In my opinion, it is time to 'cool it', because by continuing at the current level there is a risk of ruining for a long time any hope of co-operation between France and Great Britain, not only outside Europe, but also in Europe where, like it or not, they now have a common destiny.

It would be appropriate therefore, to complete this analysis of the future prospects for Franco-British co-operation outside Europe, to touch upon their common future in a finally united Europe. Here again, incantation is the done thing. If however, by a miracle, this grand design were to take shape one day, I believe that co-operation in security matters outside Europe would no longer pose serious problems. It could be put into practice according to the principle of the distribution of tasks, as regards both the nature of the missions and the region in which they were implemented, and both between Europe and the United States and between the European states themselves. Of course, in this hypothesis, Great Britain would remain free to choose between more defence for Europe and less out-of-area deployment, as at present, or the opposite, depending on the perception she then had of the threat to her own interests. She would also be able to handle carefully and to her liking her 'special relationship' with the United States, since I again personally believe that this will remain a priority in her preoccupations for a long time.

### *Personal conclusions*

To conclude this paper, I would like to add a few purely personal conclusions.

The first is that there is in France a large, permanent consensus on the importance of out-of-area deployment, after of course nuclear deterrence, but as a conceptual extension of it. There is currently no such consensus in Great Britain, and it is even less likely in the event of a change of government.

My second observation is that all of the technical and regional problems posed by possible Franco-British co-operation outside Europe can be solved in practice, and consequently they could all be settled in practice with a minimum of political goodwill.

As a third conclusion, I note that the problems of principle posed to the two countries by co-operation in security matters outside Europe basically concern their respective relations with the United States. Although it is often difficult to co-operate with the United States in this at a political level, because of its often Manichaean vision of relations with the Third World and also the lack of continuity in its government policy, it is generally easy to do so at a technical military level.

My fourth observation returns to what I have already said concerning the pointlessness of institutionalization, or even of too great a formalization of the prospects for triangular co-operation overseas. France will be more effective by remaining diversified and practical, which can only please the British, provided, however, that France shows total solidarity in the event of a serious test.

The fifth and last of my personal conclusions returns, once again, to the need to 'cool it' in Franco-British rivalry in the area of arms sales. There now seems to be very great danger of the situation getting out of control, which could seriously damage Franco-British relations both outside Europe and in Europe itself, possibly for a long time.

Unfortunately, there remains between the French and the British a historical memory that is dangerous because it is marked by suspicion. By fighting each other for centuries, they have become weaker, whereas by fighting side by side on two occasions they saved each other. Now they are 'in the same boat', if you will allow me, a sailor, to use this expression.

For the rest, the French will remain French and the English English, as General de Gaulle would have said. That is to say, the French will remain arrogant and even sometimes 'as insolent as Bonaparte', as a British newspaper has recently recalled, and the British will not cease to be 'practical', which is a great quality as I have stressed, refusing to add, even jokingly, 'treacherous' as they used to say in Napoleon's time.

To conclude this study, I will borrow this typically British humorous remark from an English writer, a talented observer of France: 'The English like to be told that they are absurd, but admirable; the French like to be told that the English are admirable, but absurd.'

Let both sides therefore satisfy this twofold wish. Then let them work together to improve co-operation in security matters between France and Great Britain, since it can only contribute towards maintaining world peace.

Chapter eight

# The prospects for military co-operation outside Europe: a British view

Jonathan Alford

At first sight, Britain and France would seem to share an overall approach to out-of-area issues that, within the Alliance, is a great deal closer to that of the United States than that of almost all other West European states. Both admit that they have substantial security interests beyond the Atlantic area, both accept in principle that safeguarding those interests can on occasions require the use of military force, and both have diverted some of their limited stocks of military resources to that end. This tends to mean that it is not difficult for British and French politicians, officials, and military men to find a common vocabulary when speaking about out-of-area problems. There is at least a minimum of common understanding and even appreciation of what each is trying to do in the Third World to safeguard western interests.

But it would be wrong to conclude that this is going to lead to close co-operation between French and British contingents outside Europe, not least because the opportunities for practical co-operation are likely to be quite limited. In part this is because most residual British and French interests are geographically separate, in part because Britain and France are as often competitors as they are allies (especially in the matter of arms sales), and in part because political calculations as to the consequences of acting in the Third World in particular circumstances are likely often to be quite different. Lastly, it must be said, it is in part because there are political barriers to co-operation over security in the Third World. Even to get the subject onto the political agenda appears to be extraordinarily difficult. It seems to be — like nuclear co-operation — a 'no-go' area for British and French politicians (and more, it would appear, for the French than the British).

## The record so far

If one looks at the record to date of French and British military involvement outside Europe in the post-war period, one has to search hard to find instances of co-operation, whereas the list of unilateral actions by each power is a long one. Moreover, when the need to seek assistance has arisen, Britain and France have more often co-operated — when they have done so — with third parties than with each other, and most often with the United States.

The obvious exception is Suez in 1956, an attempt at Franco-British military co-operation which left scars that took many years to heal, chiefly because the Suez operation was politically divisive within both countries but also because the two countries tended to draw very different conclusions from that ill-starred venture. Britain drew the lesson that there were very large risks in going against the clearly expressed opposition of the United States; Roger Louis has spoken of Suez as the low ebb of the 'special relationship'.[1] France, on the other hand, concluded that it was better whenever possible to maintain total freedom of action in the Third World.

Only one other instance of attempts at military co-operation springs to mind — and that instance arose because of a curious post-colonial anomaly. Britain and France shared reponsibility for the New Hebrides prior to the assumption of independence of this group of Pacific islands as Vanuatu. When a major challenge to law and order arose there in 1975 (and again in 1980) the British and French governments had jointly to consider what response to make. The matter was further complicated by linguistic divisions within the New Hebridean population and differing aspirations between these linguistic groups. While there was in 1980 what could reasonably be described as a 'joint' intervention (French gendarmerie from New Caledonia and 200 British marines), which served more or less to restore law and order pending independence, the episode did not reflect much credit on either Britain or France, who found it extremely difficult to work together either at government level or on the ground. The episode hardly registered on any political scale but it illustrates nevertheless that Anglo-French co-operation in the Third World is sometimes fraught with peculiar difficulties. The *Europa Yearbook 1985* remarks laconically that 'The French would not permit Britain's unilateral use of force on Esperitu Santo.'

Perhaps the chief of these difficulties arises from a fundamental political difference of approach. France has reasons to preserve her position in certain parts of the world (especially in West and Central Africa and in the Pacific region) and will go to some lengths — including the use of military force if necessary — to do so. Britain, on the other hand (and virtually regardless of which political party is in power), is anxious to divest herself of such external responsibilities as remain, providing that this can be achieved with honour and with due regard for the wishes of the people directly concerned. This is not intended as a judgement on the wisdom of policies but rather as a statement of fact. France goes to considerable lengths to maintain a unique relationship with her ex-colonies in Africa, extending now to growing links with other francophone (and even lusophone) states in Africa such as Zaire on the one hand and Angola on the other. In part this relationship is cemented by military links, arms transfers, forces in place, frequent joint exercises, and intervention in the last resort. The establishment of France's Force d'Action Rapide (FAR) (as with its predecessor, the Force d'Intervention) is justified partly on the basis that France must be capable of coming to the aid of African friends threatened by external (and, less often stated, internal) enemies. France sees this web of dependency and influence as in some way bolstering her self-image, as defining her global status.

In the Pacific region, France's position is closely linked to her nuclear test programme and Mururoa atoll, which is seen as vital to French continuance as an independent nuclear power. 'Mururoa est déjà depuis longtemps une des clés de la crédibilité de notre dissuasion,' according to Admiral Yves Leenhardt, Naval Chief of Staff.[2] While authoritative statements are hard to find, there is a strong suspicion that France will go to considerable lengths (as in New Caledonia) to prevent the growth of independence movements that would take any French colonies away from French control for fear that such a general tendency would snowball, deprive France of privileged access to important minerals, and generally undermine France's position in the region.

Britain, on the other hand, appears to be doing all that she can to divest herself of responsibility for the security of the remnants of empire, sometimes with what some would regard as indecent haste. There is very little sense anywhere in London that Britain should retain garrisons abroad for strategic purposes, with the possible exception of the sovereign base areas (SBAs) in Cyprus, which serve several general purposes (intelligence gathering, logistic support for peacekeeping, and staging). Plans have been laid for a transfer of sovereignty in Hong Kong; the garrison in Belize remains only at the urging of the Belizean government (and, latterly, the US) because of the Guatemalan claim and not because Britain has any particular desire to retain influence there; if either the Gibraltarians or the Falkland Islanders could be persuaded to go with Spain or Argentina respectively, Britain would shed few tears. In short, these remnants of empire are generally seen as an embarrassment rather than as important assets to be retained by force if need be.

It follows that not only are these residual interests geographically rather far apart but the attitudes of the two metropolitan governments towards their responsibilities are quite different. That seems a rather poor basis on which to build Franco-British co-operation in the Third World.

Futhermore, as noted earlier, in some respects Britain and France are in direct competition outside Europe. That is particularly the case in arms sales and particularly evident in such countries as India or regions such as the Gulf where there are no 'natural' or privileged markets and where arms contracts have to be worked for. Such competition is to be expected between major arms exporters and it is not necessarily unhealthy, but it has to be recognized as one factor militating against Franco-British co-operation outside Europe. The French are seldom less than explicit about the connection between military assistance and arms sales. The British tend to be less forthright, but a careful reading of government statements can discover a close link. For example, the British Defence White Paper of 1981 states:

> The British Armed Forces have a history of close contact with the forces of a number of countries, both within and outside the Commonwealth, which leaves us well placed to help in their training and development . . . Decisions . . . must take account of . . . whether . . . their armed forces use British equipment . . . Provision of British defence equipment can help to build up the self-defence capability of states which may have little or no manufacturing capacity of their own.[3]

## A possible agenda for co-operation

Language and historical connections will largely determine the patterns of co-operation in the Third World, but this does not prevent both countries from attempting to establish privileged positions in new areas and in new potential markets. While it is perhaps desirable in principle that Britain and France should co-operate in determining in advance who should operate where, in practice it seems most unlikely that this will happen.

Yet, although the arguments as to why Britain and France are unlikely to co-operate positively in the Third World seem quite persuasive, the fact remains that these two countries do share certain instincts which might lead them to take rather similar positions with regard to certain Third World developments and even under some circumstances to work together. At its most basic, this instinct could be formulated as a belief that military power does have some utility in securing or extending western interests in the Third World. Both countries, together with Italy and the US, contributed to the multinational peace-keeping force in Lebanon in 1982–3; both countries contribute to UN peace-keeping forces — Britain especially in Cyprus, France to United Nations International Force in the Lebanon (UNIFIL); both retain some capacity to deploy forces outside NATO; both accept that maritime power can — and should — protect western maritime interests, most recently with respect to possible interference with shipping in and around the Straits of Hormuz and in the Red Sea.

While stopping well short of integrating their forces with those of the United States, both have shown themselves prepared quietly to co-operate with the US. Britain, after all, facilitates American power projection very substantially by making Diego Garcia available to the US. France certainly co-ordinates its naval deployments in the Indian Ocean with the US. All three maintain a naval presence in troubled waters which, while not under unified command, presumes at least a minimum of joint communication and co-operation at the operational level. Although not without some acrimony, France and the US combined in Chad to frustrate Colonel Gaddafi. In the Shaba interventions in Zaire, the United States facilitated French (and Belgian) deployment with airlift. Again perhaps belatedly, the US provided substantial support to the UK in the South Atlantic in 1982.

In short, Britain, France, and the US are quite likely to end up on the same side of the argument. This is not to say that the US will always support British or French military actions out-of-area or that Britain and France will always back the US (witness British pique over Grenada and the French withdrawal from the UN Contact Group attempting to solve the Namibia issue) but, in the debates within the Western Alliance which relate to the diversion of American resources from NATO to Third World contingencies, Britain and France are likely to show more sympathy with the American position than are most other European governments.

## Flexibility

In a sense this is an argument about flexibility and the need to build a degree of flexibility into at least some western military structures. Much of NATO's planning tends in the direction of excessive rigidity and most Western European states like it that way because it tends also to ensure that forces must stay where they are or proceed only in the one direction that is planned for them; alone among the western allies, Britain, France, and the US reject such total rigidity and argue that there may be a need to provide some forces for unforeseen contingencies in the Third World.

Flexibility in a military sense is not, of course, cost free. Indeed it can turn out to be a very expensive attribute and that is why even British, French, and American flexibility of deployment is in practice quite limited — but some there is. Transport to facilitate rapid deployment is particularly expensive; so too is an airborne intervention capability; and so too are the communications needed for global coverage. The training and exercising out-of-area, essential if an intervention is to retain any credibility, are likewise costly. In the worst case, equipment may have to be purchased especially for this purpose which is unsuited for a conflict in Europe. Anecdotally, one might cite the case of the 'air portable spanner' which, when made in common steel, cost £2 but which, when made in light alloy to reduce weight for air portability, cost £35 (as long ago as 1975). This may be an extreme case but the point remains relevant to force planning and procurement decisions. True flexibility costs money and no one can nowadays afford much of it. As an added political point, France and Britain's European allies will tend to view too much flexibility with alarm, sensing that the US, Britain, or France may be losing interest in continental security in favour of global assertiveness or a maritime strategy, although, to be fair, there are some gains to the Alliance from the experience gained out-of-area — especially in terms of air mobility and air-to-air refuelling. Lastly, true flexibility is the attribute only of highly professional forces and probably beyond the reach of all but long-service troops, for the demands of intervention in the Third World are not at all the same as the demands of a European war. To retain the skills for both at the same time requires extensive and intensive training; time will simply not allow such training to be given to any but those on long engagements operating within a stable military structure. Britain's recent experience in combat in the South Atlantic stands as testimony to that assertion. By no means all of the forces deployed acquitted themselves well, despite the fact that all were professional. This is not intended to denigrate the courage and determination of any, but simply to state that some were not ready for action because this action was not foreseen. Some were neither fit nor prepared for combat in that distant and unusual theatre. Indeed, some were not expected to have to fight, only to garrison a reconquered territory.

This underlines a necessity well understood by those who have experienced action in distant and unusual places — the necessity for acclimatization. European man, accustomed to temperate climates and forgiving terrain, does not translate easily to desert, jungle, altitude, or extreme cold. Experience shows that he can do so and, with time, he can become extremely effective, but the time for adjustment can be considerable. We ought not to believe that servicemen can be transported rapidly to a hostile environment and be expected at once to operate at anything like optimal efficiency. That too places limits on flexibility.

## Anglo-French co-operation

What then might France and Britain in practice do to achieve a somewhat greater degree of co-operation in their out-of-area activities? What concrete steps could be taken now to make their actions more effective?

A modest ambition is to ensure that, at the least, they do not get in each other's way. In many cases of possible involvement in the affairs of the Third World, geography will ensure that they do not, but there are imaginable cases where both might wish to become involved. In such cases active political consultation will be called for both on a bilateral basis and, because the friends and allies of both may have an interest in what is intended, they should be prepared to relay their intentions to a wider forum, presumably the NATO political authorities. This would not breach NATO's self-imposed geographical boundaries because it is not intended that NATO should act, only that NATO authorities should be informed of the actions contemplated. Both France and Britain clearly reserve the right to act in pursuance of their interests outside the NATO area, as does the United States, but it would be wrong — in today's interdependent world — to deny the rights of allies to be informed of actions which might also affect their interests. Moreover, both France and Britain might well find it to their advantage to secure the political support of allies prior to some intervention in the Third World, especially if the issue is likely to be brought before the UN Security Council or General Assembly.

Second, it is my impression that experience is not often shared between the armed forces of the two countries. There could be everything in favour of confidential seminars between staffs and operational commanders. Surely there is much that each can learn from the other, as much from exercises as from operations. Both will produce lessons (of a positive as well as of a negative sort) that could usefully be shared in confidence and not in public.

Third, there could be times when either would welcome specific assistance from the other. This could well be in the area of communications if there are particular difficulties in establishing communication channels for the control of operations. It could also occur in the provision of base facilities or transit arrangements. While the world-wide network of military air routes that once existed for both countries has been considerably reduced, it is still not negligible. Given that loads carried by transport aircraft can be considerably increased by more frequent fuelling stops, the offer of transit facilities (in, for example, Cyprus or Ascension Island or Diego Garcia or Djibouti) could greatly ease the difficulties of getting quickly to awkward places (it is worth recalling that France found the Cyprus SBAs invaluable during the Lebanon crisis of 1982–3). There is a strong case for some mutual discussion of the range of contingency plans that both Britain and France undoubtedly maintain in order to see whether some might be made easier to implement through this kind of co-operation. Realistically neither should seek commitment, only that such possibilities could be identified in advance and explored. I do not know that this is not already being done; however I judge it to be unlikely, based upon my own experience with British contingency planning. I see no harm and some good in sharing concerns of this kind.

Fourth, there might be cases where intelligence could usefully be shared. This is obviously an area of great sensitivity, but it is again at least imaginable that either might gain or have in their possession intelligence useful to the other. Indeed we have on record one case where France was of great assistance to Britain with regard to technical intelligence during the Falklands war and one can quite easily imagine similar cases arising in future. It is to be hoped that intelligence is not so jealously guarded that it cannot be shared with an ally.

Fifth, and at least as promising as any of these, one might hope for some improvement in co-operation at sea. It is generally the case that maritime operations are those least burdened with political baggage, less in the public eye, and so least contentious of all types of military co-operation. At the same time, it is at sea that British and French interests might be assumed often to run in the same direction — usually to assure unimpeded transit of international waters.

It is as well to admit at the outset that more of this may go on than we know about but, if that were the case, one can see no obvious reason to conceal it. Therefore I suspect that it happens only rarely if at all. A search of the last six British defence White Papers reveals no reference at all to joint Anglo-French naval exercises (in the Indian Ocean alone, joint exercises have involved the Royal Navy exercising with the US fleet, the Omani Navy, and the Australians). There is a single reference to the mine-clearing operation in the Gulf of Suez in 1984 where five navies, including the British and French, sent mine-clearing units to assist the Egyptians, but it is notable that in this case France elected not to work through the co-ordinating committee that the British and Americans set up with the Egyptians, preferring instead to act bilaterally with Egypt. That would seem to be carrying to extremes the desire to be independent.

It would be interesting to know, for example, whether the Royal Navy has even considered asking the French whether the small group of vessels on patrol close to the Straits of Hormuz (one destroyer, one frigate, and one Royal Fleet Auxiliary (RFA)) could use Djibouti as a forward operating base or even for a 'run ashore'. Logically one might suppose that Britain could dispense entirely with the RFA if Djibouti were available for routine resupply. It has, after all, probably the best-equipped dockyard on the western shore of the Indian Ocean and a good airfield.

The chief point is that naval co-operation is unlikely to be very effective in operations if it has not been exercised. There are a great many procedural differences and language barriers to be overcome and without regular practice it is hard to imagine that Britain and France *could* work together at sea to some common purpose.

It would be comforting to be told, for example, that Britain and French naval units on station in the Indian Ocean have instituted regular joint exercises. It may be happening, but we are, for whatever reason, denied official knowledge of it. Again the point is that one can take the *ad hoc* approach to contingency planning too far. Given that there are several imaginable circumstances in which both countries would very likely wish to act to keep open maritime routes (e.g. the Straits of Hormuz, the Bab-el-Mandab Straits, the Red Sea and even the Mozambique Channel — to name only four Indian Ocean choke points), the confidence that this could be done effectively would be a great deal higher if it had been thought about. Without wishing unduly to labour the issue, common sense would suggest that, at the least, co-operating navies need to think about communication, procedures, control of strike aircraft (including IFF — Identification Friend or Foe), control of helicopter flying, anti-submarine warfare tactics, and emergency resupply at sea. More specialized operations, such as mine clearance, require rather detailed technical and procedural discussion.

None of this can happen without political authorization, but there seems no obvious reason why this should not be given. It is the kind of prudent contingency planning that ought to be taking place. Beyond that, Britain has retained privileged access to some Third World states, particularly in the context of the Indian Ocean with Oman, the Gulf Emirates, and to a lesser extent Kenya. France most obviously has the same kind of relationship with Djibouti, Réunion and Mayotte. Each could therefore use its good offices to facilitate a degree of joint maritime co-operation with littoral states in the Indian Ocean region. This would be particularly the case with Oman, given its vital interest in policing the Straits of Hormuz and its apparent willingness to promote general western interests in the region.

Finally — and very speculatively indeed — there could well be some parts of the world where military assistance could be co-ordinated. Generally the patterns are well established and this very important function neither permits nor demands co-operation between Britain and France, but it is at least imaginable that countries exist in the Third World which could benefit from a joint approach that offers to provide military assistance. One such is the Federation of Senegambia where Britain has traditional links with the former Gambia and France with Senegal. Any serious attempt to integrate the security forces of the two ought, on the face of it, to involve Britain and France working together. Not all of Africa falls neatly into francophone and anglophone countries and a carefully co-ordinated offer to provide training assistance to those who, for whatever reason, desire to turn neither to the US nor to the eastern bloc could provide a balanced alternative.

## Conclusion

It should at once be admitted that this is indeed a modest agenda. Britain and France are not about to form a joint rapid deployment force for Third World intervention. That would make very little sense, given the disparate nature of their out-of-area interests and commitments. Nor, for political reasons, is either likely to sign up for the US Rapid Deployment Joint Task Force (RDJTF), although one can imagine circumstances where some bilateral co-operation might occur.

Yet rather more quiet co-operation could usefully take place than seems now to be the case. Quite why it does not remains unclear. It may well be that the historic sense of rivalry between Britain and France, especially in the Third World, infects the relationship. There does not seem to be political endorsement to such co-operation, for it may seem to imply a greater degree of collaboration than either would wish publicly to acknowledge. This may be taking the desire to maintain freedom of action in the Third World too far.

In what has been suggested here, I do not intend to imply any commitment to future co-operative action, but my views are distinctively coloured by the belief derived from experience that co-operative action will prove impossible, even where it is seen to be desirable, if some thought has not been given to it beforehand. In a military sense, co-operation is not easy: it takes longer to bring off effectively than most people imagine; and it requires some practice. If there are circumstances — and I suggest that they can be imagined — where Britain and France find convergence in their interests and can reach agreement as to the military actions that it is appropriate to take, it would be better to have thought about the matter beforehand. Admiral Leenhardt would seem to agree. In the article quoted earlier he said also 'En dehors des zones géographiques de l'Alliance, la coopération avec nos amis restera indispensable . . . les contacts qui permettent *dès avant la crise*, de préparer cette coopération sont particulièrement bénéfiques *et doivent donc être encouragés*' (emphasis added).[4]

In his evidence to the House of Commons Defence Committee on 8 May 1985, the then secretary of state, Michael Heseltine, stated in answer to a question put to him by the Committee:

> I think it would be quite wrong for major powers such as ourselves — not superpowers but major powers, for all that — to see no role for themselves on a world stage. That is not to say that you can have an orchestrated policy of working automatically with your allies. You cannot get that, it is not real. There is no way in which the Americans, or ourselves, or our European allies, are going to say in advance that they will co-operate in certain fields; they will not do it. However, there are countries of world significance, of a general good-neighbourly disposition, who will see if there is anything they can do to help and try to work together.[5]

It will be interesting to see what comes of a political attitude to co-operation with allies out-of-area as apparently sensible and forthcoming as that expressed in this statement. It defines what is essentially (and, in my view, correctly) an *ad hoc* approach incorporating a high degree of (typically British) pragmatism. The dangers of such an approach are hidden in the language. Unless something rather concrete now takes place in terms of staff talks, shared intelligence, joint exercising, and procedural accommodation, Anglo-French co-operation out-of-area will be practically impossible. *Ad hoc* can all too easily be used as an excuse for inaction.

## Notes

1. *International Affairs*, 61 (3), Summer 1985, p. 416.
2. 'Reflexions pour une stratégie navale d'avenir', *Défense nationale*, August/September 1985, p. 13.
3. Cmnd 8212, para. 405.
4. *Défense nationale*, August/September 1985, p. 26.
5. Third Report from the House of Commons Defence Committee, Session 1984–85, vol. III: *The Defence Estimates, 1985–86* (London: HMSO), p. 52, col. 1.

Chapter nine

# Defence costs and budgeting in France

Jacques Fontanel

Defence costs have always been the subject of considerable theoretical and political debate. However, since the mid-1970s, apart from a few fringe movements, the French political parties have not basically questioned the strategy of deterrence, or the nature of the defence expenditure proposed by successive governments. Of course, there remain some disagreements about the implementation of military planning, the evolution of the military expenditure/Gross Domestic Product ratio, and the distribution of the sums committed between the various types of weapons. The military plan put forward in 1987 by the President of the Republic and the Chirac government seems, at least on the face of it, to satisfy everyone, in spite of the inevitable arguments about detail that crop up here and there to mark differences or reopen doctrinal disputes. Within the space of a decade, defence has ceased to be a subject of discord.

Does this mean then that the general public accepts the expenditure that the current strategy implies, that there are no problems with costs or the apportionment of defence spending, that no cloud of discord lies over future options? The answers to these questions have to be heavily qualified. To understand the importance of costs and budgets in the actual implementation of a country's strategy, it is sufficient to recall that no French long-term defence programme[1] has ever been fully implemented. Moreover, with the new technological challenges in the military sector, fundamental choices are going to have to be made which may well, in the next five years, shatter the strategic certainties and political consensus on the defence of France.

The basic question for a democracy is to know what financial burden the nation is prepared to accept for what defence. It is fundamental in particular to consider defence costs since, for a given budget level, they have a direct effect on the choices made by the General Staff in defining the optimum methods of defence. There is in practice constant interaction between costs and budget, but, alongside the irreducible expenditure necessary to provide a minimum level of defence, there are numerous choices that are heavily dependent on the economic constraints of the costs of existing hardware or of hardware to be ordered for the future. Costs are both initial constraints in the determination of the military strength to be established bearing in mind the available budget, and factors that govern choices, when the desired level of security cannot be fully provided by the government. There is thus constant interaction between costs and the budget, but costs are first of all fundamental constraints on the budget. I will therefore first of all analyse costs, then the budget.

## Costs

There are two main types of costs: operating costs and capital costs. However, economists also like to reason in terms of opportunity costs, i.e. the real cost of choosing military expenditure to the detriment of other possible forms of expenditure (social expenditure, investment, etc).

### *Operating costs*

Operating costs consist of personnel costs and current expenditure (purchase of office equipment, travel costs, repairs to weapons, maintenance of installations, etc.). Current expenditure is controlled by the same rules as the state's corresponding civil expenditure. Studying them specifically is therefore of no particular interest. On the other hand, it is interesting to analyse personnel costs, because of the existence of conscription and because of the different value each country puts on military service, both socially and economically.

*Conscription* Conscription poses a two-fold problem: the determination, on the one hand, of its real cost and, on the other, its military effectiveness.

In 1981, a General Staff report estimated the respective annual costs of a conscript and an enlisted man to be 21,849 francs and 43,200 francs.[2] It would therefore have cost the state budget almost 7,000 million francs more to make the French army a professional one. This estimate is, however, not entirely satisfactory for at least two reasons:

(1) conscripts are not immediately as effective militarily as volunteers; and
(2) it is probable that the choice between personnel expenditure and capital expenditure would be modified if the army were made a professional army.

Thus, France's new military planning law has to face an overall reduction in the army's manpower, while, for political reasons, the number of conscripts is not to be reduced significantly, as André Giraud, the former defence minister, reminded us.[3] Under these conditions, the indirect cost of conscription is considerable, assuming that it prevents the development of modern forms of defence.

International comparisons of military expenditure suffer from the heterogeneity of personnel situations. How conscription should be handled was the subject of a discussion paper by the United Nations' Group of Experts on the Reduction of Military Expenditure.[4] It envisaged several solutions: (1) to consider that conscription was a very special form of military expenditure, the conscript fulfilling a function that could not be compared with that of enlisted soldiers; (2) to interpret the military role of the conscript as being equivalent to that of the enlisted soldier; (3) to say that the true cost of a conscript lies in his opportunity cost. An intermediate solution was adopted: conscripts with six months' service were classed as voluntarily enlisted soldiers, whereas conscripts with less than six months' service were considered as trainees. Under these conditions, it is possible to compare the actual military expenditure of different states. Indeed, it is sufficient to calculate the number of conscripts likely to be classed as professional soldiers and to substitute their actual budget cost for the corresponding cost of voluntarily enlisted men, at equivalent grades. This is a legitimate calculation, since military expenditure would be higher in the absence of conscription, other things being equal. From an economic point of view, conscription is generally analysed as a tax which the state makes each conscript pay; this tax is equal to the difference between the sum that the conscript would have earned as a professional serviceman and his total budget cost. Under these conditions, France's military expenditure should be increased by 5,000 million francs, i.e. a little over 3 per cent of the military budget, for it to be comparable to the military budget of an army of voluntarily enlisted men. It must however be remembered that, in the absence of conscription, the pattern of expenditure would be different and the forces would be both reduced and distributed very differently among the armed services. Moreover, it should be noted that there are almost three times more civilian personnel employed at the British Ministry of Defence than at the French, and that they are better paid (20 per cent more on average in 1981). The reasons for these differences can be found in conscription, which provides France with low-paid staff who act as substitutes for expensive civilian employees, and in a difference in evaluation of the civilian jobs available in the two countries.

*Voluntarily enlisted men* In two recent studies,[5] it was shown that regular servicemen in France were generally less well paid than most of their counterparts in the developed western countries, except for Italy. If one uses the exchange rates determined by the International

Monetary Fund, a French colonel earned respectively 3 per cent and 15 per cent less than his British and American counterparts (2 per cent and 14 per cent in the case of captains). It should be noted that armies that have conscription tend to have lower pay for their regular servicemen, as if National Service reduced the pressures on the employment market in the military sector. However, the salaries mentioned above do not concern the categories affected by conscription. Jacques Aben and Ron Smith indicate that in 1981 a British serviceman cost on average 90,200 francs whereas his French counterpart cost 71,000 francs at the most. Moreover, the high salaries paid to British servicemen are apparently confirmed by the study carried out by the United Nations' Group of Experts on the Reduction of Military Expenditure.[6] From an economic point of view, two explanations could be given for this: either British colonels have a higher productivity than their French counterparts (which is very difficult to prove), or there are imperfections in the market for servicemen (which is indeed the case, bearing in mind the particular arrangements for service pay in the two countries and especially the impossibility of a Frenchman being an English colonel and vice versa). The notions of military effectiveness and economic effectiveness are of a different nature, which makes it very difficult to produce a comparison of the military strength of different states just based on estimates of defence expenditure.

### *The cost of arms*

France has a powerful arms industry; it is generally considered to be highly competitive on international markets, as export sales show. The organization of arms production in France is very centralized and the costs of hardware seem competitive, in spite of sometimes archaic management and a policy of systematic protectionism.

*Organization of arms production* Not only is the state the only customer of the armaments industry on the domestic market, it also controls exports. The armaments market is in the first place a monopsony (characterized by the existence of a single buyer). In addition, competition between arms firms tends to become eroded by the action of the Délégation Générale pour l'Armement (DGA). Through the awards of study contracts and the supervision of major programmes, the DGA has promoted the existence of 'bilateral monopolies', i.e. the presence, in each market, of a single buyer and a highly specialized single seller. In fact, the competition between arms firms has moved away from simple competition for the sale of a product to competition for research contracts or programmes for arms that complement or replace other arms. The DGA[7] finances the development of hardware and guarantees a market, especially as it exerts a definite influence on the nature of the requirements defined by the General Staffs and on the sale of military hardware abroad, which it controls through the Direction des Affaires Internationales. In fact, the existence of the DGA very often eliminates the contractor's risk and it is rare for the latter to commit himself to a programme without having received prior financing from the state. However, the government's own armaments factories are in latent crisis and they criticize the state for a policy that favours private companies, which reduces their own market correspondingly.

For the time being, the status quo seems to be accepted, but in a crisis situation, if conventional arms sales were to fall, the situation could well undergo further changes in the years to come. Specifically, change is possible with regard to the status of the workers classed as civil servants in public establishments, procedures for the award of military contracts, the restructuring of the naval shipyards, and the automatic balancing through the defence budget of the operations of the Direction des Armements Terrestres (DAT) and of its establishments.[8]

*Price formation* The prices of military hardware do not therefore reflect the influence of a competitive market and they very often relate to a project under development rather than an immediately available product. There are two main situations: controlled expenditure contracts where the price is determined retrospectively on the basis of the accounting cost plus a profit margin, and fixed-price contracts in which the prices are fixed at the outset.[9] The first form of contract is more common when the sums involved are considerable and uncertain. This method of fixing contracts shows the secondary place of price in the decision to buy. Moreover, it is not uncommon for fixed-price contracts to undergo significant price changes, either because the customer wants the initial project to be modified or because of an unforeseeable factor which calls into question the continuation of the project. The DGA has set up a body of price auditors, the practical usefulness of which has sometimes been questioned.[10]

Since it is costs which, controlled retrospectively, fix the price, performance criteria mainly depend on the efficiency of the industrial sectors close to the armaments industry. There have been numerous cases in France where costs have overshot forecasts but they have not often been the subject of public debate. It must be said that military secrecy is more developed in France than in the Scandinavian or Anglo-Saxon countries. Arms firms are for the most part nationalized, they have in their own production sector a high degree of monopoly, and they are dependent on a price formation system that reduces risks but also reduces the dynamism necessary for enterprise. Costs do get out of control, but such cases are not affected either by direct competition or by the desire to obtain the government contract at all costs. They are due to cumbersome bureaucratic management, sometimes looking to prolong a contract at an additional level of activity during a period of economic recession, to research or technological difficulties which are partly the state's responsibility, to the modification of the project during its execution, or to the risks inherent in any industrial activity. Normally, military products tend to have high costs because of the importance of the research and development element, which is about 30 per cent of the cost of military aeronautical products, compared with 4 per cent of the cost of a car, because of poor economies of scale (doubling the sales of an aircraft would reduce its cost by only 10 per cent on average, which is certainly less than the economies likely to be achieved by strict management of the project), and because of the specific nature of arms production equipment.

*Trends in equipment costs* In fact, in the case of two similar pieces of epuipment, the more sophisticated (and also the more expensive) piece is always chosen; sometimes, the purchase itself is deferred in order to meet simultaneous technological and budget constraints. This behaviour certainly does not lead to the definition, for a known budget level, of optimum security choices; in effect, over-bidding on technology certainly occurs, which promotes the development of inflationary pressures. The marginal costs of research and of technology would therefore seem to be very high for limited military effectiveness. In other words, it would be preferable to eliminate these costly improvements in order to increase the amount of equipment available and, on the whole, to improve security. The question of the choice and characteristics of equipment should be clearly put, since there are obviously budget constraints.

Is equipment chosen on the basis of lowest cost or under conditions comparable to those that prevail outside France? It does seem that the continual increase in prices is a modern feature of military equipment. The studies which have been carried out on this subject have indicated real rates of growth of prices of 8 per cent and 5 per cent per annum.[11] Military aircraft experience very considerable cost increases, as do fighting ships, and, to a lesser extent, tanks.[12] It should be noted, however, that it is very difficult to compare the prices of arms of different generations.[13] These figures are moreover only significant as illustrations, since, in military conflicts, an unsuitable weapon is an obsolete weapon with a low degree of effectiveness. Under these conditions, even if the price of an aircraft has increased five-fold in five years, if this aircraft is capable of destroying more than five aircraft of the previous generation, its effectiveness is undoubted. The key question is whether the General Staffs are over-concerned with the technology and so, anxious to have the best aircraft, end up unwittingly reducing the country's defence capability by reducing the amount of equipment available, by renewing the equipment less often, or by drastically reducing operating costs.

Compared with other countries, France does not seem to have high production costs. In particular, French military R & D costs seem far lower than those in the United States, Italy, or the United Kingdom.[14] Moreover, an armaments industry that exports is normally capable of supplying products at satisfactory prices for its own domestic market, provided it does not allow itself to be tempted by dumping or by selling at a price between the fixed cost of each unit sold and the total cost of the equipment. Conversely, the foreign buyer sometimes pays for part of the research expenditure, particularly when the product concerned is much in demand, when the arms market is not too saturated by competitive tenders, or when the export contract is awarded even before the product concerned has been developed.

*Imports or national production?* France imports few arms: about 1 per cent of the equipment bought each year according to the US Arms Control and Disarmament Agency's (USACDA) estimate. However, these figures are misleading because they do not take into account equipment manufactured collaboratively, or arms manufactured under licence, or imported components necessary for the manufacture or assembly of arms. In fact, much of France's production is dependent on imports. 'For every 1,000 million francs' worth of armaments exported, induced imports amount to more than 300 million.'[15]

The question is whether national arms production is still justified. Several economic arguments are generally put forward: the importance of military research is fundamental to the competitiveness of national R & D; national industries need military orders in high-technology sectors (like computers or aeronautics); imports are subject to price fluctuations stemming in particular from erratic exchange rate variations (at a time when the value of the dollar was continually increasing, Sweden had to increase her defence budget to satisfy her military planning); national production saves on foreign currency and improves the balance of payments; and the arms manufactured exactly meet the nation's defence requirements.

These arguments are difficult to evaluate from a strictly economic point of view, especially since the French industry has definite handicaps – like the limited domestic market which leads it to look for outside outlets on which it becomes dependent; the inadequate productivity of the space and aeronautics industry compared with the American space and aeronautics industry;[16] and the dispersion of industrial efforts in all types of arms. If the domestic market is not adequate in a depressed market, the risks of selling at a loss abroad and of paying the research and development costs and part of fixed costs for one's customers are considerable; in this case, it is the desire for independence and security that leads to the additional costs. Some exports impoverish a country. It is not obvious that, over the long term, France's arms exports do not come into this category.[17]

Arms sales abroad are only a very imperfect indicator of the competitiveness of the arms industry, since closely related political, economic, and industrial factors do not give comparable analyses of the costs and advantages of the various situations. It is therefore difficult to conclude that the arms industry is a prerequisite for France's economic development or even that it is essential to her immediate security. Indeed, if the prices prevailing in the national economy are significantly higher than those of international competitors, the army will receive fewer arms for the same amount spent. This is the choice that has been made, for example, by Sweden in her aircraft construction activities. Under these conditions, the country's defence is less well provided for, in the short term, by national production than by imports. However, all aspects of security and industrial development must be taken into consideration, such as embargos, national independence, the development of the national industrial fabric, etc. It is probable however 'that we could not finance on our own electronic warfare weapons and space defence systems'.[18]

National economic self-sufficiency and independence in arms is a policy which can prove both expensive and dangerous. That is why, for cost reasons, it will be necessary for France to call for co-operation or specialization with her European partners, unless she wishes to increase her defence spending to achieve the same level of security, with the consequential risk of burdening the national economy with inadequate industrial productivity which, in the long term, would reduce growth opportunities and national security. Good defence is never built, in a democratic country, on an economy in crisis or in recession. The Délégation Générale pour l'Armement is directing France's military policy towards the twin goals of independence and solidarity. Independence implies autonomy as regards decision-making, in spite of the great complexity of current weapons systems; it is therefore striving to harness national energies and skills with a view to providing the foundations of its defence from the nation's own resources. Solidarity implies that once a large measure of autonomy as regards decision-making has been obtained, France is required to collaborate with her allies, at least in the design and introduction of new weapons. Under these conditions, the decision to develop an arms industry primarily satisfies the requirements for national independence. The economic aspect sets the limits of industrial activity, in order best to control the investments committed and also to involve the arms firms and sectors in the modernization and industrialization of France.

### *Opportunity costs*

There are few studies on the opportunity costs of France's military expenditure. The United Nations' Group of Experts on the Reduction of Military Expenditure asked states to estimate the opportunity costs of conscription. France gave no reply on this point. Generally speaking, studies in terms of opportunity costs test the influence of military expenditure on the economy and consider, other things being equal, the strictly economic impact of other forms of expenditure.

Several highly aggregated economic models have tried to show the opportunity costs of military expenditure in the French economy.

In a six-equation model,[19] we have shown how little economic growth depends, in the short term, on a variation in military expenditure, which however can be seen as a substitute for investment and therefore a factor that reduces private consumption (a modern resurrection of the famous dilemma of guns and butter). As public expenditure, military expenditure exerts a positive influence in the fight against unemployment, but its effect is, with the appropriate time-lags, negative overall. Finally, it improves the foreign trade surplus, whilst having a very small direct influence on inflation.

In a three-equation model,[20] the highly negative effects of military expenditure on investment and the poor job-creation performance of the types of military expenditure undertaken since 1960 have been shown for the economies of France and the United Kingdom.

Using a theoretical model, Percebois[21] tested four hypotheses on the direct effect of military expenditure: (1) on productive investment via a 'crowding-out effect' (negative effect), (2) on inflation (positive, indirect effect), (3) on economic growth (negative effect), and (4) on the foreign trade surplus (positive effect because of arms exports). The first hypothesis was econometrically validated, as was the fourth. However, the other two hypotheses were not proved, given the small general impact of military expenditure on economic growth and on inflation, in view of its great stability.

Finally the use of an input–output table enabled Aben[22] to show the influence a reduction in military expenditure would have on employment in France. In all the hypotheses tested, a drastic reduction in military expenditure would lead, in the short term, to an increase in unemployment. The question one should ask oneself, however, is whether any public activity undergoing, within a very short period, such a reduction would not have obtained an even more adverse result.

These simple studies must be properly understood. They give an account of what has happened in the recent past and they can help one to understand the impact of defence budgets on growth in the next two or three years, assuming that expenditure and its structure evolve smoothly and do not produce indivisibilities or thresholds preventing the usual inertia effect of military expenditure from expressing itself normally. Under these conditions, the impact of military expenditure has to be examined together with the existing economic situation, requiring the conditions of other things being equal for a satisfactory interpretation of its effects.

## France's budget

France's military budget is both a cost which the nation must bear and an indicator of the country's defence effort. However, analysing it correctly involves breaking down the expenditure sufficiently and in a way likely to provide interesting information on the strategy implemented by the government and on the comparative cost of weapons.

### *The volume of the defence budget*

France's military expenditure is generally estimated using the budget of the Ministère de la Défense. There is however defence expenditure that does not come under this ministry's budget, involving particularly the Prime Minister's departments (including the Secrétariat Général de la Défense Nationale) and certain defence activities of the Ministère de l'Intérieur. For this reason, definitions differ according to the information sources, the definitions chosen, and the methods adopted for international comparisons and comparisons between periods.

*Definitions* Most of the time, analysts use the military budget as the main indicator of the cost of defence, but this proves inadequate if, for internal or external reasons, a country transfers to the civil budget expenditure that properly belongs to the military sector. Regardless of the notion of opportunity cost, which applies rather poorly to the area of defence (where the main expected benefit in France is protection through deterrence, preventing an attack by the seriousness of the response, without knowing exactly what is necessary to dissuade the possible enemy), the military budget does not cover the whole of the defence effort. It would be advisable therefore to introduce the expenditures included in the various ministries for national security or the civil defence programme.[23] France's total military expenditure according to official sources is as shown in Table 9.1.

*Table 9.1* France's defence expenditure (including pensions) in '000 million francs

| | *Expenditure* | *1982* | *1983* | *1984* | *1985* | *1986* |
|---|---|---|---|---|---|---|
| 1 | Total operating expenditure of which | 89.1 | 99.4 | 106.2 | 112.4 | 122.0 |
| | Budget of Ministère de la Défense | 88.1 | 97.9 | 104.4 | 110.3 | 119.6 |
| | Defence (other budgets) | 0.9 | 1.4 | 1.7 | 2.0 | 2.3 |
| | Civil defence programme | 0.1 | 0.1 | 0.1 | 0.1 | 0.1 |
| 2 | Total investment expenditure of which | 56.5 | 61.3 | 68.1 | 72.8 | 77.0 |
| | Budget of Ministère de la Défense | 56.3 | 61.0 | 66.6 | 71.7 | 75.7 |
| | Defence (other budgets) | 0.2 | 0.3 | 1.5 | 1.1 | 1.3 |
| | Civil defence programme | — | — | — | — | — |
| 3 | Total military expenditure | 145.6 | 160.7 | 174.3 | 185.2 | 199.0 |

*International estimates of France's military expenditure* There are traditional sources of quantitative information on military expenditure: SIPRI (the Stockholm International Peace Research Institute), USACDA (the US Arms Control and Disarmament Agency), NATO (the North Atlantic Treaty Organisation) and IISS (the International Institute for Strategic Studies). To these should be added the World Bank and especially the International Monetary Fund (which very often serves as a reference basis for the other international sources of statistics). The definitions and methods of comparison used are not always homogeneous, thus making it difficult to compare the military expenditure of the various states precisely.[24]

The differences in estimates are usually fairly considerable and they obviously depend not only on definitions and methods for international comparisons and comparisons between periods, but also on the varying degree of transparency of the information in the various countries studied and on the actual possibilities of checking the statistics provided by the various states. It is rather interesting to note that the figures published by USACDA[25] and by NATO show the superiority, as far as military expenditure is concerned, of the Warsaw Pact countries and especially of the Soviet Union. The same is not true of SIPRI,[26] which, however, is the only international information source incorporating paramilitary forces (very important in the eastern bloc countries) in the concept of military expenditure. Table 9.2 shows the estimates of France's military expenditure produced by two large information institutes as compared with official publications. One can see that the differences are small and that there is fairly general agreement in the world on France's total military expenditure. The differences arise basically out of the defence

*Table 9.2* Estimates of France's military expenditure (including pensions) in millions of constant dollars (1980 value)

| *Source* | *1980* | *1981* | *1982* | *1983* | *1984* |
|---|---|---|---|---|---|
| USACDA | 27,193 | 28,202 | 28,604 | 28,990 | — |
| SIPRI | 26,425 | 27,066 | 27,623 | 28,094 | 27,896 |
| French Ministry of Defence[27] | 24,940 | 25,710 | 26,950 | 27,033 | 26,945 |

activities existing in the other ministries. The three estimates for France are far closer than for most other countries.

*International comparisons* In spite of the accuracy of the estimates of France's military expenditure, the use of the exchange rate is inadequate for comparing the defence efforts of various countries, especially in the context of negotiation on the reduction of military expenditure. The studies that have been done by the United Nations' Group of Experts show the serious errors that such a method introduces.[28] Thus, using the average exchange rates determined by the International Monetary Fund, the United Kingdom's military expenditure emerges as 7 per cent lower than what it is estimated to be when measured using purchasing power parities. Comparison between France and the United Kingdom[29] shows differences of the order of 10 per cent depending on the method used (Table 9.3). Under these conditions, as part of any agreement on the reduction of military expenditure, it will be necessary for all states to define the strictest possible homogeneous method of comparison.

*Table 9.3* Comparisons between French and British military expenditure in 1982 in millions of francs

| *Method* | *United Kingdom* | *France* |
|---|---|---|
| IMF exchange rate | 166,232 | 144,305 |
| SIPRI | 164,140 | 145,155 |
| USACDA | 179,808 | 168,271 |
| Purchasing power parity (bilateral method) | 161,640 | 144,305 |
| Purchasing power parity (multilateral method) | 149,198 | 144,305 |

*Comparisons between periods* Though in the United Kingdom there is a military sector price index, the same is not true in France. When French parliamentary reports show military expenditure in constant francs, they use, more often than not, the Gross Domestic Product price index as deflator. This deficiency is fairly serious, since it prevents one from knowing the actual growth of military expenditure. Let us suppose that prices in the military sector increased by 10 per cent compared with 5 per cent for the general price index. An increase in nominal military expenditure of 5 per cent does not therefore result in maintenance of military expenditure, as the parliamentary reports would indicate, but in an actual reduction in the defence effort. France is the only developed market economy country (apart from the Federal Republic of Germany) not to calculate its price index, which makes interpretation of comparisons between periods very tricky and perhaps incorrect. If, as some authors claim, the arms sector is more vulnerable to price increases than the national economy as a whole,[30] this amounts to saying that France's actual armament effort is less than the official financial figures seem to indicate.

### *The characteristics of this budget*

France's military budget can be analysed from four main points of view: its size in relation to the major economic aggregates, the distribution between operating expenditure and capital expenditure, expenditure according to the different types of weapons, or expenditure according to the types of expenditure.

*Military expenditure and Gross Domestic Product* France's military expenditure increased in constant francs by almost 5 per cent between 1981 and 1986. This was a smaller increase than that which had been planned by the defence programme for 1984–8. If one confines oneself to the forecasts in the new law (Loi de Programmation Militaire 1987–1991), an additional increase is planned for the coming years, particularly as regards equipment.

*Table 9.4* France's initial military budgets compared with GDP and the state budget

| *Year* | *% GDP* | *% GDP at factor cost* | *% state budget* |
|---|---|---|---|
| 1959 | 6.62 | 5.90 | 28.20 |
| 1964 | 4.93 | 4.41 | 23.00 |
| 1969 | 4.22 | 3.76 | 17.80 |
| 1974 | 3.37 | 2.99 | 17.40 |
| 1976 | 3.39 | 2.98 | 17.10 |
| 1978 | 3.62 | 3.16 | 16.97 |
| 1980 | 3.67 | 3.20 | 16.87 |
| 1982 | 4.00 | 3.44 | 15.58 |
| 1984 | 3.92 | 3.37 | 15.15 |
| 1985 | 3.85 | 3.29 | 15.15 |
| 1986 | 3.80 (est) | 3.23 (est) | 15.40 |

Table 9.4 shows that the percentage of the Gross Domestic Product devoted to military expenditure, which had fallen regularly from the end of the Algerian war, increased in the years 1977–82. However, this trend was reversed in 1983. The trend at present is unclear. It is difficult to know whether the new reduction will continue or whether the aims expressed by the government will again reverse the process. It is interesting, however, to note that the process of continual reduction of military expenditure in the state budget was interrupted in 1986.

*The distribution of military expenditure between operating expenditure and capital expenditure* As can be seen from Table 9.5, after the Algerian war France gave priority to her capital expenditure, mainly in order to develop her nuclear deterrent. From 1968 onwards, this trend was reversed principally on account of the re-evaluation of military conditions,

*Table 9.5* France's military budgets since 1958 in 1970 francs ('000 million)

| *Year* | *Capital expenditure* | *Operating expenditure* | *Total expenditure* |
|---|---|---|---|
| 1958 | 7.74 | 14.70 | 22.44 |
| 1959 | 9.49 | 15.71 | 25.20 |
| 1960 | 9.08 | 15.70 | 24.78 |
| 1961 | 8.58 | 15.37 | 23.95 |
| 1962 | 7.99 | 15.00 | 22.99 |
| 1963 | 10.48 | 14.32 | 24.80 |
| 1964 | 11.70 | 13.73 | 25.43 |
| 1965 | 13.01 | 13.06 | 26.07 |
| 1966 | 13.73 | 13.03 | 26.76 |
| 1967 | 14.45 | 13.42 | 27.87 |
| 1968 | 14.67 | 13.57 | 28.24 |
| 1969 | 13.80 | 14.03 | 27.83 |
| 1970 | 13.08 | 14.11 | 27.19 |
| 1971 | 12.77 | 14.48 | 27.25 |
| 1972 | 12.89 | 14.71 | 27.60 |
| 1973 | 13.61 | 15.09 | 28.70 |
| 1974 | 13.18 | 15.02 | 28.20 |
| 1975 | 12.48 | 16.20 | 28.68 |
| 1976 | 12.52 | 17.36 | 29.88 |
| 1977 | 13.17 | 18.98 | 32.15 |
| 1978 | 14.65 | 20.15 | 34.80 |
| 1979 | 15.29 | 20.07 | 35.36 |
| 1980 | 15.87 | 19.42 | 35.29 |
| 1981 | 17.60 | 20.95 | 38.55 |
| 1982 | 18.58 | 21.96 | 40.54 |
| 1983 | 18.58 | 22.02 | 40.60 |
| 1984 | 18.67 | 21.16 | 39.83 |
| 1985 | 18.93 | 20.73 | 39.66 |
| 1986 (est) | 19.27 | 21.06 | 40.33 |

which did not however prevent the famous 'unrest' in the barracks. From 1978 onwards, in the face of new international strategic situations, the modernization of the army's equipment became a priority in spite of the not inconsiderable delays that were being experienced compared with the objectives of military planning. It is interesting to note that, in constant francs, operating expenditure has remained relatively stable in the medium term, since 1981.[31] The figures are obviously fairly rough estimates, since, as we have seen, France does not have an official military expenditure price index.

*Military expenditure according to types of weapons* France's arms policy since 1979 has moved towards reinforcing the credibility of the nuclear deterrent. More than 30 per cent of military expenditure allocated to equipment (or nearly 15 per cent of the capital expenditure in the whole of the state budget) is regularly devoted to nuclear forces. From 1980 to 1985, greater importance was given to nuclear forces, total expenditure devoted to them having increased by 4 per cent in volume terms, especially favouring the tactical nuclear forces (see Table 9.6). However, the credibility of the nuclear deterrent will depend in the next few years on a continuation of this effort.

*Table 9.6* Capital expenditure devoted to nuclear forces in millions of current francs

| *Year* | *Strategic nuclear forces* | *Tactical nuclear forces* |
|---|---|---|
| 1980 | 11,850 | 730 |
| 1981 | 13,730 | 870 |
| 1982 | 16,190 | 740 |
| 1983 | 17,830 | 1,470 |
| 1984 | 19,300 | 2,440 |
| 1985 | 20,214 | 3,172 |
| 1986 | 20,967 | 4,301 |

It can be seen in Table 9.7 that, over a decade, the army has taken a large and relatively constant share of total military expenditure, which is surprising given the major new technological challenges that France will have to face. On the other hand, the navy has seen its share increase regularly, particularly at the expense of the joint section. It is obviously very difficult to alter the distribution of expenditure between the forces and, apart from a few movements arising out of particular economic conditions, which were rapidly contained by the General Staffs, a general form of agreement has been established to provide 26.5 per cent of expenditure to the army, a little over 21 per cent to the air force, between 18 and 19 per cent to the navy and a little over 9 per cent to the gendarmerie, the rest being devoted to the joint section, which basically combines the sections common to the four forces.[32] One can certainly reflect on the rationality of such a distribution.

*Table 9.7* Expenditure on the various forces as a percentage of total military expenditure

| *Year* | *Joint section* | *Army* | *Air force* | *Navy* | *Gendarmerie* |
|---|---|---|---|---|---|
| 1974 | 26.2 | 26.9 | 21.0 | 16.8 | 9.1 |
| 1977 | 26.0 | 27.2 | 19.8 | 17.2 | 9.8 |
| 1980 | 25.0 | 27.5 | 21.4 | 17.9 | 9.5 |
| 1981 | 25.0 | 27.1 | 21.3 | 17.6 | 9.1 |
| 1982 | 24.3 | 25.8 | 21.9 | 18.7 | 9.3 |
| 1983 | 24.3 | 26.9 | 21.5 | 17.9 | 9.4 |
| 1984 | 24.1 | 27.0 | 21.2 | 18.3 | 9.4 |
| 1985 | 24.2 | 26.8 | 21.2 | 18.5 | 9.3 |
| 1986 | 24.3 | 26.7 | 21.1 | 18.7 | 9.2 |

*Military expenditure according to the major categories of expenditure* Table 9.8[33] shows very roughly the priority given to nuclear forces (expenditure on which has increased by more than 4 per cent a year by volume since 1981), to the development of the major programmes specified in the Loi de Programmation Militaire, and to military research spending in the last six years. On the other hand, the other categories of expenditure increased more slowly (development), were maintained (infrastructure) or decreased (munitions and personnel maintenance). According to Frédéric Tiberghien, 'this table shows that choices have been made: accelerated modernisation of nuclear forces, modernisation of conventional forces through major programmes and arms production, preparation for the future by studying and developing the hardware of tomorrow'.[34]

However, by calculating expenditure in constant francs on the basis of the GDP deflator, it is possible to discover only the financial effort made by France distributed among the different elements in defence. In fact, it is difficult to assert that the government's choices were to modernize nuclear and conventional forces without knowing the respective inflation rates of the types of expenditure. Thus, because of an equipment demand which marked a break with the previous trend, the massive purchases of arms from the United States at the beginning of the 1980s ran up against budgetary limits compared with what was planned (because of the inflation that they had themselves contributed to in the industrial sectors concerned). If the nuclear sector experiences an inflationary process, either more money is needed to meet strategic

*Table 9.8* Capital expenditure by major category in '000 million constant francs (1981 value)

| *Expenditure* | *1981* | *1982* | *1983* | *1984* | *1985* | *1986* |
|---|---|---|---|---|---|---|
| Nuclear forces | 14.3 | 13.9 | 15.7 | 16.6 | 16.9 | 17.6 |
| Major programmes | 11.8 | 13.0 | 9.1 | 9.3 | 9.9 | 11.1 |
| Basic research | 1.8 | 1.8 | 1.8 | 2.1 | 2.4 | 2.4 |
| Development | 3.5 | 3.5 | 3.1 | 3.6 | 3.8 | 3.9 |
| Other production | 5.9 | 5.0 | 9.6 | 8.6 | 8.1 | 7.2 |
| Munitions | 3.1 | 2.8 | 2.9 | 2.5 | 2.7 | 2.6 |
| Maintenance of equipment | 2.8 | 2.8 | 3.2 | 3.5 | 3.4 | 35 |
| Personnel maintenance | 1.3 | 1.3 | 1.2 | 1.2 | 1.2 | 1.1 |
| Infrastructure | 3.2 | 3.3 | 3.1 | 3.3 | 3.3 | 3.2 |

objectives, or it is necessary to limit its scope. An increase in expenditure may reflect only an increase in the state's financial effort and not a substantial improvement in the country's nuclear capability. Conversely, one can very easily imagine that priorities may be met while maintaining or reducing the corresponding military expenditure, if the productivity of the arms industries improves and results in lower costs. In France's case, it is probable that the inflation rates of the various types of military expenditure were not very different, but intuition can hardly replace concrete evidence.

Finally, Table 9.9 shows the stability of the total wage bill after the sharp increase in 1982, the stability of maintenance, supplies, and even operating expenditure (in the medium term), as well as the reduction in fuel costs, largely owing to the fall in oil prices.

*Table 9.9* Military expenditure by cost categories in '000 million constant francs

| *Expenditure* | *1981* | *1982* | *1983* | *1984* | *1985* | *1986* |
|---|---|---|---|---|---|---|
| Salaries and employers' NI contributions | 38.0 | 39.6 | 39.5 | 38.9 | 38.8 | 39.2 |
| Supplies | 2.0 | 2.0 | 2.0 | 2.0 | 1.9 | 1.9 |
| Fuel | 3.8 | 4.3 | 3.9 | 3.3 | 3.2 | 3.3 |
| Maintenance of equipment | 4.0 | 3.8 | 3.9 | 3.8 | 3.7 | 3.8 |
| Operating | 9.1 | 9.7 | 9.7 | 9.5 | 9.0 | 9.2 |

## Conclusion

France has not really been marked by a general revision of the objectives of defence policy, as has happened with the United Kingdom. Parliamentary debates have centred rather on the proportion of GDP that should be devoted to defence, on the application of long-term plans (which have never been fully implemented), and on the long-term credibility of the deterrent forces. Like Great Britain, France has not gone in for heavy cuts in major programmes. Since 1970, changes have occurred slowly and smoothly. When it has been necessary to reduce expenditure, most programmes have been affected, except where indivisible elements or threshold effects were involved. Strictly speaking, there were no significant changes of course, but rather slightly different ideas about the potential use of tactical nuclear weapons and about military co-operation with the European countries, particularly as regards the joint production of arms.

If France has given priority to strategic nuclear forces and if she has, according to Ron Smith,[35] sacrificed her conventional forces, it should also not be forgotten that the structure of her expenditure does not reflect a financial priority, since the direct costs of the nuclear forces represent only a fifth of total military expenditure. In other words, France's general defence principles are not limited to nuclear deterrence; they include in particular the retention of National Service, implying a particular type of defence which is not always compatible with the priority given to nuclear deterrence. Nuclear deterrence is a highly centralized process, making use, in the last resort, of the highest authority in the state and, at intermediate levels, of specialists trained in secrecy and discipline. Though there is a large consensus to permit the development of deterrent forces, it is none the less true that the choices between conventional forces and nuclear forces have not yet reached a critical stage in their development. The modernization of France's strategic nuclear strike force can be achieved without too much difficulty, bearing in mind the relatively small percentage of her GDP devoted to defence and the possibility of temporarily holding conventional forces as they are. In 1982, France spent more than 15,000 million francs on her conventional weapons (not including research and development), while Great Britain devoted more than £4,000 million pounds to this end (37,000–49,000 million francs according to purchasing power parity calculations).[36] In this situation and even if one can assume that the French arms industry is more efficient than its British counterpart,[37] it is probable that France had to limit her ambitions as regards conventional weapons.

However, in future, with changes looming in the international strategic environment, it is probable that the pursuit of the nuclear strategy will be accompanied by painful financial choices, which are liable to call into question certain basic components of France's defence. The answers provided by the Loi de Programmation Militaire 1987–1991 are not yet very explicit, even if there is talk of increasing capital expenditure, especially nuclear, in order to continue fitting out missile-launching nuclear submarines (with the M-4 system), to strengthen the communication and command systems of the nuclear forces, to construct a new generation of missile-launching nuclear submarines, to develop a new ballistic missile (M-5), to construct a nuclear aircraft-carrier, and to introduce the Hades tactical weapons system.[38] At the same time, the political parties and the government are considering the functions of National Service and especially a new definition of its role. It is probable that France's military strategy will soon be the subject of new debates, because real choices are going to have to be made, particularly if the US Strategic Defense Initiative (SDI) quickly obtains convincing results. The famous consensus that surrounds nuclear deterrence will then be threatened. The government will have to face this new strategic challenge, either by significantly increasing military expenditure — particularly on nuclear, naval, and space hardware — or by making difficult and questionable choices concerning the restructuring of the military forces and of the resources put at their disposal. The financial and economic implications of this new stage in the arms race will have repercussions that are difficult to measure on France's strategy and defence policy. Though it is always possible to increase the defence effort and therefore to prefer defence over the needs of education or health, for example, it could also be necessary, in a crisis situation, to accept a possible temporary reduction both in economic growth and in the collective well-being of the citizens; these are, however, the guarantees of the national unity and security of tomorrow.

## Notes

1. The French government puts to the legislature a five-year defence programme known as the Loi de Programmation Militaire.
2. *Le Monde*, 13 December 1981.
3. André Giraud, interview in *Revue Heraclès*, no. 34. June 1986.
4. United Nations, 'Reduction of military budgets; construction of military price indexes and purchasing-power parities for comparison of military expenditures', *Disarmament*, Study Series no, 15, A/40/421 (New York, 1986).
5. Service d'Information et de Diffusion du Premier Ministre, 'l'Organisation de la défense de la France', *Dossiers de la Lettre de Matignon* (Paris), no. 15, November 1985; J. Aben and R. Smith, 'Défense et emploi au Royaume-Uni. Une étude comparative des résultats disponibles', in J. Fontanel and R. Smith, (eds), *L'Effort économique de défense. France et Royaume-Uni*, Grenoble and Lyons: ARES, Défense et Sécurité, December 1985).
6. United Nations, 'Reduction of military budgets', op. cit.
7. H. Martre, 'Les Perspectives des activités françaises de l'armement dans leur environnement international', *Défense nationale*, June 1982.
8. J.-F. Faure, 'Les Arsenaux de la France', *Mémoire DEA Défense et Sécurité Internationale* (Grenoble, 1986).
9. P. Dussauge, 'L'Industrie d'armement en France', *Economica* (Paris), 1985.

10. ibid.
11. B. Bonavita, 'Progrès matériel et politique militaire', *Défense nationale*, November 1977. J. Fontanel and R. Smith, 'Les Industries d'armement de la France et du Royaume-Uni', in Fontanel and Smith, *L'Effort économique de défense*, op. cit.
12. J.M. Treille, 'Progrès technique et défense militaire dans le monde contemporain', *Défense nationale*, September 1980.
13. The United Nations' Group of Experts on the Reduction of Military Budgets looked into comparisons between military hardware and had to give up most of its efforts because weapon characteristics proved so different.
14. The purchasing power parities of military research and development are distinctly in favour of the French industry compared with that in the United Kingdom, Italy, and the United States. J. Fontanel and R. Smith, 'La Comparaison des dépenses militaires de la France et du Royaume-Uni', in Fontanel and Smith, *L'Effort économique de défense*, op. cit.
15. Claude Lachaux and Christian Lamoureux, 'Commerce extérieur et défense', *Défense nationale*, May 1986, p. 39.
16. The study of the United Nations' Group of Experts on the Reduction of Military Budgets put forward the difference in the costs of military hardware purchased by the American government and those of similar hardware by the governments of Sweden, Norway, Finland, Austria, Australia, the United Kingdom, and Italy. The ratio is often 1 to 2, especially for very high-performance hardware exported by the United States.
17. R. Smith, A. Humm and J. Fontanel, 'The economics of exporting arms', *Journal of Peace Research* (Oslo), 2 (3), 1985.
18. G. Chacornac, 'Les Conditions économiques du financement de l'effort de défense', *Défense nationale*, October 1984, p. 66.
19. J.Fontanel, 'Military expenditure and economic growth, Morocco and France', United Nations, *Disarmament Affairs*, 1980.
20. J. Fontanel and R. Smith, 'Estimations macroéconomiques de l'impact des dépense militaires sur les économies de la France et de la Grande-Bretagne', in Fontanel and Smith, *L'Effort économique de défense*, op. cit.
21. J. Percebois, 'Dépenses militaires ou croissance économique: effets d'entraînement ou effets d'éviction?' in J. Fontanel and J.F. Guilhaudis, *Le Désarmement pour le développement*, (Lyon and Grenoble: ARES, Défense et Sécurité, 1986).
22. J. Aben and M. Daures, 'Défense nationale et emploi en France', *Problèmes de Défense Nationale*, vol. XV, (Montpellier: Les Cahiers du Séminaire Charles Gide, 1981).
23. Mensuel du Service d'Information et de Diffusion du Premier Ministre, *Dossiers de la Lettre de Matignon*, op. cit.
24. J. Fontanel, 'Le Concept de dépenses militaires', *Revue de Défense Nationale*, December 1980.
25. USACDA, *World Military Expenditure and Arms Transfers 1974–1983* (Washington, DC, 1985).

26. 'World Armaments and Disarmament', *SIPRI Yearbook* (London: Taylor Francis, 1986).
27. The conversion from francs to dollars was done using the average exchange rate calculated by SIPRI.
28. United Nations, 'Reduction of military budgets', op. cit.
29. Fontanel and Smith, 'La Comparaison des dépenses militaires de la France et du Royaume-Uni', op. cit. See also: Ministère de la Défense, *Regards sur la Défense, 1981–1986* (Paris, 1986).
30. Dussauge, op. cit., p. 97
31. Fontanel, 'Les Dépenses militaires de la France 1919–1986', *Cahiers du CEDSI*, no. 7 (Grenoble, 1985).
32. A. Humm and J.-P. Matière, 'Une Analyse comparative des dépenses militaires en France et au Royaume-Uni', in Fontanel and Smith, *L'Effort économique de défense*, op. cit.
33. F. Tiberghien, 'L'Effort de défense depuis 1981', *Défense nationale*, November 1985, pp. 48–9.
34. ibid., pp. 48–9. This study has however the merit of correctly approaching the financial burden of defence according to various criteria and types of expenditure.
35. R. Smith, Chapter 10 of this book.
36. Fontanel and Smith, *L'Effort économique de défense*, op. cit., p. 54.
37. Aben and Smith, 'Défense et emploi au Royaume-Uni', op. cit., pp. 145 onwards.
38. It should be noted that in France, in contrast to Great Britain, the medium term defence plan is approved by the pasage of a law; this gives it a special force and improves the democratic debate on the future necessities of national defence.

Chapter ten

# Defence costs and budgeting in Great Britain

Ron Smith

In May 1985 the House of Commons Defence Committee published a report *Defence Commitments and Resources*[1] which drew attention to the 'substantial pressure developing on the defence budget over the coming years'. It is not to disparage the report, which is an essential source of information and analysis, to say that almost any review of Britain's defence commitments and resources over the past thirty years would have come to similar conclusions. Because of Britain's poor economic performance, the resources available to the defence budget have been systematically less than the costs required to meet declared security commitments.[2] Thus the central problems of defence budgeting have been seen as deciding where to economize and how to manage the process of trimming costs.

The outcome that has emerged from this process of economizing can be characterized in a number of different ways. Critics present it in almost dialectical terms, in which the thesis of budgetary inadequacy confronts the antithesis of cost escalation. But rather than being resolved in a synthesis which produces the defence policy appropriate to a relatively poor European middle power, they have generated a series of unresolved contradictions. Britain spends too much on defence, has incurred too many commitments, buys weapons which are too expensive, and has failed to elaborate a security doctrine that can be sustained over the medium term. Defenders have a more Newtonian vision in which British defence policy represents a dynamic equilibrium, which manages to maintain a subtle and impressive balance between the opposing forces operating on it.[3] I shall briefly review the main forces, or contradictions, influencing costs, budgets, and strategic objectives.

## Costs

Cost growth has been a recurring issue in British defence discussions. There are a number of different aspects to the problem, each of which has caused concern, not merely in the UK.[4]

The first aspect is the rising unit cost of weapons. It is estimated that, between generations, the unit cost of major systems tends to rise at 6–10 per cent faster than the general rate of inflation. This means that each new generation costs, in real terms, about four times the system it replaces. This cost growth, which partly reflects increased performance in response to the development of technology and threat, is dealt with by reducing the number of units in service, extending the gap between generations, and making economies elsewhere in the budget. At some stage, the interaction between the budget constraint and the trends in unit cost pushes the affordable force size, for weapons of the desired performance, below some threshold of military viability. Thus, when the existing generation is withdrawn, the choice is between ceasing to field that type of system or substituting a cheaper, lower-performance, alternative.

This choice provokes controversy about the minimum viable size for the force and about the right balance between quantity and quality of systems: the trade-off between the contribution of unit performance and number of units to force effectiveness. Comparison with France is illuminating on this account. The two countries deploy similar numbers of the main types of conventional systems, the French ones apparently having been acquired considerably cheaper. The lower cost might be related to higher productivity in the French defence industry; weapon specification and performance; or export orientation. Of course, comparison cannot be made in terms of numbers and cost alone; capability and performance also count.

Where the British have managed to keep costs low, by comparison with the French, is in nuclear systems. Britain has acquired a lot of technology and all the missiles relatively cheaply from the US. Proportional to their total budgets, which are similar, strategic systems have cost Britain perhaps a quarter of what they have cost France: 5 per cent as against 20 per cent of the budget, averaging over time. Currently France devotes about a third of her equipment budget to strategic nuclear systems, while the UK proportion never seems to have been more than about 15 per cent. This occurred during the building of the Polaris submarines, and the proportion projected during the building of the Trident submarines is similar.

However one views the desirability, suitability, independence, or utility of the Trident system, at £10 billion it costs only a fraction of what would be required if Britain were to attempt to develop a similar system independently. The $116 million, at fiscal 1982 prices, that the UK is paying towards research and development is a negligible contribution. The expense of independent development was illustrated by the cost of over £1 billion that Britain incurred in developing the new Chevaline front-end for the Polaris missiles. Despite being cheap relative to performance, the cost of Trident is regarded as excessive, even by many who are not unilateralist, because it is pushing Britain towards a 'French' posture, where conventional forces are sacrificed to maintain the deterrent. Such a posture is in accord with French strategic doctrine, but conflicts with British doctrine.

Project overruns are a second aspect of cost growth which have given concern. In the UK, there are many famous examples of projects that are delivered late, at many times their forecast cost. The development of the Chevaline nuclear system, the Torpedo programme, and the Nimrod AEW (Airborne Early Warning) are recent examples. When the US AWACS (airborne early-warning aircraft) was offered to NATO in 1977, the British share of the cost would have been about £460 million in 1985 prices and it would have, by now, been operational and compatible with the rest of the NATO system. It would also have generated considerable employment through offsets and the basing of the NATO force in the UK. Instead the domestic alternative, the Nimrod AEW was ordered, on which £816 million has already been spent, and the total cost would have been over £1.5 billion had the MoD not eventually decided to buy AWACS after all. The Torpedo programme (Mark 24 Tigerfish, Sting Ray, and Spearfish), costing over £5 billion at 1984 prices, has run into repeated problems and represented bad value for money, according to parliamentary enquiries.

The factors contributing to time and cost overruns were clearly diagnosed by the Ministry of Defence during the 1960s, and published in the Downey Report.[5] The factors include underestimation of the technological difficulty of the project, changes in project specification during development, lack of clear project direction, and dispersal of responsibility between MoD and contractors. Diagnosis is easier than treatment however, and the problems of cost control have persisted. Cost control raises a number of distinct, though related issues. First, there is the potential sourcing — what range of companies, domestic and foreign, are allowed to tender and on what terms. Second, there is the method of pricing — from cost-plus through various incentivised contracts to fix-price, each with their associated forms of risk sharing. Third, there is the process of monitoring progress and attributing responsibility between MoD, prime contractors, and sub-contractors.

Even when they are accurately estimated in advance, defence production and development costs tend to be high, compared to civilian projects, for structural reasons. On the one hand, short production runs mean that not only are the advantages of economies of scale and learning curves not obtained but contractors have less incentive to invest in process innovation and equipment since capital costs will be spread over relatively few units. On the other hand, lack of competition and cost-plus contracts reduce the incentives for the contractor to minimize costs. The dilemma is that the concentration of production that gains scale economies and avoids duplication of capacity creates monopolies, which have little incentive for cost minimization. The threshold levels at which it is economic to have no domestic producers — a single one, or many — for a particular system, are debated. Sometimes, government policy has encouraged concentration in the defence industry, creating national champions like British Aerospace and British Shipbuilders from lots of smaller companies, in order to gain the scale advantages of long production runs. At other times the government has encouraged competition to gain the advantage from incentive effects.

Costs for personnel tend to grow, over the medium term, in line with wages in the general labour market. In economic terms, Britain's choice of small professional forces, rather than large conscript forces, does not seem to make a lot of difference to total defence costs; it is a matter of political, social, and military priorities. Although conscripts are paid lower wages than volunteers, infrastructure costs are incurred to provide barracks, etc., and a large proportion of the experienced troops must be devoted to training the constant flow of short-service conscripts. It is unlikely that the conscripts are as effective, in military terms, as professionals; but this assessment depends on a judgement about the relative importance of quality against quantity of manpower in likely conflicts. Because of the problems of recruitment and retention of volunteers, Britain tends to economize on scarce military manpower. Functions that in France would be carried out by the armed services are done in Britain by Ministry of Defence civil servants or private firms. This difference is most noticeable in the number of defence civil servants, of which France has fewer than half the British total.

In the UK the various aspects of cost growth are combined in a defence-specific price index, which is used to deflate nominal budgets to obtain defence expenditure in 'real' terms. This is often contrasted with another constant price measure, where the nominal budget is deflated by a general price index (usually the GDP deflator) to obtain defence expenditure in 'cost' terms.[6] The difference between the rate of growth of the defence price index and the GDP deflator, called the 'relative price effect', provides a summary of the adverse movement in defence inflation relative to general inflation. Of course, the difficulties involved in defining the price of defence, which in the UK is measured by input costs, means that the interpretation of this measure is subject to dispute. On average, the relative price effect for total defence expenditure has tended to be about 2 per cent per annum, with large year-to-year variations. The relative price effect on the non-pay component is rather less, in the range 1–1.5 per cent per annum.

**Budgets**

This rising cost of capability has had to be met from a constrained budget. By European standards Britain has devoted a high proportion of income to defence, and there is evidence that her economy has suffered as a result. In 1984, Britain spent 5.3 per cent of GDP at market prices on defence as compared to 4.1 per cent in France. The historical path of the defence share of GDP in each country is shown in Figure 10.1. The British share is greater or equal to that of France throughout the period, and the major influences on the budget of each country can be seen in the graph. In the UK the effect of the Korean war rearmament can be clearly seen, as can the effect of the Sandys Defence Review in 1957 and the reviews of the 1960s and the late 1970s. The growth in the

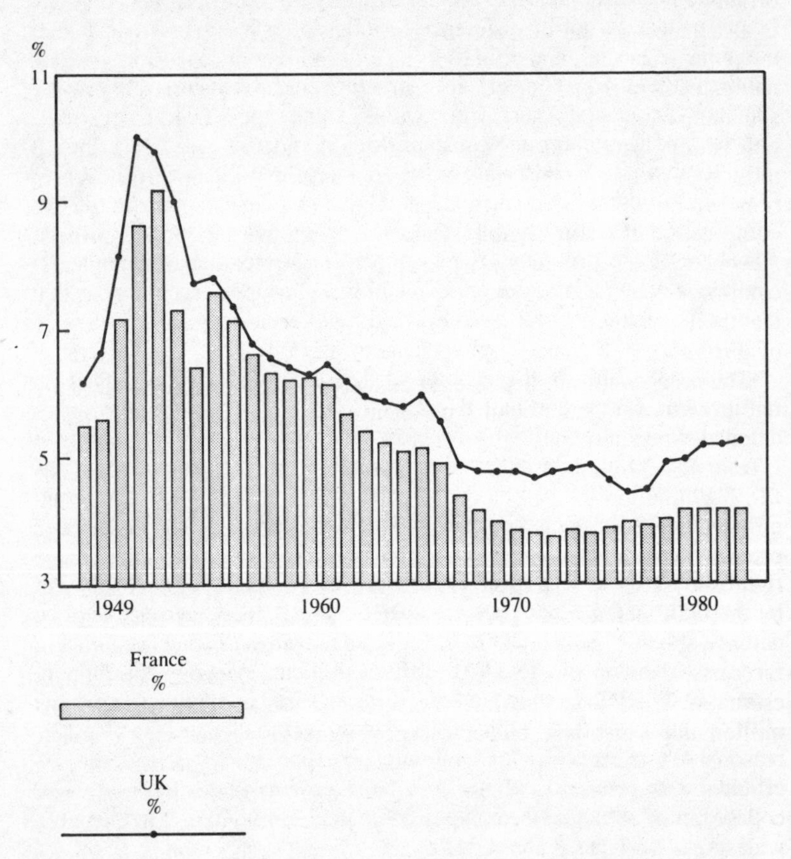


*Figure 10.1* Defence expenditure as a percentage of market price GDP, UK and France, 1949–84

defence budget since 1979 is also apparent. In France, the share shows less variation; the impact of the Indo-Chinese and Algerian wars is noticeable, followed by a gentle decline to an almost constant share.[7]

The graph shows the proportion of GDP that each country devotes to military expenditure. The actual level of military expenditure then depends on the level of GDP. The French economy has grown faster, perhaps partly because of the lower share of military expenditure. For instance, between 1973 and 1983, GDP in France grew at 2.3 per cent a year, whereas it only grew at 1.0 per cent a year in the UK. As a result of the faster French growth, the total defence budgets are now very similar in the two countries: $22.7 billion in the UK against $20.1 billion in France in 1984. This comparison is based on official British figures, official French figures may give a different ranking. The comparison is also based on the average market exchange rate for the year, and movements in the exchange rate can make large differences in international comparisons of level, as can differences in definition. Per person in the country, the UK spent $406 and France $367 in 1984. Population is very similar in the two countries: 56 million in the UK, 54.6 million in France. Real French military expenditure (i.e. after correction for inflation) grew by 27.2 per cent over the period 1975–82 compared to 18.4 per cent in the UK, according to the IISS estimates. Anyone who has been following the debate about adherence to the NATO commitment to 3 per cent real growth in defence expenditure will know that there is a lot of scope about how one corrects for inflation. The use of different price indexes will give different results for real growth.

The prospect for the UK defence budget is that, after six years when real growth averaged around 3 per cent per annum, from 1985/6 real defence expenditure will fall somewhat. In current prices the movement is from £14.5 billion in 1982/3 to a planned £18.1 billion in 1985/6 and £18.8 billion in 1987/8, of which the Falklands components are £785 million, £552 million and £300 million. Figure 10.2 shows actual and projected defence expenditure in 1983/4 prices. Two constant price figures are shown: for 'cost', expenditure in current prices is deflated by the GDP deflator to remove the effect of inflation; for 'real', by a defence-specific price index. The cost projections use government forecasts, the real projections House of Commons Defence Committee estimates. The Committee describe the 1987/8 real estimate of £15,271 million as a worst case, but in historical terms it is based on perfectly reasonable assumptions. The government hopes that improvements in efficiency, the effects of competition, and the benefits of international collaboration will slow the adverse trend in defence costs. But there is widespread scepticism about the significance of such savings. In addition, if the government is to keep the Public Sector Borrowing Requirement under control and cut taxes, as it has promised, then public

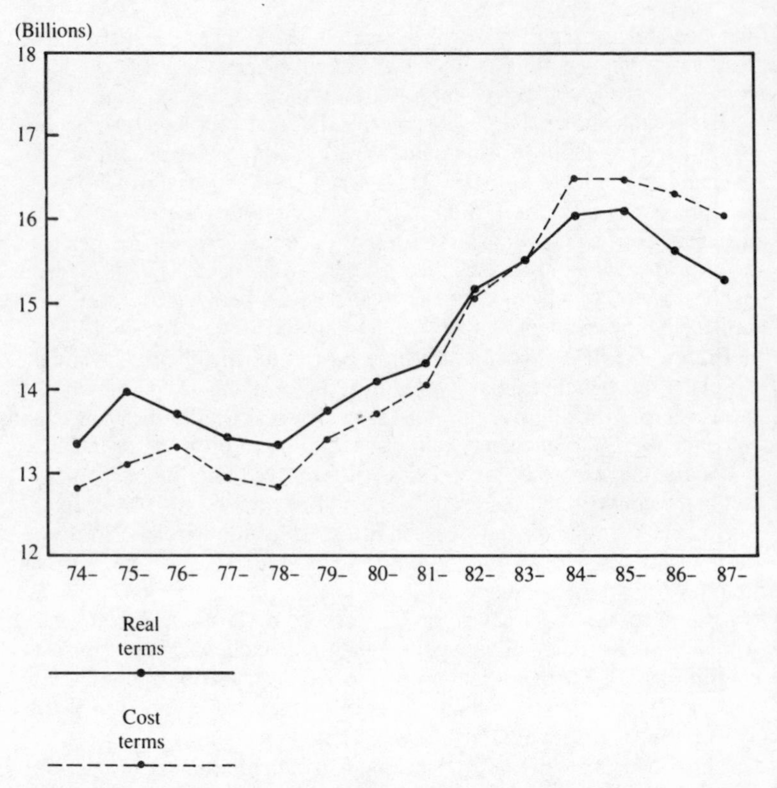


*Figure 10.2* Defence expenditure in cost and real terms, 1983/4 prices, 1974/5 to 1987/8

expenditure will come under further pressure. In these circumstances, defence may have to accept cuts.

Within the defence budget, there has been relative stability in the distribution between the services, as Figure 10.3 shows. The category labelled 'other' comprises reserves, training, repair, stocks, and other support functions. Except in the early period, when Polaris was under construction, the nuclear component has been small. The large research and development component has been a source of continued concern, partly because R&D is such a high proportion of total equipment costs, and partly because defence absorbs around half of total public R&D expenditure, with little apparent benefit for the civilian economy.

The management of inter-service rivalry within the budgetary process has been a matter of continued concern. There has been a trend over the post-war period, albeit slow and strongly opposed, for a movement from a single-service to a defence-wide approach. The 1964

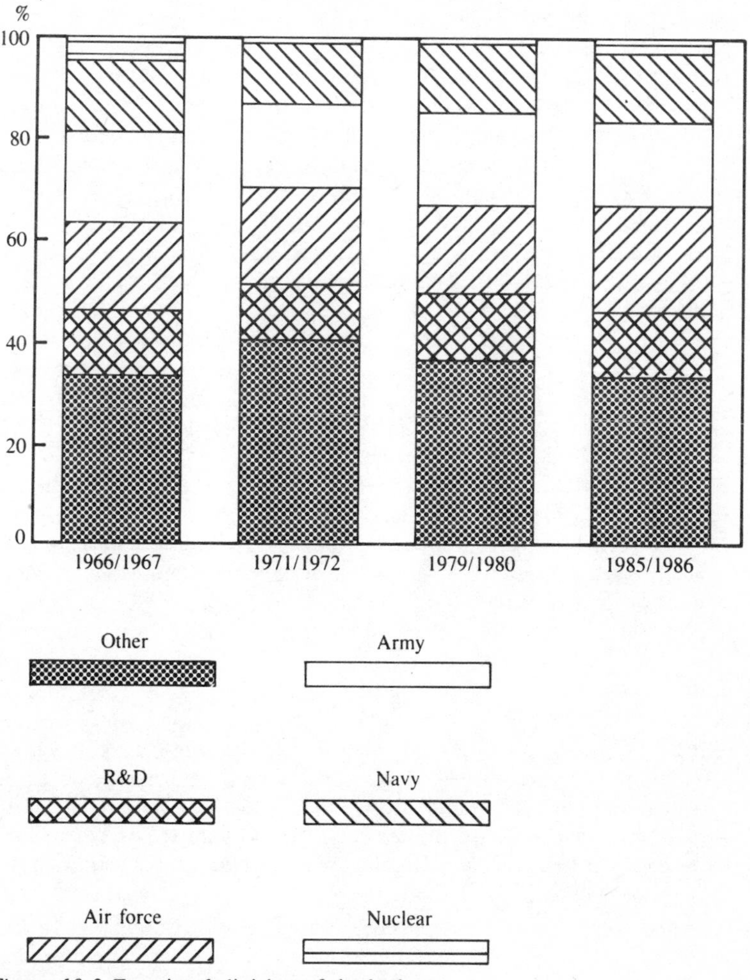


*Figure 10.3* Functional division of the budget

reorganization of the ministry marked one important step along this route, as did the establishment of a central procurement executive in 1971. It is too early to know the significance of the 1985 reforms of the central organization for defence. There is sometimes a tendency to regard the budgets as the final and ultimate statements of policy: commitments memorialized by money. This may be true in terms of inter-service competition, but it should also be remembered that important British military commitments, particularly Ulster, hardly show in the defence budget, being relatively cheap. The main financial cost of Ulster falls on the civilian budget.

Within the framework of a budget balanced between the services there have been considerable movements in the proportion devoted to equipment (as against personnel costs, etc.). The comparisons with France are illuminating in this respect. Around 1960 France spent about 30 per cent of the budget on equipment, compared to around 40 per cent in the UK. By 1966 the position had reversed, France spending 47 per cent (over half of which went on strategic nuclear equipment) and Britain 45 per cent. The equipment shares then declined in both countries, bottoming at 30 per cent in the UK in 1971 and 37 per cent in France in 1977. The share of equipment in both budgets has risen since, faster in Britain, and by 1983 the ratios were 46 per cent in the UK and 43 per cent in France (of which 32 per cent goes on strategic nuclear equipment). The share of equipment in France is intended to rise towards 50 per cent; in the UK plans are for the share to stay just under 50 per cent.

Budgets vibrate in response to a series of cycles of different frequency and amplitude. There are the long technological waves, running over decades, as major projects such as Trident or Tornado go through their life cycle of specification, development, production, deployment, operation, and disposal. Within decades, there are economic cycles with their impact on resources as budgetary, monetary, or trade crises bite; political cycles as governments come, go, or reverse their policies; and bureaucratic cycles as influence shifts. Within years there is the annual budgetary cycle of the Public Expenditure Survey Committee. Central to the process of tuning these fluctuations are the long-term costings – projections ten years ahead of how much might be needed to meet expected commitments and of how much is likely to be available. At regular intervals what will be needed starts to get grossly out of line with what will be available, a 'funding gap' appears, and objectives have to be reconsidered.

## Objectives

In Britain the broad adjustments in the objectives of defence policy which seemed needed in order to trim costs to match resources and commitments have been associated with recurrent agonizing reappraisals. Time and again, the balance between nuclear and conventional forces, Europe and the rest of the world, maritime and continental commitments, appearance and readiness, have been debated. Some of these reappraisals became embodied in defence reviews.

The line between a formal defence review and a mere reorientation of priorities announced in the annual White Paper, the Statement on the Defence Estimates, is a very fine one. In its report on the 1985

*Statement of of Defence Estimates*, the House of Commons Defence Committee feared 'that the cumulative effect of managing the defence budget in the manner endorsed in the White Paper may result in a defence review by stealth'. Historically, the more explicit reconsiderations have been the 1957 Sandys review, which abolished conscription; the 1964–8 Healey review, which planned the withdrawal from East of Suez; the 1974–5 review, which further reduced non-NATO commitments; and the 1981 Nott review, which planned to reduce naval forces.

In practice, these defence reviews often did no more than outline a future policy that failed to materialize or chart a way forward that was rapidly reversed. However compelling their analysis, and commendable their vision, their implementation was never more than partial. Illustrations of the subsequent failure to implement declared policy can be found in each of the defence reviews. For example, in February 1966 it was declared that the UK would not undertake major operations without allies; provide military assistance outside Europe unless invited in good time and given every facility; or commit herself to any operation beyond the range of land-based aircraft. Yet in 1982, Britain did all these things.

The constant reconsideration and policy change characteristic of British defence decisions is often contrasted with the French pattern of continuity and policy confirmation.[8] However, behind this appearance of change the British adjustments have, despite the proclamation of defence reviews, been balanced: cutting across the board, while preserving the overall shape of the defence posture. Again the contrast is drawn with the French, where, instead of balance, a clear priority is attached to nuclear strategic forces, and the cuts, when required, fall asymmetrically on the conventional forces.

The choice between balanced cuts and setting priorities arose again during the enquiry by the House of Commons Defence Committee. Members of Parliament asked the witnesses from the armed forces whether they would prefer to deal with the financial pressures that seem likely in the near future by cutting thin 'salami slices' from the whole spectrum of capabilities or by drastic surgery in particular areas. The witnesses preferred salami-slicing to amputation. Similarly, in an earlier episode, Greenwood[9] defends the January 1968 measures, which trimmed all major categories of expenditure, as being economically sound in removing the marginal items from each programme, against the criticism that their evenhandedness showed the government's lack of clear priorities.

The conventional theory of defence budgeting suggests that, if costs have to be constrained within a given budget, the cuts should be applied to the marginal expenditures, those that provide the least strategic utility. The dispute about slicing and amputation, or balance and priorities, is about whether the marginal category should be defined between programmes or within programmes. Is the margin a major programme such as strategic nuclear forces, North Atlantic navy, troops in Germany, air defence of the UK, or out-of-area commitments to the Falklands; or is it the marginal components from each of these programmes?

Conventional defence budgeting would suggest that, in general, intra-programme cuts are better than cutting a whole programme, unless there are significant indivisibilities or threshold effects. These intra-programme cuts can be made by cancelling projects not regarded as central to the programme; delaying delivery of equipment or reducing system-sophistication; short-term economies in support, maintenance, logistics, and training; or finding efficiency savings in the budget. These options are valued in the Ministry of Defence as providing flexibility in budgeting. Ironically, they often involve extra costs. Rescheduling production raises unit costs, cancellation and redundancy charges are incurred, and so on.

In any event, if flexibility involves cutting a programme below a threshold level of viability, beyond which it is useless, then money spent on that programme is wasted and it should be cut completely. Thus, much of the discussion of British defence budgeting has centred on the issues of threshold effects. At what level do the forces allocated to a programme become so small and poorly equipped that they are not worth having? At what stage does the cost of maintaining appearances in terms of sophisticated systems require such economies on support, training, and logistics that readiness and capability are sacrificed? At what burden do the costs imposed on the rest of the economy by the defence budget become intolerable? The debate is about whether Britain crossed these thresholds long ago, or has successfully managed to keep balancing on the edge.

## Acknowledgements

I am grateful for financial support from an Economic and Social Research Council–Centre National de Recherche Scientifique collaborative project on the British and French defence efforts and for comments and advice from Jacques Fontanel.

## Notes

1. House of Commons Defence Committee, *Defence Commitments and Resources*, Third Report 1984–5, HC 37, (London: HMSO, 1985), vol. I.
2. Both the Freedman and Greenwood chapters in J. Baylis (ed.), *Alternative Approaches to British Defence Policy* (London: Macmillan, 1983) give this account as do D. Smith and R. Smith, *The Economics*

*of Militarism* (London: Pluto, 1983). The Chief of Defence Staff described, to the House of Commons Defence Committee, the essence of defence policy as 'fitting commitment quarts into resource pint pots', which expresses the same idea.

3. The chapter by Williams in J. Roper (ed.), *The Future of British Defence Policy* (London: Gower, 1985) describes British defence policy in these terms.
4. The cost issues are discussed more fully in my chapter in Roper op. cit.
5. Report of the Steering Group on Development Cost Estimation under the chairmanship of Sir Gordon Downey (Ministry of Technology, London, 1966).
6. Unfortunately there is no standard usage, even within the government, to distinguish constant price measures based on specific and general price indexes. I have used real and cost for convenience.
7. A series of articles comparing the defence efforts in Britain and France can be found in J. Fontanel and R. Smith (eds), *L'Effort économique de défense. Les Experiences de la France et du Royaume-Uni* (Lyon and Grenoble: ARES, Défense et sécurité, Special issue, 1985–6).
8. Jefferies in D.J. Murray and P.R. Viotti (eds) *The Defence Policies of Nations* (Baltimore, Md: Johns Hopkins Press, 1982), p. 356, makes this comparison.
9. D. Greenwood, *Budgeting for Defence* (London: Royal United Services Institute, 1972), p. 69.

Chapter eleven

# Co-operation in arms procurement: a British view

Farooq Hussain

For Western Europe, co-operative development of defence equipment is worth pursuing because of the escalating costs of weapons systems. From one generation to the next, these costs represent an average increase of 400 per cent in real terms for any given weapon system, placing an increasing burden on defence budgets with intolerable long-term consequences for the quantity of weapons that need to be procured and the level of national expenditure that this requires. It is also a means by which a nation may maintain a defence industrial base larger and more diverse than otherwise would be possible. Co-operative development of weapons reduces wasteful duplication of effort between the Allies. It provides significant economies of scale, spreading the technical risks and costs of weapons development projects between partners. This is said to provide a more secure passage for a project from its research and development stage to production. It is also a means by which European defence industries may join forces to compete on more equal terms with those of the United States, especially to further develop skills in the application of advanced technologies to the design of new weapons systems. Last, and perhaps most important, co-operative development of weapon systems is the only viable long-term policy by which NATO Europe can be expected to procure adequate quantities of conventional weapon systems to maintain a balance of forces between NATO and the Warsaw Pact.

The aims of co-operative procurement are designed to lead towards a rationalization of NATO's defence industrial base and to improve the level of standardization and inter-operability of weapon systems. This would permit the Alliance's European members to meet their future security requirements better and provide for an equitable distribution of its economic burden within Europe, and between Europe and the United States. The worth of these objectives may be self-evident. However, the extent, character, and manner by which co-operation in the procurement of defence equipment has been and should be pursued is the subject of divergent interpretation between the nations, industries, and military services. For the United Kingdom, co-operative development of weapons with European partners is primarily a choice of economic necessity rather than one of political inclination. Past experience with joint projects is mixed and the attitudes towards future ones apprehensive — though the factors that influenced British decisions to embark on the earliest co-operative ventures are powerful and still effective today.

The most significant Franco-British defence projects of the past have been the Jaguar fighter-bomber and the Lynx helicopter. Other important programmes have included the licensed production in Britain of the Gazelle and Puma helicopters, the Milan Anti-Tank Guided Weapon (ATGW), and the jointly developed Martel air-to-surface missile. These and other programmes, especially the Tornado multi-role combat aircraft (MRCA), have shaped British views of the future of defence co-operation both with France and with other European partners. In its *Statement on the Defence Estimates* for 1985 the Ministry of Defence lists twelve co-operative projects in service and fourteen under study or in development; about half of the total are co-operative ventures that have included French participation. Future projects include the important European fighter aircraft, the NATO NH-90 and other helicopters, the NATO NFR-90 frigate, the multiple launch rocket system (MLRS), and TRIGAT, the third generation anti-tank guided missile.

Although Franco-British co-operation in the crucial aerospace sector of industry began in November 1962 with the agreement to develop the Concorde supersonic airliner, the agreements to develop jointly the Jaguar and the Lynx, Gazelle, and Puma helicopter package were very substantial programmes which followed in May 1965 and October 1967 respectively. These were followed in October 1976 with British entry into the Franco-German Milan ATGM programme. The agreement to develop the Martel (also made in the mid-1970s) was the last of the exclusively Franco-British defence co-operation agreements. Subsequently all co-operation between Britain and France relating to the development and procurement of defence equipment has been within multinational European programmes. Clearly, the present extent of co-operative weapons development programmes under way in Europe is significant. But do these projects represent only a portion of the potential for co-operative ventures or, as seems more likely, do they constitute the widest available range of programmes until the late 1990s? Even though co-operative programmes in defence equipment procurement between Britain and France now have a twenty-year history, to what degree can these be seen to have fulfilled all or any of the idealistic aims of co-operative procurement set out above?

It would seem that a level of intra-European co-operation in the procurement of defence equipment will be sustained irrespective of the more general ideological aims of such projects. This is especially so in the light of past experience where the criteria that establish success of a co-operative project can rarely be seen in terms of its fundamental objectives of reducing costs and progress towards a better-integrated European defence industrial base. The pressures for co-operative defence projects arise when comparable military requirements occur in phase between two or more countries. They also require a prospect for an equitable distribution of technological and industrial skills. These conditions are brought about only by a willingness to apply political pressure to overcome parochial interests for the common good. All co-operative projects have to resolve conflicting interests by acceptable compromise. Past experience has shown that this process does not take place between the industries of European nations without government initiative. The role of governments is all the more important since they dictate the market requirements for defence equipment and have national interests in the preservation of the defence industrial base.

The Cabinet crisis precipitated by the resignation in 1986 of the Secretary of State for Defence, Michael Heseltine, arose over significant differences between Mr Heseltine and the Prime Minister. At the centre of these differences was the dispute over the extent of government intervention in the affairs of industry that would be appropriate for the sake of European defence co-operation (EDC). While British participation in co-operative defence projects is unlikely to collapse following Mr Heseltine's departure, the high profile given to EDC by his personal commitment to it is gone. The implications of this may be only that the character and extent of future British participation in EDC programmes will follow the pattern of the past ones.

## The industrial base

The United Kingdom maintains a large and diverse defence industrial base. However this base is notoriously lacking in competitiveness. For instance, if the government were to buy foreign equipment when this offered a better economic solution to procurement requirements then British defence industrial capacity could be expected to contract substantially. This kind of policy carried out in the extreme is, of course, politically unacceptable now, and probably in the future. For Britain, co-operative ventures are the imperfect but only available means of maintaining her wide-range defence industrial capabilities, since the cost of programmes she could not otherwise afford are spread over time with partners. Co-operative ventures that are pursued with the objective of maintaining otherwise over-expensive domestic industrial capabilities inevitably create conflicts of interest between partners and result in uneasy project development.

But Britain, France, and West Germany, who constitute the upper tier of the European defence industrial base, share a common concern to preserve and further develop their defence industries. The FRG, the UK, and France (representing about 54 per cent of the population of NATO Europe) account for roughly 80 per cent of its defence industrial output. They are also the most significant net exporters of arms. Thus, in Britain at least, co-operative defence programmes are not just for improving NATO's capability to defend itself (perhaps this is the least important concern); they are also for preserving national capabilities. It is recognized that, with some sacrifices, these capabilities can be best maintained through an emphasis on greater co-operation. But the sacrifices are politically extraordinarily difficult to make.

In view of this it is not surprising that Franco-British co-operative ventures have essentially been confined to aerospace projects, since this sector of the defence industrial capability is the most important for both countries. The ground armaments industry, by comparison, exhibits quite different characteristics. For example, ground vehicles are developed and produced within the large civil automative industry as well as by government-owned companies. However, in the UK the government-owned Royal Ordnance Factories have by now been privatized. Guns and artillery as well as small arms and ammunition are developed and produced by independent companies with substantial experience in the field, by the subsidiaries of large diversified conglomerates, and by nationally owned companies and government establishments. The market for this equipment is well defined and the world market highly competitive. The only co-operative project in this field in which Britain has participated is the SP-70 self-propelled howitzer. Begun in the 1960s, this project was originally planned to deliver a system that could enter service in the 1990s but at a cost grossly in excess of original estimates. As a co-operative project between Britain, West Germany, and Italy it will be some fifteen years or more behind schedule and was estimated to cost $450 million at the time of its cancellation in 1986.

In the 1970s, West Germany and the United States tried jointly to develop a main battle tank, the MBT-70. Sadly, the project failed, but not because conflicting military requirements could not be entirely resolvéd rather because satisfactory industrial development and production arrangements could not be achieved. The United States and Germany went on to develop the M-1 Abrams and the Leopard II independently; though the positive results of this attempt to develop a common tank have been the adoption of the German Rheinmetall 120mm gun for the M-1 and the MTU diesel engine that powers the Leopard II. However, the British experience during this period of sharing the 'Chobham Armour' technology with the United States has brought no special rewards.

While light armoured vehicles, main battle tanks, and artillery are important candidates for future collaboration, past experience suggests that this will be very difficult to achieve. It will be difficult to form a common military requirement for these three pieces of ground forces equipment both within Europe and between Europe and the United States, although experience with the MBT-70 and the SP-70 shows that it is feasible with sufficient effort to develop common requirements. These experiences also show that the development costs are difficult to control and that savings compared to national development have not resulted. More importantly, these projects have shown that, in addition to establishing common requirements, it is essential to control industrial interests. Nations need to be willing to make sacrifices, forgoing the national capacity to develop and produce new generations of equipment independently. This is politically unlikely but it is the only means by which economic efficiency can be brought to these projects.

Co-operative development of naval platforms has been very limited. Collaborative ship construction programmes, such as the standard frigate of the Dutch Kortenaer and German Bremen classes and the tripartite minehunter, between the Netherlands, Belgium, and France have been undertaken. However, neither of these programmes has the scale or the scope of the NATO NFR-90 frigate replacement project. The requirement for the NFR-90 is for a ship of 3500 ton standard displacement (called the Atlantic baseline), whose primary mission role is divided between the eight participating nations. The need to configure the NFR-90 for an anti-aircraft and anti-submarine role to suit the specific requirements of the participating nations has led to the adoption of a modular construction method. Three types of modular construction exist, the MEKO from Blohm and Voss, the American Ship Systems Engineering Standard, and the British Cellularity System. The system to be adopted for the NFR-90, though, is predicted to draw from the best features of all three. This approach will prevent the dominance of any one national technique, but the adoption of a new modular construction method adds to the overall development costs of the frigate.

In October 1985 the final report of the NFR-90 feasibility study was submitted to the NATO Project Steering Committee. After evaluation by the governments of the participating nations, further negotiations were required to arrive at a detailed NATO Staff Requirement. Eventually, agreement was reached in 1988 and Statements of Intent signed by a number of NATO governments. Even though the future of the programme is fraught with difficulties it represents an important step forward, for the development of naval vessals in Europe has been subject to *de facto*-specialization between nations. The requirements of both the Alliance's European members and the world market will be primarily for ships of the NFR-90 displacement. Although the hulls could be built anywhere, no one European nation could configure the sub-systems and weapons suite of the ship independently. Thus the NFR-90 carries also a symbolic importance for future co-operation in the development of naval platforms. Current estimates are that, for a requirement of some fifty frigates, the costs would be in the region of $200–$300 million per unit, representing savings of the order of 15–20 per cent when compared with individual national procurement. But past experience with co-operative projects has shown that such savings are extraordinarily difficult to achieve in practice.

Thus of the three main fields for defence co-operation — aerospace, ground forces equipment, and naval systems — only the aerospace sector has a significant past and an ambiguous though probably assured future. Another field, that of defence electronics, is of growing importance. Having overcome previous difficulties in developing a compatible IFF (Identification Friend or Foe) system and in establishing a wide range of communication frequency standards, the path is open to important future co-operative ventures in this field. One great opportunity for co-operative development between France and Britain in this field that has been missed is that of ground forces communication systems. Each nation developed national systems independently (RITA for France and Ptarmigan for Britain), the consequences of which are discussed later in this paper. Even though no substantial co-operative programmes have evolved thus far, the promise of the defence electronics sector for a rationalized co-operative development of sonars, radars, and communications systems within Europe is great, and, in the commercial sector at least, co-operative research and development is being actively sought.

## Managing co-operative programmes

Past experience has helped determine the most profitable methods of co-operation. But this experience has left different impressions not just between France and Britain for example, but between government, the military services, and industry. From a national perspective the British military services broadly view co-operation as the only long-term means of obtaining the equipment they require in relevant quantities. This does not though extend to a preference for the development of a European defence industrial base. Rather, they see a balance of co-operative ventures and licensed production between Britain and America and Britain and Europe. Only recently have British efforts had a distinct European preference and these were looked on with considerable scepticism within the Ministry of Defence, especially by those with previous experience of major Franco-British projects. The British aerospace industry, which is the sector with by far the most experience of Franco-British and other European co-operative ventures, is distinctly apprehensive about co-operative development. Partly as a result of the experience with the Jaguar and helicopter development programmes, future bilateral co-operation between Britain and France on major defence equipment items is not a likely prospect. Instead the British aerospace industry has sought to pursue co-operative defence programmes with a number of European partner nations, including France. Though this pattern predominates in programmes for major items of defence equipment, it has not excluded significant bilateral activity for the development of weapons sub-systems.

The Westland helicopter affair brought government attitudes towards the European or American option for the procurement of defence equipment into sharp relief. But the policy of successive administrations, including that of Prime Minister Margaret Thatcher, has shown a high degree of consistency in balancing the importance that British governments have historically placed on the value of the special relationship with the United States, especially in defence, with the value to Britain of inter-European defence co-operation. In the area of conventional weapons procurement the special relationship has provided the opportunity not only to manufacture under licence but to absorb American technological expertise into the British defence industrial base. It has also provided, in the case of the AV-8B advanced Harrier jump-jet, the opportunity to develop jointly an aircraft incorporating advanced American and British technologies which Britain could not have afforded to undertake alone, and for which a European partnership was not in prospect. Other areas of importance are associated with the supply of spares and replacements.

British purchase of the US Harpoon anti-ship and anti-submarine missile and the AIM-9L air-to-air missile has left her dependent on the United States for the supply of these systems in conflicts such as the Falklands. In these circumstances British governments place greater confidence in the United States than any other European nation not just for perceptions of political dependability, but for the ability to arrange beneficial methods of repayment in difficult circumstances.

Thus British governments, the military services, and the defence industry in general see the continued development of Britain's defence industrial base with both American and European co-operation programmes. While France, West Germany and other European nations also seek to maintain a balance of this kind, they see a greater ideological purpose to the creation of an independent competitive European defence industrial base than Britain does. In part this is because in the past Britain has been much more successful in the American defence market place than other European nations. In recent years this dominance has certainly diminished but it is still substantial and considered worthy of further cultivation and if possible protection.

Since France and Britain are closely comparable in the size and diversity of their defence industrial base, direct co-operation in weapons procurement raises protectionist sentiments in the respective defence industries of both countries. These industries are usually in direct competition and will not readily forfeit the opportunity to gain dominance in Europe, or at a very minimum maintain their existing capacity to compete in the European and world market for weapons systems. The only way to overcome this kind of difficulty would be to encourage the development of strong with weak industries. Though this has a great potential and is pursued in the development of sub-systems, it assures the continued inferiority of the weaker industry. Politically such policies have proved extremely difficult to pursue in high-profile programmes such as the development of combat aircraft.

The influence of these factors and the experience of the past has driven French and British defence industries towards two distinct models for the successful management of co-operative projects. One is preferred by France and the other by Britain. The French approach requires designating one of the international partners as the lead manufacturer for the joint project and minimizing any international organizational superstructure. Collaboration with the UK on the Jaguar aircraft and on the helicopter package, as well as with West Germany on the Alpha Jet and the Milan, Hot, and Roland missiles followed this model. Such arrangements have been successful when they have brought complementary capabilities together — an airframe manufacturer from one country with an aero engine manufacturer from another, for example. However, this was not quite the case with either the Jaguar or the helicopter family projects, where work was divided between the respective airframe and aero engine manufacturers of the two countries. The project leadership was similarly divided, with France having the lead for airframe design and Britain engine development in the case of the Jaguar.

The model of co-operative development preferred by the British is that established for the German–Italian–British Tornado aircraft. In this case significant international organizations and staffs were formed to manage the programme. Panavia was formed as the international company for managing the airframe development, and Turbo Union for managing the aero engine. Both of these companies are jointly owned by the main manufacturers in each country, Germany and Britain being the majority shareholders with a stake of 42.5 per cent. This approach, with joint international staffing and development leadership, is preferred by British industry at least in part because it allows manufacturers with greater expertise to maintain a dominant role behind the international management agency. This is of special concern to British Aerospace in particular because Rolls-Royce so thoroughly dominates aero engine design in Europe that the French approach severely limits their opportunities to take the design lead where these two components are divided between the two countries.

The British aerospace industry argues that this problem is averted by using the international organization to select relevant capabilities from the different sources. However in the case of Tornado this approach worked because the partners were not equally capable and the choices were therefore uncomplicated. Germany and Italy implicitly accepted the greater British expertise, while the British gratefully accepted the joint financing of the programme. Thus neither the French nor the British approach to the management of co-operative defence programmes is trouble free, nor are they necessarily representative of an ideal means of conducting co-operative aerospace programmes in Europe. But these approaches have been tried and have worked in different programmes by both Britain and France. Thus when the time came to consider the co-operative development of the next generation of the European fighter aircraft to replace existing Jaguars and F-4 Phantoms in the 1990s the differing French and British approaches to the management of co-operative aerospace projects became a matter of serious contention once again.

## The European fighter aircraft (EFA)

Both Britain and France developed prototypes for their next generation fighter aircraft requirements before a joint European Staff target was firmly established. The principal combat aircraft manufacturers of both countries are fiercely competitive and suspicious of each other. Each would wish to maintain the lead in any co-operative development of combat aircraft in Europe. The British aircraft was developed to meet the RAF Air Staff Target 403. The French aircraft was similar in performance specifications but 20 kg lighter in its BME (basic mass empty), and 10 kN (kilonewtons) less powerful in thrust. With the exception of one requirement, that of French CAP (Combat Air Patrol) and German air superiority, the French design met all EFA criteria within 8 per cent of stated requirements. The British aircraft met or exceeded all requirements except that of German air superiority. Thus the two aircraft were closely comparable in design specification. But British Aerospace, which led efforts by the Anglo–German–Italian consortium for the EFA, objected to the French configuration. This objection was based on the now-familiar theme that French weapon systems are designed primarily with export markets in mind to the detriment of national and NATO military requirements. In fact, EFA was not an ideal candidate for merging French requirements with those of Britain, West Germany, and Italy. These countries require a high-performance interceptor to replace Lightnings and Phantoms, while the French requirement is for a lighter-weight fighter-bomber to replace the Jaguar. The French interceptor, the Mirage 2000, is still entering service and will not need replacement until the turn of the century.

But even if it had been possible to combine the requirements, future co-operative combat aircraft development between France and Britain rather than between these two countries as members of a broader European consortium is not a likely prospect. France and Britain are too similar in aerospace technological and industrial capabilities for their respective industries to accept the kind of division of work that would be necessary for economically sensible co-operative projects. Past experience has borne this out and set the present pattern. The only way this might be changed is by political intention to alter the character and structure of the European defence industrial base, which also does not seem likely in the foreseeable future.

## The RITA/Ptarmigan case

Though Franco-British co-operation in the development of future military aircraft is unlikely, this will not necessarily prevent a general pattern of improvement in the level of co-operative activity for the development of other weapon systems. A high degree of *de facto* specialization has taken place between European manufacturers of naval weapon systems, although France, Britain, and Italy still maintain a high level of independent capability to develop modern warships. A similar pattern exists in the military electronics industry, with a few large industries dominating the European market. In such circumstances the importance of identifying common requirements and military specifications is overwhelming. The natural inclination of national industries is to go it alone, for, without the political pressure to undertake co-operative development, independent national development will always be the preferred option. In the case of the French RITA and British Ptarmigan military communications systems these factors resulted in the now-familiar stories of duplication of development effort and competition for export markets, all of which would have been better rationalized by co-operative development. The tragedy of the RITA/Ptarmigan case is that sufficient political pressure did not exist at a time when common requirements and military specifications could have been accomplished. These could have been established only by the political determination to do so, not by waiting for the natural coincidence of military and industrial interests between nations, which rarely, if ever, occurs.

## The helicopter affair

A persistent theme throughout the Westland affair was the need for Britain to maintain an independent capacity to develop military helicopters as part of her defence industrial base. This is in spite of the fact that neither the European option nor the Sikorsky bid really offered this prospect. Now the political and economic consequences of an MoD decision not to purchase the Blackhawk are likely to be dramatic (especially for Westland). Equally a decision to purchase the Blackhawk could have damaging consequences for future British interest in co-operative weapons development with her European allies and will place further strain on the national defence budget. It would seem that here, as in other cases before it, concern with maintaining the defence industrial base will impact on the capacity to meet future military requirements.

After the board of Westland helicopters finally succeeded with their recommendation to join forces with Sikorsky, the two companies restated their hope that the Ministry of Defence would consider the purchase of the Sikorsky Blackhawk helicopter. This helicopter, though liked for its rugged military construction, is too small for the RAF requirements and was previously rejected for this, and for its high cost. Westland propose to re-engine the Blackhawk, perhaps stretch it to meet the seating capacity requirement of the RAF, and install largely British avionics. On the basis of past experience, all of this will further increase the costs and probably result in delayed delivery. Additionally, Sikorsky/Westland hope that the RAF will purchase some 150 of these helicopters, which is three times the stated MoD requirement. This expenditure falls at a time when the RAF is in the middle of the largest and most expensive modernization plan in its history. This modernization includes having to correct for the failures of the Nimrod AEW (Airborne Early Warning), problems with the radar of the Tornado, and forthcoming expenditure associated with the EFA (European fighter aircraft), the Tornado mid-life improvement programme, and the procurement of the GR-5 (AV-8B) V/STOL aircraft.

The Westland affair illustrates many of the issues with which we are concerned. The company is Britain's sole manufacturer of helicopters and has depended on the MoD for most of its business. It is one of four European helicopter manufacturers who must compete for NATO military requirements barely large enough for one major company. The minimum for a newly developed helicopter to be commercially viable is considered to be in the region of 1,000 aircraft and the NATO requirement for the NH-90 utility helicopter in two versions between four or five European participating nations is around 700. Consequently, European manufacturers have forged partnerships (in Westland's case first with Aerospatiale and then with Augusta) in order to be able to develop helicopters for joint national requirements. Thus the helicopter design, development, and manufacturing base in Europe represents a substantial overcapacity that ought logically to be rationalized in the interests of both the future security of the industry and military requirement. Another aspect is the extent to which the defence industrial base has sought links with that of the United States through direct purchase, licensed production, and co-operative development. Westland, for example, has maintained a long relationship with Sikorsky, and the MoD purchased the Chinook medium support helicopter directly from the United States. Neither industrial management nor the workforce has ever held a high view of greater integration with Europe. These views are by no means uncommon in other British defence industries.

## Conclusion

Thus the past and future of Franco-British co-operation in the procurement of conventional weapon systems is a story of accommodation. It ought perhaps to have been one of a pooling of resources to strengthen the European defence industrial base for both local requirements and to provide a stronger basis for competition with the United States. It may be regrettable that this has not been the case and especially that it is unikely to be so in the future. However, both Britain and France are too similar in defence industrial capability for co-operation to follow simply from the commonsense idea of a rationalization of the European defence industrial base. Rather the inclination to rationalize the defence industries of Europe can follow only from far more substantial changes in the political outlook of successive British and French administrations. Changes that would accept the sacrifice of some domestic capability (albeit inefficient) for the sake of a common European defence industrial base.

The prospects for effective Franco-British defence co-operation in the future then rest on the capacity for national governments to recognize the limits of economic and political usefulness of a national defence capability when better capabilities exist elsewhere within Europe. This will be at best a slow prospect for Britain, not least because she is still determined to divide her interest between the European partnership and the American 'special relationship', but equally because British defence industries can still steal a cloak of protection for independent development on the basis of the requirement to protect a national defence industrial base. The political rationalization for such a base will need to be more clearly identified before domestic sacrifices will be made by British governments towards the collective European interest.

Chapter twelve

# Co-operation in arms procurement: a French view

Pierre Menanteau

The general problems posed by European co-operation in arms production acquire an additional dimension when applied to Franco-British co-operation alone.

It is necessary to go beyond the passionate reactions often aroused by some aspect or other of this co-operation and examine objectively the facts of the matter. If European co-operation is to be developed, it must be based initially on the two main defence industries, aerospace and electronics. There will be no meaningful Europe and no European defence without France or without Britain and even less so if either of them is against it. Circumstances force us into a marriage of convenience. It will be a difficult marriage but its success is a prerequisite to the construction of Europe.

## The constraints

For two countries to co-operate, other than sporadically and in piecemeal fashion, in the very sensitive area of arms production, they must first have harmonized their defence policy, their strategy, and their tactical concepts. They must also have resolved the industrial problems which are inevitable in the case of co-operation between countries with developed armaments industries. In these two major areas, the divergences between France and Great Britain are not unimportant.

### *The political and military constraints*

France and Britain are both nuclear powers, the only nuclear powers in Europe. France is continuing to modernize her nuclear forces at considerable expense. Her defence policy is based on the existence of this strategic nuclear force. The inherent independence conferred by a nuclear force, over which control cannot be shared, led France to leave the integrated military organization of NATO. As a nuclear power, France could not be bound by the automatic obligations of an integrated command. She thus insisted on retaining its autonomy in decision-making.

The British approach is quite different. Although strictly national as far as its use is concerned, the British strategic nuclear force, perhaps because it was set up as part of a certain Anglo-Saxon private agreement, has never appeared likely to lead Britain to adopt an independent defence policy. On the contrary, the integration of British forces in NATO, where Britain has a privileged position because of her nuclear forces and her special ties with the United States, remains central to British defence policy.

Britain has been able to establish a nuclear force for approximately a quarter of the cost of the French strategic nuclear force. The British strategic nuclear force has always taken a relatively small proportion of the defence budget. Unlike the situation in France, the emphasis in Britain has always been on equipping and modernizing her conventional forces, particularly her air forces.

Although the defence budgets of the two countries are of the same order of magnitude overall ($28.7 billion for Britain, compared with $27.7 billion for France in 1986 — see Table 12.1), the distribution of spending is in fact very different. In France, the largest proportion of money goes on the nuclear forces (21.3 per cent of the overall budget in 1987). These nuclear items have priority; spending cuts are always at the expense of the conventional forces. As far as French conventional forces are concerned, the army has the largest budget (19.3 per cent of the total), way ahead of that of the air force (11.8 per cent) and the navy (12.2 per cent). In Britain, the strategic nuclear forces account for a very modest proportion of the budget (2.7 per cent), the Royal Air Force receiving the largest share (20.5 per cent), compared with 16 per cent for the army and 13 per cent for the navy.

*Table 12.1* Defence spending in Britain and France

| | *France* | *Britain* |
|---|---|---|
| 1986 defence budget | $27,715m. | $28,011m. |
| Share of budget in 1986 devoted to equipment | 50.7% | 47.0% |
| Share of budget in 1986 devoted to R & D | 12.7% | 12.4% |

This asymmetry, arising from different political choices, is a source of difficulty. As the two countries have neither the same defence policy nor the same priorities, they cannot devote the same funds to the same weapons systems. This makes bilateral co-operation difficult and more risky, as with the programme for the joint construction of helicopters. Having a much smaller domestic market, the French arms industry has to turn to exports far more than its British counterpart. This necessity leads it to promote its own products for export in preference to collaborative products, and also to favour the development of systems that compromise between purely French requirements and satisfying the export market, rather than systems that are specifically designed for the requirements of the European theatre.

### *The industrial realities*

The French and British arms industries, the largest in Europe, have very similar capabilities. They both cover all sectors, including all the high-technology sectors; they are direct competitors in all areas (aircraft, engines, helicopters, missiles, electronics, ship-fitting, weapons systems, etc.). Being equally strong, each naturally tends to look for co-operation to a third party (preferably West Germany), in order to establish superiority over the other. There have however often been instances of co-operation between the French and the British, the French and the Germans, and the British and the Germans, which shows that strong, lasting European co-operation can only be established around these three European industrial powers.

It is also important to highlight the major differences in the relationship between the arms industry and government in each of the two countries.

In France, there is far greater osmosis between industry and government. The arms industry is very much under the wing of the Délégation Générale pour l'Armement (DGA), which draws up a policy, selects from a number of industrial competitors, and nominates the main contractor. Close contacts are established between manufacturers and the state, through the design and technical departments of the DGA. Most major projects are the outcome of study contracts at least partly financed by the government (though the proportion of self-financed studies is tending to increase) and are largely jointly discussed. Export and collaborative operations are monitored very closely, even directed, by the government.

In Britain, the government certainly pursues a deliberate, aggressive export strategy, and all the ministries are made aware of, and involved in, this strategy, which includes the possibility of compensation deals. However, on the domestic market, less government intervention leaves far more scope to competition between firms. It is apparently paradoxical that the defence industrial sector, while dominated by competition within Britain, still strives in the export market to appear above all as essentially 'British'.

These differences in approach, linked to the fact that British manufacturers often do not fully appreciate the nature of the nationalized defence companies in France, are a source of difficulties for bilateral co-operation.

They can even lead British manufacturers to prefer to co-operate with countries such as the USA which have similar approaches.

It is essential to mention the importance attached in Britain to collaborative programmes, perhaps owing to the impetus given at the beginning of the 1980s by the defence secretary Mr Heseltine (40 per cent of the equipment budget since 1980 has concerned collaborative projects). In addition, British officials always stress that any proposal for the purchase of new equipment which does not consider European alternatives is automatically rejected.

## The legacy of the past: balance sheet of Franco-British co-operation

Franco-British co-operation in defence procurement really began in the 1960s with three major programmes: the Jaguar aircraft, the helicopter family, and the Martel missile.

### *The Jaguar programme*

It was difficult and took a long time to define this programme. The Jaguar experience confirms, if confirmation were needed, how hazardous it is to set up a joint programme when the operational specifications of the participants are different. However, in retrospect, one can say that the programme was implemented very satisfactorily, as far as industrial co-operation is concerned, with regard to both the airframe and the jet engines. Britain was in fact obliged to participate in this project for financial and industrial reasons. The success of this co-operation raised hopes for the future. Relations between the manufacturers were excellent and the arrangement that had been set up highly suitable: France was the executive agency for the airframe, and Britain for the jet engines, through two European companies created by the grouping, respectively, of Breguet and British Aerospace, and Rolls-Royce and Turbomeca.

Commercially, the remainder of the programme was not so satisfactory because, once Dassault had taken over Breguet, it quickly emerged that Jaguar was competing for exports with the other aircraft produced by Dassault. The resulting difficulties and tension were bound to create resentment between the partners, which was of significance for the future.

### *Puma–Gazelle–Lynx helicopters*

These ambitious programmes were the subject of a protocol signed in 1967 on co-operation in the helicopter field and were launched to meet the pressing needs expressed by the armed forces of both countries. They enabled machines to be developed under good industrial conditions. The arrangement was a very good model in terms of industrial management, but budgetary problems did not enable France to buy as many helicopters as had been initially forecast and this led to an imbalance which was very damaging to the health of collaborative ventures.

*Martel missile*

This programme was carried out fairly satisfactorily, but did not lead to work on a new generation of missiles.

These three major programmes, which could have been the starting point for much wider and longer-term co-operation, in fact marked the end of Franco-British bilateral co-operation, partly for reasons specific to each programme, partly for structural reasons attributable to the political, economic, and industrial constraints, and perhaps also to a large extent for psychological reasons — the prejudices were too great, the rivalry too strong, and the will to find a compromise absent. The decisive development was the failure at the end of the 1960s of the Franco-British variable geometry aircraft programme.

*What co-operation is possible between Britain and France?*

Past experiences show the difficulties and the limitations of Franco-British bilateral co-operation on major projects. Bilateral co-operation is certainly easier to set up, but in the case of major systems there are market pressures in Europe for wider co-operative partnerships; these are inevitably more difficult to implement. To make a success of these large programmes for the development of major systems requires a combination of shared political will, common military interests, and an appropriate industrial arrangement; but the efforts are justified by what is at stake. This was the case, for example, when Britain joined with France and West Germany for the improvement of the Milan missile (by the provision of a night sight) and then to develop the future anti-tank weapons system (TRIGAT).

In spite of the difficulties, the need for co-operation and the advantages accruing from it seem obvious. Very often particular projects have emerged from the wish of specific countries to 'do something special' for political reasons; projects in these cases have not come from an overall European view or concerted action by all the European countries. But there are some signs of change. In particular, in Britain, it is currently considered that co-operation in Europe must be achieved through a structure that permits the various requirements to be summarized, all the possibilities to be examined, and initial co-operation then to be set up. The Independent European Programme Group (IEPG) seems to be the most suitable existing structure for this task and in Britain the current tendency is to prefer co-operation through the IEPG to the past pattern of co-operation between two or three participants. This approach is largely shared by the other states.

British officials also stress the fact that the development of co-operation in Europe must above all aim to reinforce the capability of the Atlantic Alliance as a whole, and can under no circumstances be considered as an anti-American activity. On the contrary, the Conference of National Armaments' Directors (CNAD) must, jointly with the IEPG for the European countries, remain NATO's consultative body for arms programmes.

Though it is accepted in Britain that the IEPG should on a number of projects enable Europe to speak with one voice, for other special projects there is a desire to be able to continue, or to develop, bilateral transatlantic co-operation. However, both in Britain and in France, it does seem that the IEPG should be the preferred forum in Europe, bringing together the thirteen Euorpean members of the Alliance. It now meets at defence minister level and enables European ideas, particularly tactical concepts and their repercussions as regards arms, to be enlarged upon and promoted. It also enables countries with advanced and comprehensive defence industries to be combined with those countries that, having less developed defence industries, are the favourite customers of the USA in Europe. Finally, the IEPG can serve as a framework for agreements between manufacturers joining forces bilaterally or multilaterally.

Since we are concerned particularly here with co-operation between France and Britain, it must be admitted that, in spite of a willingness on both sides to co-operate, the reasons remain which have in the past given mixed results or even partial failure. These reasons, which include competing industries, different policies, and aspirations to leadership, contribute to the fostering of a degree of mistrust or at least a certain wariness.

This is why, at the same time as supporting multilateral co-operation on major systems devised within the European framework, it seems desirable more specifically to promote Franco-British co-operation in order to avoid the pitfalls inherent in the constraints, particularly the industrial constraints.

This co-operation should be developed in the area of components and research in key technologies. Rather than attempting spectacular groups aimed at developing complete systems, it seems preferable, by means of agreements between manufacturers, to create first of all a form of technological community, which is the only way in the long run to preserve Europe's independence from the USA and Japan. Because of their industrial and scientific capabilities in leading military technologies, France and Britain seem particularly suited to becoming together the centre and the driving force of this European technological community.

The agreements already concluded to date between French and British manufacturers in the field of military components and sub-assemblies should also be noted, together with the many instances of participation of firms from both countries in civilian programmes such as Esprit and Eureka.

## Conclusion

If it is to last, co-operation in arms production must be built on as wide a base as possible and must be organized and controlled by a suitable European structure which specifies where the main efforts should be directed and what major equipment should be developed jointly. At the moment the IEPG seems to be the most suitable structure to promote this intra-European co-operation and also to restore the balance in transatlantic co-operation.

Though it seems that the construction of major systems (aircraft, ships, communication detection systems, etc.) must inevitably fall within the scope of multilateral co-operation, for which it is necessary to have suitable structures, key research and the development of components and sub-assemblies can and must be the subject of fruitful bilateral co-operation.

In this respect, France and Britain seem particularly suited to forming a privileged technological axis in Europe. It seems that this pooling of the research capabilities of the two countries in the field of key military technology, mainly through agreements between manufacturers, should in the future be the most appropriate way for bilateral co-operation between the two countries to avoid past errors. This bilateral technological co-operation should not replace the other major European technological research programmes. On the contrary, it must be the driving force behind them.

## Author's note

Although this article was written two years ago, it remains basically up-to-date, despite problems such as those involving the European fighter. One important decision has, however, been made: the agreement in 1987 between the British and French Defence Ministries to open their national armaments markets to companies from both countries for arms procurement proposals for all types of equipment. It is too early to say how this will work, but it will probably not be easy to implement this fully until the structure and rates of government support for R and D in both countries have been harmonized, and a substantial understanding of procurement procedures on each side has been achieved.

Part three

# Towards a new entente cordiale?

Chapter thirteen

# A new step in Franco-British co-operation

Ian Davidson

If there is one strand which is common to most if not all of the contributions to this Anglo-French study, it is a clearly conveyed sense of regret. Co-operation in the field of defence between Britain and France ought, in some sense, to be much closer than it is; the two countries are, in so many respects, complementary to each other, with similar policies and overlapping interests and yet, alas, there are practical difficulties, historical legacies, political suspicions, and *arrière-pensées*, which mean that the situation is not likely to change very much.

In so far as this is a consensus judgement, it is remarkably interesting, because the tone is new. It is not long since such a collection of authors, assembled to debate this self-same question, would have failed to get beyond an exchange of ill-humoured recriminations, with the British accusing the French of being bad allies, and the French accusing the British of being bad Europeans. Here, by contrast there is a clear desire to accentuate the positive, to emphasize common interests, and even, in some cases, a tendency to overstate the degree to which existing policies of the two countries already coincide more closely in reality than divergent rhetoric would suggest.

To that extent, I am not sure that the pervasive sense of hopeless regret is not overdone. If such an authoritative group of experts is able to go beyond the mutual recrimination that used to block any sensible discussion, and is prepared to engage in an earnest debate on the premise that more co-operation would be desirable, then that already is progress.

On the other hand, progress is bound to be very limited if more defence co-operation is perceived merely as something 'desirable' or 'helpful', or 'useful'. If that were the full extent of the potential driving force behind Franco-British defence co-operation, I should certainly subscribe to the mournful consensus of most of my fellow authors. Defence is a policy area which is vibrant with nationalist resonances, with historical associations, with implications for national survival. Governments are unlikely to tamper with their defence arrangements just because more co-operation might be desirable. Peter Nailor discusses the issue in terms of the concept of 'advantage', and, while he is quite right in one sense, in another he has chosen an inadequate benchmark: governments co-operate on life and death issues not when it seems advantageous, but only when it becomes *necessary*, and is perceived to be necessary.

The studies contained in this book are disaggregated into discrete aspects of possible defence co-operation — nuclear, conventional, out-of-area, equipment procurement, and so on. This is logical, especially with a number of authors, each with a specific speciality. But there is a sense in which it may be a misleading approach, because it can appear to suggest that defence is like a display of goods in a do-it-yourself shop, where the shopper can pick and choose the most useful items.

In the autumn of 1986, Dr David Owen and Mr David Steel, the two leaders of Britain's centrist Social Democratic Liberal Alliance, visited Paris to discuss the idea of Anglo-French defence co-operation, including among other things perhaps co-operation on nuclear matters. The popular press in Britain immediately interpreted this as a proposal for an Anglo-French nuclear bomb — whereas, of course, an Anglo-French nuclear bomb is almost unimaginable; if it could be imagined, it would need to be preceded by an enormous chain of other co-operative steps.

Only one aspect of defence co-operation can usefully be treated on a supermarket basis, and that is co-operation on defence procurement, because it does not necessarily impinge on the political aspects of defence doctrine; but the benchmark of *necessity* rather than mere 'advantage' remains the critical test. Here the augeries are relatively encouraging in European rather than narrowly defined Anglo-French terms. There seems to be greater impetus behind the attempt to create the structural conditions for co-operation in the Independent European Programme Group, because even France and Britain are concluding that they can no longer be self-sufficient in the manufacture of defence equipment at an acceptable budgetary cost; therefore they must co-operate with others.

But in all other aspects of defence the key to co-operation lies not in ingenious discussion of the workaday opportunities, but in the evolution of central political ideas; in the head, not in the headquarters of practical men. We are now told that the co-operative arrangements between France and NATO launched by Ailleret and Lemnitzer were much more far-reaching than anyone has previously been prepared to admit. Perhaps; but the incontrovertible fact is that the Franco-German defence debate has followed the pace laid down by François Mitterrand after his election to the French Presidency, not that implicit in the practical arrangements of the generals, because it is the French President who would decide on the use of French forces — conventional and nuclear. François Mitterrand launched the Franco-German defence debate, intervened to endorse the deployment of cruise and Pershing II missiles in West Germany, and set up the Force d'Action Rapide, because he believed these steps were necessary. So far there is little sign of corresponding necessity driving analogous co-operation between France and Britain.

The main obstacle to real defence co-operation between France and Britain is the survival in both countries of an atavistic belief in the possibility of a national defence policy. National defence seems one of the most glorious attributes of national sovereignty; in neither country do politicians care to admit that this sovereignty is entirely contingent on others.

In fact no European country *can* have an independent defence policy if the potential adversary is the Soviet Union; for fighting the Argentines in the South Atlantic, perhaps, or the Libyans in Chad, but not for keeping out the Russians. The independence of any European country is contingent on the independence of its neighbours. Therefore the starting point for any European defence policy is the concept of alliance. Not just a purely declaratory alliance either; nor an alliance whose practical arrangements are maintained *sub rosa* by the military while denied by the political elite; nor an alliance where total loyalty is somehow combinable with total independence of national decision-making; nor, because of the speed with which danger could erupt, can it be an improvisatory alliance. A real alliance means integration in advance.

I think it follows that the opportunities for France and Britain to co-operate on the hard, political aspects of defence policy will be contingent on the ability of each to subordinate their defence thinking to the claims of the alliance. In this sense, it is obvious that the most material obstacle to Franco-British defence co-operation has been the absoluteness of the French claim (going back to General de Gaulle and the break with NATO in 1966) to a nationally independent defence policy.

That obstacle has diminished since President Mitterrand activated the military chapters of the 1963 Franco-German Treaty, and it continues to diminish the closer leading French politicians get to an admission that French security is indissolubly linked to German security. Encouraging markers here have been the formation of the Force d'Action Rapide, which *could* be used in the forward defence of Germany, and the suggestion that France might consult Germany before using any short-range nuclear weapons, if time allowed.

Ostensibly, Britain's military posture is more naturally susceptible to a co-operative mode, because Britain has from the beginning of NATO committed herself, both in practice and in rhetoric, to the concept of an integrated alliance. Politically, however, the position is very different: the traditional blind spot in the mentality of post-war British governments has been their instinctive assumption that the relationship with the United States must have priority over, and in some sense determine, the relationship with Europe.

At one level this may seem a logical preference. The US is a superpower, and none of Britain's European partners comes remotely into the same league; America's vast nuclear arsenal is what deters the nuclear threat from the Soviet Union; America's commitment of 300,000 troops to Europe is what helps to make up part of the shortfall in Europe's own defence; so the top priority must be to cultivate the American guarantee for Europe's security.

In purely psychological terms, however, these are just plausible rationalizations for an instinctive preference, based on nostalgia and the ease of common language and shared political values. After the Second World War, the Anglo-American relationship was prolonged by the British in the belief that a victorious war-time partnership of moral equals could be kept in being in peace-time, despite the vast and ever-widening gap in economic resources. At first, indeed, while continental European governments were launching the early experiments in political integration, Britain stood aloof as if she could command great power status.

Britain's most extreme pretensions have shrivelled in the face of cruel reality and uninterrupted economic decline; over the years, successive governments have been driven by *la force des choses* into a closer relationship with Europe. On the whole, however, this is an evolution that has been followed without enthusiasm, and where national security is concerned officialdom continues to give top priority to the American relationship.

Such a priority clearly militates against the deepening of defence co-operation on a specifically European basis, including closer co-operation with France. Beyond a certain point, defence co-operation must depend on an implicit assumption that no relationship in the security field takes precedence over that with co-operative partner or partners. The British are not likely to take any really significant steps towards European defence co-operation until they accord the top priority to their relationship with their European partners, starting with France, Germany and the Netherlands.

From this point of view, the British are, if anything, less naturally predisposed to the possibilities of mutual defence co-operation with the French. The conservative half of the country still clings to Atlanticism as the top priority, and is supported in this by the Whitehall elite; in the general election of 1987 the Labour Party adopted an anti-nuclear policy which would put Britain at odds both with the United States and with the other NATO allies in Europe; only the centrist Alliance parties were searching for a Euro-centric defence posture. By contrast, the political elite in France, both on the left and on the right, has started to wake from twenty years of Gaullist self-delusion to the beginnings of an explicit recognition that the top priority for the security of France is the security of West Germany.

The second precondition for the deepening of defence co-operation beyond a certain point is an agreed understanding of military doctrine and the practical arrangements required to implement it. For twenty years France virtually ruled herself out as a possible partner in defence co-operation in Europe, partly because non-cooperation was General de Gaulle's *political* objective, partly because Gaullist *military* doctrine was at variance with that of the rest of the Alliance.

If French attitudes appear to be evolving in a more European direction, it is partly for political but also for military–technological reasons. On the one hand, the political turbulence in West Germany over the Euro-missile crisis in 1979–83, the consequent rupture of the German consensus on defence policy, and the fear that Germany might move towards neutralism, all exposed the absurdity of the pretension of French claims to the right of non-engagement. On the other hand, the growing anxiety of the rest of NATO about undue dependence on tactical nuclear weapons, and the search for hi-tech conventional weapons which could be used instead of nuclear weapons, exposed the nakedness of the French doctrine that the magic power of the nuclear could be counted on to guarantee a state of *non-guerre*.

General de Gaulle broke with NATO in 1966 because he rejected the adoption of the 'flexible response' doctrine, which he regarded as an unacceptable reduction in the emphasis on nuclear deterrence. The paradox is that NATO's exploration of high-tech options for further raising the nuclear threshold is inducing the French to reconsider whether their nuclear doctrine may not place them in a dangerously exposed position. The rupture of 1966 was a piece of politically significant theatre, which was unlikely to lead to any meaningful difference in the use of nuclear weapons if hostilities should break out; however much General de Gaulle may have objected to the apparent softening of NATO's nuclear threat, there was virtually no chance then, and none at all now, that France would be prepared to cross the nuclear threshold on her own. The significance of the formation of the Force d'Action Rapide is that it is a tacit acknowledgement that quarrels about nuclear dogma are sterile, unless they are placed in their proper context: that the security of Western Europe is indivisible, and depends first on adequate conventional defence. If there is to be any European co-operation on defence, it must start with an attempted convergence of views on the role of conventional forces.

It follows that, if France is to co-operate with anyone on central defence issues, she must do so either bilaterally with West Germany, or multilaterally with a wider group of NATO partners. It is much less clear what role there could be for bilateral co-operation between France and Britain on central defence issues except within the context of multilateral co-operation. The main stumbling block is the institutional symbolism of NATO. The French, for reasons of pride as well as concern for the domestic political consensus, are most unlikely to recant on twenty years of rupture; their European partners will continue to insist on the operational primacy of the NATO framework; neither side will be anxious to side-step the issue, for example by a real strengthening of Western European Union, to a point where it would risk upsetting the Americans.

The paradox is that America's commitment to the defence of Europe is increasingly being linked to the demand that the Europeans bear a larger share of the burden. However, given the stringency of defence budgets on both sides of the Atlantic, it is probable that Europe can make a bigger contribution to its own defence only through political synergy: through a more united and more specifically 'European' approach to the problems of the defence of Europe. Yet Washington reacts in prickly fashion to anything that smacks of European caucus within NATO.

Because of these institutional and symbolic obstacles, the evolution of Europe's defence configuration is likely to be extremely slow, unless there should be a radical change in the external environment. If one looks back to the end of the Second World War, one is drawn to the assumption that radical change is unlikely: the European stand-off has been fixed for forty years, and neither side will want to run the risk of trying to upset it. On the other hand, the Reagan–Gorbachev mini-summit at Reykjavik in October 1986 ostensibly came close to agreement on a major arms control package which would certainly imply major change in the east–west relationship, and possibly even bigger change in the nature of the European security dilemma.

It is hard to tell how close they really came, since an agreement is not an agreement until it is signed and ratified. Nevertheless, European governments can no longer rule out the possibility of an international regime characterized by a sharp reduction in America's nuclear commitment to the defence of Europe. Such a regime would not necessarily imply the total decoupling of America from Europe, or a situation of great danger for Europe; but it would represent a major change, and it would require Europe to review its collective security arrangements.

Chapter fourteen

# The prospects for Franco-British co-operation

Jean Chabaud

At first sight, Franco-British relations in defence matters seem like a succession of misunderstandings and missed opportunities. In this respect, the Heath–Pompidou period (1969–73) was unusual and therefore remarkable, since it was characterized by a shared political will to overcome opposition.

Though it has become customary to consider French and British policies as irreconcilable, it is in fact the persistence of their differences which seems surprising at a time when historical rivalries already seem dated and when the two countries have faced new and similar problems: decolonization, restoration of power through possession of atomic weapons, the redefinition of relations with the United States and the Soviet Union, and the construction of Europe. Although the rapprochement between 1969 and 1973 led to Britain's entry into the Common Market, it did not lead, in the last analysis, to any result with regard to defence. After hopes had been raised, Franco-British relations once again lapsed into routine indifference, and it was not until 1982–3 that the initial signs of a new rapprochement could be seen. It would now appear that, in spite of different political and especially doctrinal choices, there are fundamental strategic convergences between France and Britain which provide possibilities for increased co-operation. I propose, therefore, after outlining the history of Franco-British relations, to analyse the approaches which have been made in recent years and to suggest possible ways in which they could be further developed.

## From the post-war years to the 1980s: a succession of misunderstandings and missed opportunities

### *1945–69: Unrealized opportunities for closer relationships*

Two major questions characterize this period: the need for Europe to provide for its security in face of the threat represented by the Soviet Union, and the choice of nuclear weapons as the basis for the strategic balance in Europe. On these two closely related matters, there were many occasions on which the French and British positions could have been identical. However, prejudices and misunderstandings prevented this.

The concern to show a united face to the growing power of the USSR explains why France and Britain were the two countries behind the Brussels Pact of 17 March 1948, which was to lead to Western European Union. At the same time, the French and particularly the British asked the United States to open talks with a view to reaching a wider security agreement; the outcome of these was the Atlantic Pact of 4 April 1949. However, from 1950 on, the first misunderstandings appeared. As the Cold War reached its height, Britain considered it more necessary than ever to strengthen her ties with the United States in order to guarantee the defence of the British Isles. Although she had signed the Atlantic Pact a month earlier, she was uncertain whether to approve of the creation of the Council of Europe (5 May 1949), causing irritation in France. The Schuman and Pleven plans in fact enabled the movement for European unity to be launched without Britain, who rejected the plans without seriously examining them. Britain felt so close to the United States that, in her eyes, European developments were of no interest; their purpose was simply to enable France and the Federal Republic of Germany to complete their reconciliation. Though France was prepared to follow this path, she could not then face its possible, even logical, consequences, which was German rearmament, without the guarantee that British involvement in a European defence organization would provide.

French demands and uncertainties, misunderstood and badly received by Britain, were among other reasons why the proposals for a European Defence Community failed. As Churchill wished, Britain then put pressure on France to agree to German rearmament within the framework of an enlarged Brussels Pact and also to the Federal Republic of Germany joining NATO. These arrangements were formalized by the London and Paris agreements of October 1954.

General de Gaulle's arrival in office was to herald a new era in misunderstandings and intransigent attitudes on both sides, with a major split coming after the Nassau meeting between Kennedy and Macmillan in December 1962. The United States and Britain had shown reluctance to reply to General de Gaulle's September 1958 plan for a tripartite directorate in NATO. After Nassau, de Gaulle was convinced that from then on Britain was the Americans' 'Trojan horse' and that Britain's path to Europe had to be blocked. His disillusion was all the greater as, at his meeting with Macmillan at Rambouillet a few days before Macmillan left for Nassau, he had believed that Britain wanted to free herself from American tutelage. Macmillan's disillusionment was no less great, as he had thought that General de Gaulle was not opposed to Britain joining the EEC. Feigned or real, this misunderstanding led to General de

Gaulle's veto of Britain's application to join the European Economic Community and his rejection of Kennedy's multilateral force (MLF) plan.

Almost symmetrically, of her own free will, France left the integrated military structure of NATO in March 1966. However, she did not close her camps, her firing ranges, and her test centres to the Allied armies and particularly not to Britain. They were made available under multilateral or bilateral agreements which have been periodically renewed since the 1960s. However, this acceptance, from a position of autonomy, of commitments to the Alliance in no way affected the Franco-British disputes: General de Gaulle was to continue to impose upon Britain a 'separate' status in Europe, just as he had assumed a 'separate' status in the Alliance for France. Though of course very dissimilar and therefore not really comparable, these exclusions none the less reflected the state of deep rivalry which led the two countries to great mutual mistrust. In 1967, General de Gaulle therefore again rejected Britain's application to join the EEC and Britain was to be irritated further by his visit to Canada in the same year. Britain found this refusal all the more difficult to understand as, since 1963, she had been engaging with France in major co-operative armaments procurement programmes: the Martel missile from 1964, the Jaguar aircraft from 1965, and the Lynx, Puma, and Gazelle helicopters from 1967.

The efforts to develop nuclear energy, which occurred at the same time as the attempts to co-operate in security matters, no doubt partly explain these failures. Rivalry was present in the civilian as well as in the military domain.

This co-operation began badly: in 1946 and 1947 the British were reluctant to agree to French demands for collaboration in the civilian nuclear domain. Apparently under pressure from the Americans, they refused in 1954 to sell France a uranium separation plant which France needed in order to continue her civilian programme.

There were, however, undeniable similarities between the French and British positions and, at that time, among most of the reasons given for the choices made. Both nuclear programmes were born out of the involvement, very different in kind it is true, in the Manhattan programme during the war. Certainly Britain had preferential treatment in her relationship with the United States. In fact, Britain and France were both concerned to guarantee their independence and to preserve their capacity to influence the two superpowers. For both countries, nuclear weapons seemed to be the guarantee against the uncertainties of American protection; the existence of independent centres of nuclear decision-making served to increase uncertainty and so reduce the probability of the Soviet Union being able to bank on American non-engagement in Europe. These convergences in approach appeared to be strong enough to lead General Gallois to write in 1962 of Britain's efforts to create a national sanctuary by the threat of massive nuclear retaliation: 'Thus, in actual fact, the London government is following the only defence policy which makes sense nowadays.'[1]

Could there have been convergence of nuclear weapons policies? In 1962, contacts were indeed made with a view to combining strategic forces and developing elements essential for setting up these forces. That same year and as part of official and private visits to Paris, the British defence and aviation ministers are even said to have had talks on an 'entente nucléaire' between the two countries. During the Rambouillet meeting of December 1962, General de Gaulle is said to have proposed nuclear co-operation to Macmillan, but without getting any answer. Then the Nassau meeting between Macmillan and Kennedy thwarted these attempts at rapprochement. The Labour Party previously had approved the Conservatives' nuclear policy, then considered that the abandonment of the Skybolt missile by the United States made the American offer to provide Polaris missiles as part of a multilateral nuclear force the best solution for Britain. They therefore accepted the American arguments while the Conservatives were still assessing the consequences of the Nassau agreements. Britain's hesitation was not exploited by General de Gaulle who rejected simultaneously the American proposals for the supply of Polaris missiles to France, the creation of a multilateral nuclear force, and Britain's entry into the EEC.

In 1964, the Labour party came to power and from then on *British policy virtually ceased to evolve*; the accent was put almost constantly on the contribution of the British nuclear force to strengthening NATO's overall deterrent (a role that was to be acknowledged for the two European nuclear forces in the Ottawa Declaration of 1974).

### *1969–73: Hopes dashed*

On 1 January 1973, Britain joined the EEC. It was the outcome of lengthy negotiations carried on since 1970 and was facilitated by the excellent relations between Mr Heath and M. Pompidou. Indeed, Mr Heath, a committed European, had been the negotiator of Britain's earlier application to join the EEC. For his part, M. Pompidou was convinced of the need for Britain to join the Common Market.

This conviction was based on two arguments which are particularly interesting since they form the basis, on the French side, of the current rapprochement. First, because Europe had to define an overall policy, particularly in relation to the United States, it was futile to keep a power like Britain out of things. Britain's exclusion from the European Community could only strengthen her links across the Atlantic. Second, there were three main powers in Europe — France, Britain, and the Federal Republic of Germany. Stability, according to M. Pompidou, could only come from a proper balance between these three states. Good Franco-British relations were therefore necessary, particularly as the prospect of too strong a Germany was feared. There was in fact in France the two-fold perception of the Federal Republic of Germany becoming increasingly powerful economically, and of increasing uncertainty about her foreign policy. Symbolizing these two elements, West German *Ostpolitik* gave rise to concern, mistrust, and irritation among her European (and American) partners. For France therefore, Britain's entry into the Common Market and the deepening of Franco-British relations seemed to be the safest way of counter-balancing Germany's increasing power. Linked to that were the intellectual affinities and mutual esteem between the two statesmen, which contrasted with the poor personal relations between M. Pompidou and Chancellor Brandt.

The result was positive as far as the first aspect of this policy was concerned, EEC membership. Could the same also have been true as regards defence? It is certain that the favourable climate that prevailed in both countries could have facilitated rapprochement in strategic matters. It is moreover probable that at the highest political level defence questions were broached, but this cannot be confirmed by publicly available documents. One can only assume that during this period the two countries in some way renewed their relations in defence matters.

On the other hand, as far as co-operation on nuclear weapons is concerned, two public declarations by the British prime ministers of the time, denying any idea of Franco-British rapprochement on this question, must be emphasized, one in October 1972 and the other in March 1976.

In October 1972, shortly after a meeting with Georges Pompidou, Mr Heath replied to a journalist that the question of nuclear weapons co-operation had not been discussed with the French President because the latter did not wish it, and that it would not be discussed at the next summit meeting. In March 1976, a Labour MP asked the then prime minister, Mr Wilson, whether his government was still opposed to the proposal for a joint Anglo-French nuclear force and whether he would continue to reject it if France were to rejoin NATO. Mr Wilson replied that he had never heard of any such plan and that he did not believe that it had ever been put forward under the previous Conservative government; moreover, he himself rejected such a plan, which was also not envisaged by President Giscard d'Estaing. The British prime minister concluded by admitting that it was an idea that might gain ground, but only in the remote future.

In fact, the absence of any real rapprochement in the area of defence means not that there were no talks on the subject, but that they failed, demonstrating the differences between two policies which were still under development. In these circumstances, it was difficult to negotiate about weapons that still only constitute the beginnings of a credible deterrent.

Unable to discuss the principles lying behind their nuclear defence policies, the two countries may then have tried to find some area of agreement on logistics, but without success. From this arose the nickname of 'the cornflakes talks' which the English gave to these talks: if even the eating habits of the two sides are so different, what can be done?

### *1979–82: Routine indifference*

From 1974, Franco-British relations were dominated by the problems posed by Britain's membership of the EEC and in particular, from 1979, by the problem of the 'repayment' of the British contribution to the Community budget. During this period, France and Britain frequently clashed and co-operation in security matters slowed down. In 1981, when M. Mitterand came to power, Franco-British relations were at their lowest ebb.

However, contacts never entirely ceased. Thus, in a joint declaration of 23 June 1976, the President of the Republic and the British prime minister established an annual Franco-British summit. Franco-German co-operation was taken as the model for these occasions, with the qualification that France did not really want to offer the British the same type of relations as she had with the Federal Republic. This is why, for instance, an annual meeting is held with the British, as against two a year with the Germans. At the same time, following the example of what is done with the Federal Republic of Germany, a Strategic Studies Group was created, in particular to prepare for the summit meetings. As for co-operation in armaments procurement matters during this period, this resulted from the implementation of previously agreed projects — no new projects were agreed by the two countries. In London in January 1980, M. Bourges, the French defence minister, met his British counterpart, Mr Pym; the two ministers touched on the defence policies of the two countries and arms control. In the same year, Mrs Thatcher repeated her desire for closer and fuller co-operation in defence matters, but this did not lead to any initiative whatsoever.

## The evolution of a new understanding

Mrs Thatcher's desire seemed to take concrete form from 1982 when France, Britain, and other NATO countries found themselves supporting projects for the design and manufacture of a third generation anti-tank missile and a multiple launch rocket system. At the same time, after a period of stagnation, bilateral security relations began to intensify.

This is why, at the 1982 Franco-British summit, it was decided that meetings between ministers and top civil servants were to be more frequent and more regular: foreign affairs and defence ministers were to meet twice a year from then on. At the 1984 summit, it was agreed that neither country was to embark upon armaments programmes without consulting the other. Moreover, the frequency of the meetings of the Strategic Studies Group was doubled and one of these meetings was to be held at foreign ministry political director level.

Similarly, informal contacts increased, particularly through the Franco-British Council, which was created when the United Kingdom joined the European Community and which now found a new momentum in this area. Although official responsibility for these contacts was not claimed on either side of the Channel, they were none the less encouraged. Finally, matters of common interest were considered in more official groups — for example, in the regular talks on the position of the 'third nuclear powers' with relation to the Geneva arms control negotiations.

The last example is not the only one, but it is representative of the processes that enabled the taboo on Franco-British relations to be lifted: the evolution of the strategic context increasingly made the French and British defence situations similar. The return to significance of the 'third nuclear powers' (a generic term, which was itself significant) made it necessary for the two situations to be compared. It was this growing realization of being in a common situation that made the visit by David Owen and David Steel to Paris in September 1986 so spectacular. Initially not much noticed in Britain, this visit subsequently received a lot of attention from the British press as a result of the warm welcome given by all French political parties to the leaders of a party grouping with a somewhat uncertain position in British politics. The bulk of the talks centred, as far as we know, on the prospects for a more united defence of Europe and on the proposals previously made by David Owen in Britain to replace the planned Trident II D-5 missiles with cruise missiles, which could be produced in co-operation with France. Further proposals, including ideas for a minimum European deterrent, are said to have been aired. While these were premature and perhaps unrealistic, they were indicative of new attitudes.

To what could this change be attributed? The new relations between the two countries were first of all due, without any doubt, to the goodwill on both sides, which resulted from the common interests of two powers with global perspectives; they were also due to the strategic environment, dominated by the two superpowers, which neither France nor Britain could ignore; finally, they were largely dependent on the implicit but omnipresent factor of the Federal Republic of Germany. In these three areas, the common approach has become increasingly recognized, although some ambiguities remain.

*More goodwill on both sides*

We have seen the way in which Franco-British relations were defined in relation to Europe in previous decades — following two symmetrical but contradictory elements: Britain's exclusion from the European Economic Community and her Atlanticist concept of defence; France's total loyalty to the EEC and her commitment to defence autonomy.

The two opposing elements have tended to merge. More goodwill and a certain mutual respect between Mrs Thatcher and M. Mitterand had something to do with this. In fact, France intervened so that the problems of Britain's financial contribution to the EEC and her disagreement with the Common Agricultural Policy could be resolved. Moreover, in the final analysis, London appreciated French support during the Falklands campaign (in spite of everything that has been said about the Exocet, which should be put into proper context by pointing out that the British themselves were about to supply the Argentinians with frigates armed with Exocet missiles).

Relations in defence matters cannot be isolated from the general framework of political relations between the two countries. When the improvements in other areas quoted above have allayed misgivings, common interests have come through more clearly.

Britain, always suspected in France of unconditional support for the Atlantic Alliance, found herself in the unpleasant position of being certainly the favourite ally of the United States, but of not always being listened to in Washington. This strengthened anti-American tendencies in British public opinion. Mrs Thatcher could not totally ignore this. She was unhappy about American procrastination at the time of the Falklands crisis, and annoyed at not having been informed of the intervention in Grenada; she found dubious compensation from the SDI proposal. While President Reagan adopted Mrs Thatcher's Four Points on SDI at Camp David in December 1985, he did not abandon his dream of a world free of nuclear weapons.

For the first time for a long time, British loyalty to the United States no longer necessarily equates with a convergence of interests between the two countries. This is particularly striking as far as European security is concerned, where Britain is being caught between her interests as a European power and her duties as a loyal ally. Following the Reykjavik summit, Mrs Thatcher did not publicly oppose the United States but she had no hesitation in strongly attacking its stance.

In all these respects, France supports and reinforces British positions and can perhaps also sometimes be used as a 'scapegoat'. Conversely, France too can benefit from this rapprochement, which legitimizes her strategic philosophy at a time when her national consensus on defence is strong enough no longer to require the claims for total independence that have in the past irritated Britain. Moreover, the growing current public mistrust of nuclear weapons makes the position of the European nuclear powers both more necessary and more difficult; they therefore do well to show a common front.

*Similar strategic constraints*

In spite of differences in doctrine, the French and British strategic postures are fairly similar: both countries have built up their nuclear forces with the intention of thus establishing their power status; both have aimed for a minimum deterrent to counter the Soviet threat. One should not be deceived by the 'conceptual vacuum' which seems to characterize the British deterrent; it is a question of different political styles, the British having little liking for rhetoric and declaratory policies.

The developing of strategic constraints will only reinforce the need for convergence which already exists. When the USSR gave up trying to achieve strategic superiority (1977), it inevitably re-focused its policy on Europe. France and Britain will therefore be increasingly faced with the risk of limited Soviet attacks, nuclear or otherwise, and of saturation of their airspace by bombers, tactical missiles and cruise missiles. Faced with the probable deployment of Soviet defences, they feel the same need to improve the penetration capability of their nuclear forces, to modernize them and to have at their disposal the strategic intelligence provided by satellites.

These common needs are reinforced by the American tendency to wish to raise the nuclear threshold in Europe, which is in keeping with a political environment of growing scepticism about nuclear deterrence. This is why, irrespective of their declaratory policies, the actual positions of the two countries with regard to SDI are fairly close. This seems too to be the case on the issue of the deployment of active anti-tactical ballistic missile (ATBM) systems in Europe. British and French nuclear response could be simpler than the counter-force methods of the flexible response, and a shared appreciation of this should increase still further the possibilities of convergence.

The Soviet Union is not deceived by this. It sometimes tries to class the 'third nuclear forces' as Alliance theatre forces and sometimes tries to isolate them by advocating the unconditional withdrawal of INF from Europe. In both cases, it is a question of preventing the formation of a united European grouping and also the modernization of a possible independent force which would increasingly complicate the calculations of its strategists. Although there has been no joint declaration, France and Britain have a common approach to the American–Soviet arms control negotiations and the implications for their own forces: they both refuse to dissociate the Euro-strategic balance from the whole of the east/west balance; they are both hostile towards Reykjavik; and they both refuse to include their nuclear forces in the negotiations.

In this respect, the two countries, because they are nuclear powers and therefore potentially responsible for the escalation, must pay attention to any possible conflict, particularly in the Federal Republic of Germany, and to their relations with that country.

### *Germany — the implicit pivot*

Britain, like the Federal Republic of Germany, has always thought that too great a concentration on European defence co-operation risked encouraging American disengagement. Nowadays, the problem is no longer quite the same, because American commitment will be increasingly dependent on the Europeans' own will and capacity to defend themselves. Germany's role is therefore all the more crucial. It is, however, an ambiguous role in the case of the Franco-British dialogue, owing to the British fear of exclusion from the Franco-German relationship. This fear is a counterpart of France's reproach that Britain shows excessive support for the Atlantic Alliance. France, as a nuclear and continental power, is in fact at the heart of the triangular relationship that could be established with Britain and the Federal Republic of Germany. It is not surprising then that the resumption of the Franco-German dialogue in 1982 worried the British and caused them to make some overtures towards France.

Conversely, the relative hesitation in Franco-German relations explains why France was prepared to compensate for any disappointments she might experience with the Federal Republic of Germany by strengthening her links with Britain. This was the case for example at the time of the Heath–Pompidou rapprochement.

It is nevertheless a fact that France and Britain are the two European countries most involved in Germany in the defence of the Central Front, both having approximately 50,000 men stationed in the Federal Republic.

This triangular situation, with opportunities for double-dealing, is far from being simple: it reflects areas of uncertainty but it provides possibilities of influence.

## The paths to increased co-operation

One can see, then, that ambiguities remain. One cannot repeat too often that the will to surmount past obstacles and to turn to advantage a situation that is now more favourable to Franco-British relations must not conceal the fact that there are on both sides interests to be placated, traditions to be respected, and sensibilities to be spared. The most tangible effect of these ambiguities is that the most obvious areas of co-operation — those in which the current rapprochement might be measured exactly — are not necessarily those in which progress is most likely to be achieved. This is the case in particular for co-operation in armaments procurement matters, where little is to be expected.

On the other hand, these ambiguities can no longer mask increasing convergence of strategic perceptions, which can all the more easily constitute the solid basis for increased co-operation (as the inevitable compromises are not immediately apparent). It is on the basis of convergence here, and not on the basis of some political or military preconceptions, that co-operation should be envisaged. I have initially identified three areas of such convergence: strategic constraints, the importance of West Germany, and the global interests of the two powers. These establish three fields for possible co-operation, which will be discussed in the following order: nuclear forces, operational commitments in Europe, and 'out-of-area' activities (i.e. outside the area covered by the Alliance).

### *The ambiguities over co-operation in armaments procurement*

Both the weakness of Franco-British relations and their ambiguity are reflected in the absence of major co-operative armaments programmes between the two countries. The major projects carried out jointly date back to the 1960s (the Jaguar aircraft, the Lynx helicopter). At that time, when in Europe only France and Britain had a full range of armaments industries, 50 per cent of the British co-operative programmes were undertaken with France, mainly bilaterally. Today this percentage is very low, and the French are involved with Britain only in programmes that bring together a large number of countries. This stems from Britain's political priorities, which lead her to make the United States a favoured partner, to prefer to co-operate within NATO, and to some extent to work with her most Atlanticist European partner, the Federal Republic of Germany. However, the clash of competitive industrial interests, especially at a time of economic crisis, must not be overlooked as an additional factor.

In addition to the fact that the British armaments industry has made technological choices leading it to develop projects in direct competition with those of France, especially in aerospace (such as the HOTOL spacecraft), her rediscovered dynamism since Mrs Thatcher's arrival in office should not be underestimated. This revival, helped by the Falklands war, is due to factors other than the economic situation and testifies to great adaptability; the UK aerospace industry is pragmatic and particularly quick to fill gaps left vacant for political reasons. This is reflected in a gradual equalization of France's and Britain's shares of the world market for arms: standing at 7 per cent and 3 per cent respectively in 1981, they were 10 per cent and 9 per cent in 1984. Britain's recent success in selling Tornado to Saudi Arabia, following France's success with RITA in the United States, shows that it will be difficult to overcome these economic rivalries.

Moreover, the recent trend in Europe, after a general stagnation of co-operation in armaments matters during the 1970s, is now towards greater multilateralism of both European and European–Atlantic programmes. This reduces the range of possibilities for a bilateral Franco-British approach, even though, in the areas of research and aerospace, the French and the British are well placed to co-operate and to be European leaders . . . or to compete with each other.

Several proposals should therefore be considered. They concern in particular promoting the emergence of more flexible structures for industrial co-operation, like a common European procurement agency. As partners/opponents, France and Britain could together stimulate the creation of such a body, which would enable them to seek to share the leadership of major industrial projects to their mutual benefit.

This development would be helped by preliminary but vital progress on the definition of more harmonious defence concepts. It is on this that the resumption of dialogue since 1984 has logically concentrated.

### *Nuclear co-operation*

We have seen that it is in this area that the British and French analyses show the greatest convergence. This is in spite of differences in doctrine, which primarily concern the use of tactical nuclear weapons — with a contrast between France's idea of their being used as a final warning shot and NATO's commitment to flexible response.

Beyond the joint reaffirmation of the role of nuclear weapons in the security of Europe, which has already been made but which could be given a more solemn character, joint positions could be developed, and even diplomatic action taken, on the modernization of both nuclear forces. This would at least deflect the unjustified accusation that France and Britain are preventing arms limitation. This could be an initial aim for those who are actively promoting Franco-British nuclear co-operation.

A second aim could be a joint consideration of the new responses that the two countries will have to make, given the evolution of strategic constraints and in particular the development of Soviet defensive systems. A joint analysis of the new air threat constituted by the combination of bombers, cruise missiles, and ballistic missiles will also have to be undertaken. It is a question of examining how to reinforce their air defences; if a more significant response is required, this could involve a co-ordinated increase in strategic offensive options rather than matching the 'Soviet-type' deployment of active defence systems.

Finally, a third aim could be the joint evaluation of the growth of offensive systems, which could increase the symbolic value to Europe of the British and French forces. Without calling into question the autonomy of the two centres of decision-making — Paris and London — some form of co-ordination might be possible. One could consider, for example, optimizing the total number of submarines at sea by co-ordinating their maintenance cycles, although these are fairly inflexible, or by examining new areas for co-operation, particularly in the areas of space, communications, and intelligence.

Despite its central importance, it is difficult to explore further the possibilities for Franco-British nuclear co-operation, because of its classified nature. But it may be that a first concrete step could be to put the strategists and practitioners concerned with these problems in contact with each other, so that they can talk about them together.

In any event, it is not necessary for the hardware to be identical for this co-operation to develop. The Trident II D-5 and the M-4/M-5 can coexist perfectly well within a closer nuclear relationship. It is perhaps even preferable to have different and complementary missiles at one's disposal.

### *Operational co-operation in Europe*

This search for closer co-operation on nuclear matters must be accompanied by the study of operational co-operation in the event of a conflict in Europe, since this would present common problems for the two nuclear powers. Both countries would be confronted with the same paradoxical situation of having the potential for escalation to a nuclear conflict, whilst having particular reason to fear it.

There are three possible directions for such co-operation. First, there could be a joint analysis of the situation in the Central Front in West Germany, where Britain commands the Northern Army Group, and of the possible contribution of rapid deployment forces, including the French Force d'Action Rapide. It seems in effect preferable to focus consideration straight away on new concepts which imply neither a British withdrawal (nor increased commitments on the Central Front) nor an increased French engagement in northern Germany.

Second, there could be a study of the introduction of more frequent Franco-British joint exercises which, added to the increasingly extensive Franco-German exercises, could contribute to the development of a new 'European military culture'.

Third, there could be an increase in operational co-operation between the third and fourth largest navies in the world in which French aircraft-carriers and British attack submarines could, for example, well complement each other.

### *'Out-of-area' co-operation*

It may seem surprising to mention last an area of co-operation within the province of the French and British navies, but it is clear that the historic rivalry between the British and French empires in the Near East, Africa, the Indian Ocean, etc. has left marks which do not show themselves solely in competition between the armaments industries. Because it involves general international policy considerations and the history of the two countries, 'out-of-area' co-operation has both a strong symbolic value and inevitably relatively restricted opportunities as the initial divergences are so great.

However, new threats have appeared which represent growing risks both for the security of energy and raw material supplies and for citizens living overseas. It is not surprising that Britain has developed forces with capabilities comparable to those of the French Force d'Action Rapide.

While accepting the particular interests of each side, a future crisis may therefore justify joint intervention. The clearing of mines from the Red Sea and the events in South Yemen, where a humanitarian operation could have been carried out in concert, have recently provided illustrations of this. It is better to try to anticipate such eventualities.

However, without going as far as joint intervention, bilateral co-operation could prove useful in the following areas:

— exchanges of information, particularly among navies, on the lessons learnt from out-of-area actions;
— analysis of situations and possible future scenarios. Such concerted action would, in addition to increasing the analytic capability of both partners, permit a comparison of general policy positions with regard to the geographical areas concerned.

This dual approach would in particular have the effect of contributing towards reducing the friction between the arms-exporting policies of the two countries in some regions of the world.

### *The tools for increased co-operation and the joint think-tank organizations*

All of the above analyses show that European security now requires critical decisions. While the predominance of the United States and its weapons in the Alliance is both inevitable and desirable, at least for the immediate future, it is none the less necessary for the European countries to define their own concept of security.

In this field, France and Britain, who together house the institutions of the Western European Union — the Council and the General Secretariat

— and who have fairly similar defence colleges for senior civilian and military staff (the IHEDN for France, the Royal College of Defence Studies for the United Kingdom), would seem to have an important part to play. Such bilateral co-operation would not conflict with the Franco-German joint efforts at officer training, but should of course be extended as quickly as possible to the other West European countries. It should also be accompanied by the development of closer relations between the European research institutes specializing in international relations and strategic studies, which provide the background for necessary 'day-to-day' co-operation. The various working parties bring together experts from the foreign and defence ministries of the two governments, whose pace of work, as we have said, has already quickened.

Mention should also be made of the Franco-British Council, which brings together politicians, intellectuals, industrialists, and civil servants. Since 1986, the Council has had a security commission which tackles defence and disarmament questions. Through authoritative analysis of proposals, this commission can contribute effectively to the development of co-operation in security matters between London and Paris.

## Conclusion

There is no concealing the difficulties — often the result of different political priorities as well as of different political styles — that Franco-British co-operation will encounter. Britain's position as an island and France's central position on the Continent of Europe are part of the reason for these difficulties, but so also are their former imperial and maritime rivalry. It is nevertheless a fact that recent changes in the strategic environment in Europe and the prospect of future changes have led to a convergence of the strategic situations of France and Britain, and made their co-operation more necessary. Despite all these problems, it now seems that if the French and the British do not unite their defence efforts, in agreement with the West Germans and the other Europeans, Europe will remain at the mercy of the policies of the two superpowers. Western European security will not seem effective without a nuclear dimension that is credible in the eyes of the Soviet Union. France and Britain will be the more able to be responsible for this dimension if they reach agreement on common objectives, and undertake the modernization of their respective forces in harmony.

Without doubt, it will be difficult to find a proper balance between British pragmatism, mistrustful as it is of broad declaratory ambitions, and French attitudes which are more attached to them. This means that Franco-British rapprochement will probably have to remain relatively discreet.

The period after Reykjavik gave London and Paris the opportunity to express positions that were practically the same. It is to be hoped that their positions will remain close or, better still, be identical on the major strategic questions that will come to the forefront of the international scene in the months and years to come, beginning with the modernization of their nuclear forces. The modernization task is easier for the French than for the British, since there is strong opposition to nuclear defence in Britain. Is this not another reason for France to co-operate with Britain in this area?

The conditions and tools for increased co-operation exist, but a strong and shared political will is needed for concrete results to be obtained and for such co-operation to endure. There are numerous obstacles to the translation of ideas into action; this is true on both sides of the Channel.

Finally, it is advisable to take care not to give too exclusive a character to Franco-British co-operation. On the contrary, it must be a natural complement to the American presence, which cannot be called into question, to Franco-German co-operation, and to wider special relations among Europeans, particularly within the Western European Union.

## Author's note

Revised to the end of 1987, this article does not take into account the most recent developments in Franco–British defence co-operation.

## Notes

1. P.M. Gallois, 'Deux budgets militaires, une politique de sécurité, *Revue de défense nationale*, June 1962, p. 948.

Chapter fifteen

# European security: bilateral steps to multilateral co-operation

William Wallace

Franco-British co-operation in defence and security is only one strand in the complex network of bilateral and multilateral co-operation, both among Western European countries and with the USA and Canada within the Atlantic Alliance. Much of this co-operation, bilateral as well as multilateral, takes place with the NATO framework; in NATO training schools, on NATO ranges, within NATO standing forces, in accordance with NATO reinforcement roles. Some takes place within the context of the Eurogroup. The withdrawal of France from NATO, and the absence of France from the latter, makes bilateral links between France and her major partners more important, substituting for the multilateral co-operation in which her partners are more fully and regularly engaged. French association with NATO exercises and use of training areas are of necessity informal and limited; French missions at NATO commands play a discreet (if increasingly active) role.

On security policy, the Atlantic Alliance's structure of political consultations includes *all* the member governments of the Alliance. Within that, the structures of European political co-operation and the Western European Union (WEU) bring together the major European actors. On arms procurement, the strengthening of the Independent European Programme Group and the intricate network of the Conference of National Armaments' Directors (CNAD) provide a multilateral structure within which British and French bilateral conversations are firmly embedded. Military co-operation however lacks this firm link between the bilateral and the multilateral.

The strengthening of Franco-British defence co-operation cannot be primarily a bilateral affair. Each has a close relationship with Federal Germany — closer for each than with each other. Each is committed in principle to the reinforcement of 'that side of the transatlantic bridge of which Britain forms a part: the European pillar'.[1] The aim of this paper is therefore to examine the wider European context for Franco-British defence co-operation, and to consider how *this* bilateral relationship fits in with the two countries' other bilateral and multilateral obligations and with the developing pattern of European defence co-operation as a whole.

## The pattern of European co-operation

Military co-operation among West European countries within the framework of NATO has developed very considerably since the completion of the French withdrawal from the integrated structure in 1966. American pressures for standardization and rationalization have combined with European efforts to economize on defence budgets to produce a range of common operations, standing forces, and training agreements which have eaten into the national autonomy of European NATO members in defence terms. This process has gone furthest for the smaller countries, but it has not left the United Kingdom or Federal Germany unaffected. It should be recognized how large a role American leadership and American pressures have played in this entire process. The Mansfield Amendment was as much the father of the Eurogroup as it was of the Mutual and Balanced Force Reductions (MBFR) negotiations. The determination of Helmut Schmidt and Denis Healey to demonstrate to the US Congress that the European NATO members were making a full contribution to their own defence launched the Eurogroup and the European Defence Improvement Programme, and lay behind a number of other associated initiatives taken in the late 1960s and early 1970s. American forces take part in many of these integrated activities, sometimes under European command; in others, European co-operation wears a NATO 'label'.

Co-operation among conventional forces takes place most intimately in Federal Germany, along the 'Central Front'. The intimacy of the Franco-German defence relationship is in many ways outside and alongside this multilateral framework. In southern Germany the deployment of forces and the NATO command structure makes for a very close bilateral relationship between American and German army and air force units. In northern Germany, the Northern Army Group and the 2nd Allied Tactical Air Force are more European in composition, bringing together German, British, Dutch, Belgian, and Canadian units within an integrated command.

Reinforcement roles for the northern and southern flanks also bring European defence planners, military commanders, and active forces together. The Allied Command Europe (ACE) Mobile Force (formed in 1960) provides common training and shared responsibilities for contingents from six of the seven member states of WEU — all except France — together with American and Canadian forces. Its flank-reinforcement role leads to exercises in Norway and Denmark, Greece and Turkey (and, on at least one occasion, Portugal) in co-operation with the forces of those countries. The commitment to Norway is maintained by the most remarkable example of integrated defence capability that I am aware of: the UK/Netherlands Marine Force. This spends up to three months each year in Norway, training with Norwegian forces. US and Canadian forces are assigned to support their Norwegian commitment, and exercise in Norway on a less extensive basis; one exercise ('Avalanche Express') in March 1984 included in addition German and Belgian units, Italian alpine troops, and a third of the entire land forces of Luxembourg.

Co-operation along NATO's southern front is much more limited. With neither France nor Spain within the Alliance's integrated structure, Italian defence links are overwhelmingly with the United States. Until 1983 the United Kingdom had a reinforcement role in north-eastern Italy, now transferred to American forces in exchange for an adjustment of commitments to reinforce Denmark's Baltic approaches. Portuguese troops and aircraft supply a further European element alongside Italian and American forces in regular exercises. Surprisingly, command and military exchange links between German forces in Bavaria and Italian forces in the Trentino are few; Senator Nunn's suggestion that an Italian brigade should be stationed in Bavaria to strengthen that part of the Central Front aroused no response. There have been suggestions that the Force d'Action Rapide (FAR) might play a supporting role in northern Italy; but in the absence of formal consultations and of the opportunity for joint training, Italian defence opinion remains sceptical so far.

Italian training areas are much more extensively used by other members of NATO's integrated structure. British, German, and American air force 'lodging units' are permanently based at the Decimomannu air range in Sardinia, a NATO establishment constantly in use by squadrons from those and other air forces. British and other ground troops undergo mountain training with Italian alpine forces in northern Italy.

Naval co-operation is most intense among countries within the integrated command structure bordering the North Sea; much less intense in the Mediterranean, again due to the absence of France and Spain — and to the sensitivities of bringing Greece and Turkey within a co-operative enterprise. NATO's Standing Force Eastern Atlantic, a group of frigates operating under common command, includes US ships as well as British, German, Belgian, and Dutch vessels. Standing Naval Force Channel, a force of minehunters, consisted in early 1985 of two British ships, two Dutch, one Belgian, and one German, commanded for twelve months in rotation by an officer from each of these four navies. Anti-submarine co-operation between these navies is also close; proposals to bring Dutch anti-submarine operations more directly under British command within an even more closely integrated operation, some years ago, were blocked after some discussion by objections that this would involve the automatic acceptance by Dutch officers of British command authority. Dutch, German, and Belgian ships work up their crews using British facilities at Portland. Danish and Norwegian ships join in these standing forces and associated exercises on a less regular basis. French ships also participate in a number of US-led NATO exercises, while remaining formally under national command.

Looked at from a British perspective, the pattern of European military co-operation is therefore one in which the bilateral relationship with France is only one among many. It is, furthermore, much more limited in scope than those with the Netherlands and Germany, which involve joint training, shared command, and a degree of specialization of function within a common framework. The UK/Netherlands Marine Force might serve as a model for the maximum degree of military co-operation achievable among West European countries compatible with the preservation of formal national sovereignty. The primary operational task of both countries' marine forces is defined as an integrated commitment focused upon support for other European NATO members. One of the three commandos within the brigade declared to NATO for this role is Dutch. It comes under British command for a number of activities, relies upon British logistic support, stores much of its war maintenance reserves in Britain, and relies for much of the basic training of its personnel on British facilities. A further independent Dutch marine company is stationed in Britain to fulfil associated tasks. Neither government is entirely constrained by this arrangement, which is covered by a formal Memorandum of Understanding; when Argentina invaded the Falklands the national contingents were separated and its British elements detached for service in the South Atlantic. But for normal peacetime operations — and for operations in the event of a European emergency — it functions as a binational force fulfilling multilateral commitments.

## Military co-operation, defence and security

In itself, co-operation among armed forces is only one part — and by no means the most important part — of the construction of a European defence entity. It does however link in with other aspects in a number of ways that suggest that its absence, or its inadequate development, may impede progress in other areas.

Bilateral staff talks and political–military conversations take place on a regular basis among almost all West European countries, with France as active a participant as any other. The agenda of such staff talks however varies enormously. Common operations and common concerns make for detailed discussions. *Tours d'horizon* and comparisons of separate national experiences and practices provide a much more limited field of interest. Politico-military conversations range more broadly. But they also benefit from the common concerns that follow from shared commitment to Western defence: in discussions on conventional arms control, for example.

Collaboration in military procurement also interacts, in both directions, with military co-operation. Tactical doctrines and assumptions affect operational definitions of future equipment, in general and in detail. Where these diverge, or in the absence of the process of convergence that comes from close military collaboration, agreement on common equipment may well prove impossible. The equipment procured in turn influences patterns of collaboration and tactical doctrines — particularly with respect to air forces. The Royal Netherlands Air Force, with strong links with the British Royal Air Force in the immediate post-war years, has progressively adopted American doctrines and practices as it has procured successive generations of American aircraft. Its pilots undergo much of their training in the United States (after initial training in Belgium); personal links have grown up with American officers and establishments over the years. Conversely, procurement of the Tornado is making for closer operating links between the RAF, the Luftwaffe, and the Italian Air Force. An integrated training operation has been established for the three air forces at RAF Cottesmore — recently described by Italian defence minister Spadolini as one of the most striking examples of the construction of a European defence identity.

As in a number of Franco–German and Franco–British examples of collaborative procurement, common equipment also makes for easier pilot and squadron exchange, so reinforcing shared working practices and attitudes. The sense of European identity, in defence as in other areas of co-operation, grows out of the experience of working together over an extended number of years. The useful but limited patterns of individual personnel exchanges between West European armed forces, in which the French are as fully involved as their partners, are insufficient in themselves to build such a sense of solidarity; it is rare for those who reach the top to have spent much of their careers in such exchange activities. Short-term unit exchanges, which the French and others undertake most intensively with the German forces, make for some greater familiarity. But *European* co-operation will only grow out of broader interaction on a more long-term and integrated basis, involving more than two countries at a time.

## Multilateral collaboration or multiple bilateralism?

The three most important states for West European defence co-operation, we may agree, are Federal Germany, France, and the United Kingdom. German–British and Franco–German bilateral ties are strong, across the whole range of defence, security and arms procurement issues, focused around common interests in the defence and stability of Germany. It might therefore be argued that the most important task in strengthening European defence is to thicken up the Franco-British relationship, to create a triangle of bilateral ties upon which a European entity can rest.

There are, however, a number of problems with this approach. The first is the disjointed character of such a structure, with parallel ties and separate meetings. The second is the interest of other West European states, which make contributions to the common defence, which share in the common threat — and which, it is hoped, are candidates to purchase European defence equipment produced predominantly by their larger European partners. There are therefore strong arguments for a multilateral approach, bringing together the interests and military contributions of large and small European Alliance members. But this in turn raises two further problems: the difficulties of balancing — or disentangling? — the European and Atlantic dimensions of defence co-operation, given the very close links between all European NATO members and the United States; and the equally difficult balance between the maintenance of national sovereignty and autonomy and the achievement of effective (and cost-effective) common defence.

These two problems loom largest for Britain and for France. The smaller member states have long since accepted the realities of their dependence on others for central elements of defence, and moved some way down the road towards the integration of their defence budgets and military operations with those of their partners. For Belgium and the Netherlands, for example, the advantages to be gained from integration are pressing, the costs to national autonomy not novel. The Belgian navy has no independent anti-submarine warfare (ASW) capacity; its frigates operate and train either as part of the Dutch ASW squadron or as part of the NATO Standing Force Eastern Atlantic. Its minehunters and minesweepers train in the integrated Dutch–Belgian school at Ostend. Its naval helicopter pilots are training in France, its transport aircraft crews largely in Britain; two complete crews within an RAF transport squadron are currently provided by Belgian personnel. There is a British logistical base within Belgium, with permanently stationed troops; one of Belgium's many roles within the integrated Alliance structure is to maintain the line of communications which in an emergency would bring British — and American — reinforcements up to the Central Front.

Similarly for the Netherlands the limitations on sovereignty are taken as given, with an entire training regiment of the Luftwaffe stationed on its territory, with strong defence links with Britain, with its ports and airfields committed to receive American forces in an emergency, and with ships and marines committed to the northern flank. The Benelux countries have assumed for the past twenty years and more that their national defence must be embedded within an increasingly close-knit

European and Atlantic Alliance structure. Both Dutch and Belgian defence ministries see the way forward through strengthening the European pillar within NATO, working primarily through the Eurogroup. On a Benelux basis, pressures of cost, perceptions of shared interests, and shared language have led to a gradual extension of co-operation. 'De plus, un groupe de travail intégré, sous présidence belge, a été constitué pour examiner dans quels domaines il est possible d'intensifier la coordination, la collaboration, *voire l'intégration des Forces armées respectives*. Dans ce contexte, il a déja été décidé de tester le fonctionnement d'un commandemant intégré pour la mise en oeuvre des lignes de communication alliées sur le territoire du BENELUX.'[2]

Italy and West Germany have slightly different perspectives — retaining much more of a national capability across the whole range of defence tasks, but sharply aware of their dependence on allies for support, and on the United States in particular. European defence co-operation for these two countries is partly a means of reducing their bilateral dependence on the United States, without reducing or risking the US contribution to their security, through the creation of a European entity able to collaborate with the United States on a more equal basis. For both, French participation in multilateral European defence collaboration is central to the achievement of this objective, in the Mediterranean and on the Central Front.

France and Britain do not have the same focus for intensive bilateral military links that each has with Germany. Logically the defence of the English Channel and the management of supply and reinforcement lines for the Central Front should provide that common focus. But France's withdrawal from the integrated NATO structure diverted British co-operation on both of these towards Belgium and the Netherlands. Informal contacts and conversations between London and Paris have of course covered these issues. Exercises between the two navies, without publicity, in the open waters of the Channel approaches and the Bay of Biscay have become more regular and intensive in recent years; though air and ground forces do not have the same luxury of neutral ground on which to meet. If Franco-British military co-operation is therefore to be strengthened more deliberate steps must be taken *either* to create an appropriate bilateral framework *or* to bring the armed services of the two countries together within a mutually acceptable multilateral organization.

## The Franco-British dimension

The preoccupation of both British and French land and air forces with their specific roles on the Central Front and elsewhere has left the nuclear dimension as the main focus for debate about bilateral defence co-operation. The Parisian perspective, it appears to many British observers, places conventional defence collaboration along the bilateral Franco-German axis, and would seek to supplement that with bilateral nuclear collaboration between France and Britain. From that perspective France would remain at the centre of European defence collaboration, with strong but distinctive ties to Western Europe's two other leading military powers.

The view from London sees West European co-operation in a rather different light. The British conventional commitment to West Germany, and the network of conventional military ties with Germany, are seen as both stronger and easier than the Franco-German link — because they require less political weight to underpin them. The Benelux countries are highly significant to Britain's participation in European defence, their importance being increased by the non-availability under peace-time conditions of French territory and by the positioning of British forces in Germany within the Northern Army Group. France represents from this perspective not the pivot of European defence co-operation but the hole in the middle, the reluctant partner who prefers collaboration to be limited, *ad hoc*, and largely unacknowledged.

It may well be the case that some move towards shared operation on procurement in the nuclear field is the key that can unlock Franco-British defence co-operation, without which little else of substance is possible. For all its symbolic weight, that is however a narrow foundation on which to build. Some sharing of nuclear tasks and responsibilities would bring small — if crucial — elements of the French and British services together, providing a counterweight to the intensive Anglo-American naval link to which Polaris has contributed. But unless other tasks were shared, other joint activities undertaken, the sense of distance — and of historical rivalry and mistrust — will not be overcome.

British and German servicemen work together in North Germany at least as closely as French and German servicemen do in Baden and the Rhineland-Palatinate. An increasing number of senior British officers speak German; they spend up to a third of their careers in Germany, and rules are now in force that require a command of the language as a condition of command of a brigade or above. Other shared tasks, equipment, and training arrangements (as illustrated above) bring British servicemen closely together with their Dutch, Belgian, Italian, and Norwegian counterparts.

British and French servicemen do not meet and work together so naturally; British and French defence officials thus find they have a less detailed agenda to discuss. A sense of mutual distance between defence ministries and defence forces remains, in spite of some modest but useful improvements in recent years. I have, for example, been told repeatedly by senior French naval officers — in the course of this study, as in earlier conversations — that 'We have now forgotten Mers-el-Kébir';

clear witness that the historical legacy is *not* entirely forgotten. The symbols of past Franco-British military contact are not particularly positive. Formally allies throughout the Second World War, the wartime relationship was not an easy or an equal one. Nor was the Anglo-American liberation of France without its tensions and controversies — with the Free French as junior partners, the Forces Française Internes (FFI) as independent actors, and the section of French society and the French services that had accepted the German occupation ambivalent about the blessing of liberation. The closest collaboration since the Second World War was in the Suez operation of 1956.

How then would we build a more positive bilateral defence relationship? The first point to stress is how little the question has been explored either in Britain or in France, beyond the complacent Parisian generalities about France's European 'vocation' and the continuing ambivalence within London about how far to strengthen the European dimension within (or alongside) the integrated Atlantic Alliance. There remains on both sides a prevailing assumption that any prospect for substantial progress is blocked by the conventional wisdom of the other capital. French participants see British subservience to US leadership, with a consequent insistence on working through the integrated structure, as a major obstacle; British see the Gaullist consensus, the insistence on independence, and the exclusion of multilateral co-operation or association with the integrated structure as the main block. Fresh thought is thus necessary on both sides.

The second point follows from this: the need to create alternative and positive symbols of Franco-British defence co-operation, to set the context for an easier relationship. The Franco-German defence relationship has been redefined partly through symbolic actions, from the 1963 parade at Rheims through to heads of government hand-holding at Verdun. The historical legacy between France and Britain was not so immediately bitter as to be seen to require such grand gestures; though the battle honours of British regiments, or the descriptions of Franco-British conflicts which run through the pages of the *Guide Michelin*, demonstrate the depth of past rivalries. Nuclear collaboration would itself be a powerful symbol, though not an immediately visible one without dramatization for a wider political and public audience. Joint parades, linked to royal and presidential occasions, would alter the political and emotional climate, and thus provide the context in which joint exercises would easily follow. Is it too fanciful to suggest that French troops should play their part in ceremonial duties in London, and British guards march up the Champs-Elysées?

The third point is to recognize the need for a closer defence relationship to be constructed as a coherent whole out of the sum of different joint activities and shared responsibilities. Armaments collaboration, for example, can go only so far without agreement on strategy and tactics, or without the convergence of views on operational requirements that flows from joint operations and training. Nuclear collaboration requires closer consultation on nuclear strategy, intelligence, and targeting; it leads logically on to collaboration in anti-submarine warfare, and so to naval co-operation across the board. Military co-operation 'out-of-area' may perhaps be seen as standing outside this pattern of interlocking links, though the symbolic and practical benefits from out-of-area co-operation for the relationship as a whole would be very substantial. Bilateral ties need also to be interwoven with multilateral ties, as both Britain and France come to terms with the meaning of *European* defence co-operation.

Lastly, there must be a willingness on both sides to explore new structures for collaboration, moving away from mutual intransigence over commitment to the NATO integrated structure and to national independence. The British must accept that the existing structure of European military co-operation within NATO needs to be modified in order to accommodate the French. The French must recognize in their turn the value and experience of that co-operation, and accommodate themselves to multilateral collaboration with their West European partners, in which French forces will come operationally under foreign command. The shift in 1975 from working in the Eurogroup to the IEPG, which includes France, for arms procurement matters provides a model: French acceptance that they could no longer define 'European' interests unilaterally from Paris, matched by British and German acceptance that it was politically impossible for France to join the Eurogroup as such — and by American acceptance that French participation was valuable enough for the ties that bound Eurogroup to the integrated structure to be loosened a little. It would not be impossible to alter the formal designation of the different standing naval forces, for example, to accommodate French participation on a regular basis, or to include French aircraft and support staff in 'Europeanized' NATO training areas. What is required to achieve that is goodwill on both sides, a common recognition that bilateral defence links are best placed within a broader multilateral framework, and a willingness to address both the general principles of bilateral defence co-operation and the hard detail.[3]

## Notes

1. Statement on the Defence Estimates 1985, Cmnd 91430–1, (London: HMSO, 1985), p. 15.
2. Lire Blanc de la Défense Nationale, (Brussels, 1985), p. 22; emphasis added.
3. Where not otherwise noted, information in this chapter is taken from interviews with defence officials and servicemen in London, Paris, Bonn, Brussels, Rome, and The Hague.

Chapter sixteen

# Conclusion

Yves Boyer and John Roper

At the end of the 1980s it is becoming increasingly apparent that European co-operation in security matters must be based on the firm foundations of close co-operation between Britain, France, and the Federal Republic of Germany. Co-operation between each of these pairs of countries must be effective in order for there to be a sound basis for intra-European co-operation.

In this network, at the moment the Franco-British relationship appears to be the weakest. The chapters of this book have indicated some of the reasons for that and some of the opportunities for strengthening this relationship. What we believe is now possible is a real increase in bilateral co-operation between Britain and France, making explicit certain things that have existed nominally in the past, and building on the common interest of Europe's two nuclear powers.

As a first step towards developing and strengthening the bilateral relationship it is important to develop at all levels, a common understanding of strategic questions. In the past, very often the two countries have developed different approaches or at least different language which has been used to address common problems. In the future there is a need, not merely at an official level but throughout the whole of the strategic community in both countries, for discussions to intensify in order that this common approach, indeed a common strategic culture, can be evolved. This development is one that will require a 'thickening up' of bilateral relations at all levels. It will require a political symbolic framework, but within this there must be practical co-operation in various sections, as we will suggest below.

Before arguing the case for a new formal treaty relationship between Britain and France, it is important to set out the reasons why we believe such a new treaty is both necessary and desirable. There is, we believe, a strong historical precedent for such an arrangement. The first treaty of alliance and mutual assistance between European countries in the post-war period was the treaty signed at Dunkirk on 4 March 1947 between Britain and France. Although this has inevitably been overtaken by events and changes in the nature of the threat in Europe, the precedent is important and the treaty remains in force. This historic precedent should now be brought up to date and given a new relevance.

The second reason for formalizing the relationship is the growing understanding that Europe's two nuclear powers should have a fuller basis for co-operation, as nuclear weapons become objects for debate in international relations as well as requiring closer co-operation in production and operational planning.

The third reason derives from the fact that Britain and France are the two European states that are permanent members of the Security Council. They therefore have a responsibility for security not merely in Europe but on a world scale. This can be seen still in the nature of their forces and the capabilities retained by both of them to different degrees for out-of-area activities.

Finally, as was stated above, although the development of security relations in Europe has become increasingly important, some of the traditional patterns seem to have become rather more fluid. We believe that there is a need for firm relations between the three major powers within Western Europe, but in a period of increased fluidity there is an increased argument for Franco-British co-operation in order that traditional allies can renew their long-tested association. It should perhaps be added that, from the British side, the existence of the Elysée treaty between France and West Germany leads them to feel that there should be a similar formal relationship between Britain and France.

Before considering the nature of a possible treaty between Britain and France it is perhaps worth pointing out that there are much greater similarities between Britain and France than there are between France and Germany. It could even be suggested that there is an inequality in the position of France and Germany which does not exist in the situation between France and Britain: France is a nuclear power, whilst Germany is not; France has a developed defence industrial base with substantial research capabilities, which does not exist to the same extent in the Federal Republic; France has commitments and capabilities to operate throughout the world, whereas Germany has constrained herself against such action; France has developed her own strategy, where Germany has always accepted the strategy of NATO. In the case of Britain and France there are, as we shall see, much closer parallels in national capabilities and approaches.

It is perhaps worth pointing out that, in recent years, the highest French authorities have indicated the need for developing closer conversations with Britain, paralleling those that now exist under the Elysée treaty with Germany. The same idea is taken up explicitly in the most recent law for the next five-year programme of military expenditure, which states: 'La coopération en matière de sécurité avec la République Fédérale d'Allemagne a un caractère privilégié. Son développement constitue une priorité. Elle doit s'accompagner d'une intensification de nos relations avec nos autres partenaires européens, notamment avec la Grande-Bretagne . . .' From the British side we have seen the last two ministers of defence take a much more active part in promoting close discussions with their French opposite numbers and the Foreign Secretary, Sir Geoffrey Howe, in his speeches has also indicated the need for closer Franco-British security discussions.

The case for a treaty is also to give a clear symbolic statement of the commitment of the two countries at the highest level to closer co-operation in security areas. There is no doubt that recent meetings between Presidents of France and Chancellors of the Federal Republic have given a very high profile to that relationship and a parallel is important. The existence of the Elysée treaty has obliged the administrations of the two countries to focus at the highest levels on their shared problems of security from time to time. This gives an initiative throughout the administrative machines of both countries for co-operation. The Elysée treaty of course does not restrict itself to security. Indeed, the fact that a large number of ministers covering a wide range of issues meet regularly to discuss their problems together integrates questions of security into the common approach to co-operation. While there are regular meetings between British and French prime ministers, they are not accompanied by the same obligation on the entire Cabinets to co-ordinate their activities. A treaty creates a certain automatic network between two countries which it is not possible to develop without a treaty. Having said this, it was the case that for a number of years the existence of the Elysée treaty was not enough; it took political will in the 1980s to implement the clauses that had lain dormant for a long time. We thus do not see a treaty as adequate in itself, but we do believe that the regular meetings would facilitate the development of a whole system of links between Paris and London at various levels, not merely among officials, but among others working on defence and security questions in institutions, and indeed between political parties.

It is not necessary there should be a complete parallel between the Elysée treaty and a treaty between France and Britain. Some aspects of the existing Elysée treaty were drafted in order to facilitate Franco-German reconciliation. While there is a strong case for promoting the exchange of young people between France and Britain, it is not perhaps the same as that which existed twenty years ago in the context of the Franco-German relationship. What is important however is that the nature of the Elysée treaty has led to the creation of an inter-ministerial structure in France whereby the operations of all ministries involved are co-ordinated at an inter-ministerial level including security and defence questions. In the case of a Franco-British treaty it would appear that pre-eminence should be given to the security relationship, although there are probably certain other problems such as transport and industry which would play an important part.

There are, in one respect, differences between the British and French approaches and motivations in arguing for a strengthening of the relationship. On the one hand, the British hope that France will be brought back to a greater extent into the family of European NATO members, that even if she is not brought back totally into the integrated military command this will be a process that will move in that direction. The French approach, on the other hand, relies rather more on the need for the two European nuclear powers to define together the contribution that they can make to European security without discussing so explicitly the relationship with NATO.

In parallel with this increased co-operation between governments, it is equally necessary to revitalize the other links between the two countries in order that among opinion formers there can be a much better understanding of the security approaches, and indeed the communality of interests in the security area. This would mean the development of patterns of exchange not only among academics, but among others who are involved in the development of ideas in both countries, parallel to those that already exist between France and Germany. For example, following the Elysée treaty, provision was made for there to be a German member of staff at the Institut Français des Relations Internationales (IFRI) and similarly a French member of staff at the Deutsche Gesellschaft für Auswärtige Politik (DGAP) in Bonn. This does not exist between Britain and France, and would be a very desirable precedent.

## Co-operation on strategic doctrine and practice

We need to develop together a common language and a common approach to strategy. Although Britain is part of the integrated military command, and therefore shares in the NATO doctrine of flexible response, she has her own strategic doctrine as far as the use of her own nuclear weapons is concerned. There is therefore a need to get a better understanding of the strategic doctrines of the two countries. These are often misunderstood at the moment because the language used has developed separately in the two countries without sufficient exchange. On some occasions, very similar approaches are described in different formulations in the two countries. While for twenty-five years the British tradition has been to work extremely closely with the United States, and France has followed an independent route, we are now at a point where the development of certain technologies does suggest the case for closer co-operation without Britain giving up her pattern of collaboration with the United States or France her independence. Britain and France both face the need to continue to ensure that their own national deterrent forces maintain military credibility and at the same time to keep a close watch on the defensive capabilities being developed elsewhere in order that they may maintain effective deterrents.

Most attention is inevitably given to the strategic forces — to the submarines with their ballistic missiles. As far as these are concerned, it looks unlikely that there will be any co-operation in procurement for at least another generation, as the Trident is being deployed with the British forces and the M-4 and eventually the M-5 with French forces. On the other hand, both countries have other nuclear forces in the naval field, where Britain has her own nuclear depth charges but up until now no such weapons have been developed in France.

Britain and France have both been alarmed on the one hand by Mr Gorbachev's proposals for the denuclearization of Europe, with its implication for their forces, and on the other hand by Mr Reagan's view that nuclear weapons should be made impotent and obsolete. They both believe that, for the foreseeable future, nuclear weapons have an important contribution to make to the deterrent forces of the west in Europe. They have therefore watched with some care and some concern various arms control proposals that have been put forward. There has been in recent years fairly close co-ordination between London and Paris over the definition of positions taken in debates in the United Nations and elsewhere on the situation in which the nuclear forces of so-called 'third nuclear powers' are involved in arms control. While Mr Gorbachev did not wish to have British and French nuclear weapons involved in the double zero decision on intermediate nuclear forces (INF) and shorter-range nuclear forces, there is no doubt that these will return and be an issue in any subsequent nuclear negotiations. There is therefore a need for close co-ordination between London and Paris on forthcoming nuclear negotiations between the superpowers and indeed on the implications for nuclear forces of any discussion on arms control within Europe.

As far as the technical problems of nuclear weapons are concerned, it is interesting that for the first time in the autumn of 1987 the discussions between the ministries of defence of the two countries were widely reported in the press to have concerned themselves with nuclear as well as with non-nuclear questions. While it is difficult to see that much progress can be made in the near future as far as strategic nuclear systems are concerned, it is obviously important that the ministries of defence should be in continued contact in order that both sides have a better understanding of the positions of the other.

One area in which there is a good deal of potential for co-operation, although it may be difficult to realize this, is that of intelligence and reconnaissance. Both France and Britain have their own systems for obtaining information by a variety of methods. In the case of the United Kingdom this is shared with other countries. None the less, as far as both threat evaluation in Europe and intelligence from the rest of the world are concerned, there are possibilities and opportunites for closer co-operation between the two countries. In the future, with the growing importance of space for intelligence and reconnnaissance, both in an operational sense and in terms of arms control, the two countries, together and within the wider European framework, should be endeavouring to find opportunities for co-operation.

## Co-operation with regard to conventional forces

Co-operation among conventional forces can be divided between land forces and air and naval forces. As far as land forces are concerned, there has in the past been a very limited number of joint exercises. Quite clearly it would be important in the future for the pattern of exercises that has begun between the French and German armies to be repeated in terms of exercises between the French 3rd Corps, the Force d'Action Rapide, and the British Army of the Rhine. It is not altogether clear where these should be conducted, but such exercises would give an opportunity to discuss and practise current French and British strategic and tactical doctrines.

While there is some limited exchange at the moment between Britain and France on training courses, this is relatively limited in comparison with the exchanges between France and Germany. It would therefore be useful to see rather more French students attending the courses of the Royal College of Defence Studies (RCDS) and, in the same way, British staff officers attending courses at the Institut des Hautes Etudes de Défense Nationale (IHEDN). There are other courses that could provide other opportunities for exchanges and we would particularly suggest that young staff officers should have the opportunity to work in the staffs of the other countries. There are some exchanges between the British and French initial training establishments (Sandhurst and St Cyr); perhaps more effort could be put into ensuring these produce positive results on both sides.

Britain has played an important part in developing tactical doctrine as far as the Northern Army Group in Germany is concerned. Very little has been done in terms of discussion between British and French officers on the validity of this doctrine. It would therefore be valuable to try to arrange for systematic discussions of tactical doctrine and the various possibilities for defence in central Europe to be undertaken.

A further area where exchanges could perhaps take place is that of chemical weapons. France continues to possess chemical weapons and it would be important to have discussions with British forces about their use, as well as having discussion between the arms control authorities in both countries.

While there were certain agreements between the United States and France on logistic support following the withdrawal of France from NATO, attention has not been drawn to similar agreements between Britain and France. Quite clearly, given the location of the French ports and their relationship to the United Kingdom, it makes a great deal of sense for this subject to be debated and potential arrangements exercised. Such logistic agreements will obviously take on a new dimension with the building of the Channel Tunnel, which will transform the logistic links between Britain and the Continent.

As far as air and naval forces are concerned there is a strong case for increasing the joint exercises that occur at the present. In doing so, particular attention could be given to flight refuelling, where the capacity to refuel the aircraft of the other country would be of great interest and importance. Britain and France have the largest capacities in Europe for in-flight refuelling, but very little, if anything, has been done about co-operation between these services. It would be a useful force multiplier for the west if patterns of co-operation between these two important services could be undertaken.

As we have stated earlier, Britain and France are two of the European countries with the greater capacity for deployment outside Europe. It is therefore of particular importance that, in both the air and naval areas, greater co-operation should exist over deployment and over force projection at a substantial distance from Europe. This involves not merely joint exercises but also agreements for the use of bases in other parts of the world. The use of French and British bases in the Indian, Pacific, and Atlantic oceans would give Europe a substantive capability, which would be considerably increased if they were operated on a common basis.

In looking at exercises in the rest of the world, a good deal of pooling of staff resources could usefully take place. Although in fact the deployment might be by one nation rather than by the other, there would be advantages in having done the staff work together. This would obviously facilitate co-ordination in those circumstances in which both countries deploy forces into the same area. There have been too many examples in the past when local commands have been unable to co-operate effectively. These should be avoided in the future.

As we have seen in the earlier chapters, because Britain and France have the most developed defence industrial bases in Europe, they are competitors as much as they are co-operators. It is none the less essential, in a period of constraints on defence resources and increasing technological co-operation, that as far as possible these defence industries should work in co-operation. We are therefore particularly pleased that new signs of close co-operation have appeared in 1987. The Lancaster House conference in September of 1987 is an example of positive action to create a common industrial area dealing with defence procurement between Britain and France. This will often be at the component level rather than at the total project level, but greater acquaintance and greater cross-co-operation between their defence industries can only benefit effective and economic defence.

Britain and France have shared, often in conflict but more recently in alliance, 1,000 years of European history. Both countries are now convinced that their future security lies in closer co-operation as a basis for European co-operation. They also realize that politeness is not enough; they can no longer afford the luxury of noticing each other's existence and of being polite to each other. They must realize the potential that exists for effective co-operation. They must get down to brass tacks rather than talking about generalities. They have the potential, not only to increase the security of their two countries by co-operating together, but also, through such bilateral co-operation, to provide an effective contribution to the future of European security as a whole.

# Index

NOTE: *Some of the longer entries contain two levels of subordinate entry; where this occurs, the sub-subentry is enclosed by parenthesis.*


ABM (Anti-Ballistic Missile) Treaty 36, 37–8, 41, 42
Acheson, Dean 9
Aerospatiale 138
Ailleret-Lemnitzer arrangement 58, 59, 60, 62, 150
AIM-9L air-to-air missile 134
Algerian War 108, 121
Alliance Nuclear Force (ANF) 13
Alpha Jet 135
Amery, Julian 10, 19
Andropov, Yuri 39
Angola 86
Antarctica 47
ANZUS military alliance 77
arms control negotiations 23, 39-42, 59, 163-4, 185; Geneva talks 38, 161; and SDI 37; *see also* Reykjavik summit
arms procurement collaboration: Franco-British 32, 128-46, 157, 160, 165-6, 178, 187-8; multilateral 129-30, 150, 166, 175, 179-80; (Germany's role 54, 131, 132, 142, 165)
arms sales overseas: British 142; French 55, 98, 102, 141-2; Franco-British rivalry 71, 74, 81, 82, 84, 86-7
Aron, Raymond 4
Ascension Island 47, 69, 75, 90
ASW (anti-submarine warfare) 36, 37, 176, 180
ATBM (anti-tactical ballistic missile) systems 163
Atlas missile 9
Atomic Energy Commissions, British and French 18
Attlee, Clement 6; government 4-6, 19
Augusta 138
AV-8B advanced Harrier jump-jet 134
AWACS airborne early warning aircraft 118

B-29 strategic bomber 19-20
Beirut *see* Lebanon
Belgium: and Britain 176, 178; collaborative arms development 132; defence budgets 52; multilateral co-operation 176, 177
Belize 47, 70,76, 86
Bermuda agreement of 1957 20
Bevin, Ernest 6, 19
Blackhawk helicopter 138
Blue Streak missile 8, 9
Bow Group (Britain) 22
Bramall, Field Marshall Sir Edwin 52-3
Brandt, Chancellor Willy 159
Breguet 143
Bremen class frigates 132
Brezhnev, Leonid 39
Britain: nuclear policies 3-15, 34-5; (and arms control 39-42, 59; and domestic political change 3-4, 35-6; and SDI 15, 23-4, 25); overseas possessions 47, 69, 85,

86; relationship with Germany 152, 171, 175-6, 178; relationship with United States 4-14 *passim*, 19-21, 70; (European role 18, 26, 82, 151-2, 156, 162)
British Aerospace 119, 135, 136, 143
British Shipbuilders 119
Brunei, Sultanate of 47, 70, 76
Brussels, pact of 1948 156
Brzezinski, Zbigniew 78
Buchan, Alastair 19

Callaghan, James 3; government 14
Canada 47
Central African Republic 47
Chad 47, 88
Chalupa, General Leopold 49
Channel Tunnel 187
chemical weapons 186-7
Chevaline nuclear system 14, 21, 38, 40, 42, 117, 118
Chiefs of Staff (Britain) 5, 6-7, 8, 20
Chinook medium support helicopter 139
Chirac, Jacques 23, 95
Churchill, Winston S. 5, 6, 7, 19, 20, 64, 156
CNAD (Conference of National Armaments Directors) 145, 171
Concorde supersonic aircraft 129
conscription: Britain 7, 8, 12, 13, 119; France 96-7, 112, 113
conventional forces 47-66; Britain 4, 7, 8, 12, 20, 26; France 26, 53-5, 58, 60-2; (*see also* FAR); Franco-British co-operation 26, 48, 54-5, 57, 65-6, 167, 186-8; multilateral co-operation 172-4; *see also* 'out-of-area' deployment
Council of Europe 156
cruise missiles 3, 20, 39, 150
Cuba 76
Cyprus 47, 74, 86, 87,90
Czechoslovakia 49

Dassault 143
Decimomannu air range (Sardinia) 173
defence budgets *see* military expenditure
de Gaulle, General Charles: breaks with NATO 151, 153; defence policies 23, 59, 60, 151, 153; relations with Britain 19, 78, 156-7, 158
Denmark 52
d'Estaing, Giscard 22, 159
Deutsche Gesellschaft für Auswärtige Politik (West Germany) 184
DGA (Délégation Générale pour l'Armement (France) 98-9, 102, 142
Diego Garcia 69, 75, 88, 99
Direction des Affaires Internationales (France) 99
Direction des Armements Terrestres (France) 99
Djibouti 47, 74, 90, 91, 92
Douglas-Home, Sir Alec 3
Downey Report of 1966 (Britain) 118

Eden, Anthony 7
EEC (European Economic Community; Common Market): Britain's entry 155, 158; (French opposition 19, 156-7, 158); Britain's financial contribution 160, 162
Egypt 47; *see also* Suez crisis
Eisenhower, Dwight D. 7, 9, 20
Elysée treaty between France and West Germany 182, 183, 184
Espiritu Santo 85
Esprit programme 146
Eureka programme 146
Eurogroup 171, 172, 177, 180
European Defence Community 156
European defence co-operation 171-80, 181-4 *passim*; in arms procurement 129-30, 150, 166
European Defence Improvement Programme 172

European fighter aircraft 81, 129, 136-7, 138
Exocet missiles 162

F-4 Phantom aircraft 136
F-111 bombers, 20
Falkland Islands: British presence 47, 69, 75, 86; (cost 52, 121); 1982 conflict 68, 71-3 *passim*, 78, 88, 91, 134, 174
FAR (Force d'Action Rapide) (France) 54-5, 61-2, 72, 150, 153; European deployment 26, 151, 167, 173, 186; 'out-of-area' deployment 74, 86
'first use' of nuclear weapons 50-1
flexible response strategy of NATO 9, 12, 14, 15; French opposition 50, 59-60, 153, 166
Follow-on Force Attack 57
Force d-Intervention *see* FAR
Fourquet, General 14
France: attitudes to Europe 152-3; global ambitions 70, 86; and NATO 12, 13, 26, 48, 58, 157, 171; nuclear policies 12, 17-18, 35, 58-60; (arms control 39-42; domestic consensus 3, 35, 154; and SDI 23, 24); overseas possessions 47, 69, 85-6; relations with Germany 160, 164, 169, 172, 178, 179, 182-4 *passim*
Franco-British Council 161, 169
Franco-British summit meetings 160-1
Franco-British treaty, case for 181-4
Franco-German Treaty of 1963 151

Gabon 47
Gallois, General P.M. 8-9, 157-8
Galosh defence system 37
Gazelle helicopter 129, 134, 135, 143-4, 157
General Staffs (France) 95, 96, 99, 101, 109
Geneva arms control negotiations 38, 42, 161; *see also* arms control negotiations
German Democratic Republic 49
Germany, Federal Republic of 13, 26, 51, 161, 164, 177; arms co-operation 54, 131, 132, 142, 165; European co-operation 172, 175-9 *passim*, 182, 183, 184; (British-German relations 152, 171; Franco-German relations 160, 164, 169); French security 150-3 *passim*; increasing power 158-9
Gibraltar 47, 69, 74, 86
Giraud, André 97
Giscard d'Estaing, Valéry 22, 159
*Global Strategy Paper* (British Chiefs of Staff) 6-7, 8, 20
Gorbachev, Mikhail 42, 185; *see also* Reykjavik summit
Gordon Walker, Patrick 13
Gowing, Margaret 4, 5, 6
GR-5(AV-8B) V/STOL aircraft 138
Greenham Common (Britain) 20
Greenwood, D. 125
Grenada, 75, 88, 162
Guadeloupe 76
Guyana, French 47, 69, 76

Hades tactical weapons system 26, 62, 113
Harpoon missile 134
Harrier jump-jet 134, 138
Healey, Denis 3, 13, 125, 172
Heath, Edward 26, 31; and Pompidou 155, 158, 159, 164; and SDI 25
Henderson, Sir Nicholas 17
Hernu, Charles 23
Heseltine, Michael 93, 143; *see also* Westland affair
Hibbert, Sir Reginald 22
Home, Sir Alec Douglas- 3
Honest John missile system 62-3
Hong Kong 47, 69, 72, 76, 86
Hot missile 135
HOTOL spacecraft 165
Howe, Sir Geoffrey 15, 24, 41, 183

IEPG (Independent European Programme Group) 144-5,

146, 150, 171, 180
IFRI (Institut Français des Relations Internationales) (France) 184
IHEDN (Institut des Hautes Etudes de Défense Nationale) (France) 169, 186
IISS (International Institute for Strategic Studies) 105, 121
India 74
Indo-Chinese War 76, 121
INF (Intermediate Nuclear Forces) 15, 25, 40, 41, 153; withdrawal 163, 185; *see also* arms control negotiations
intelligence and reconnaissance co-operation 185-6
International Monetary Fund 105, 106
Italy 131, 177
Ivory Coast 47

Jaguar fighter-bomber 50, 129, 134, 135, 143, 157, 165; replacement for 136, 137
Joliot-Curie, Frédéric 18

Kennedy, John F. 3, 9, 10, 11, 157, 158; *see also* Nassau conference
Kissinger, Henry 10, 59
Korean War 120
Kortenaer class frigates 132
Kourou space centre 69,76
Krasnayorsk radar station 37

Labour Party (Britain) 3-4, 9, 10, 25, 40, 152
Lacaze, General 22
Lakenheath (Britain) 20
Lancaster House conference of 1987 188
Lebanon peace-keeping force 47,74, 87, 90
Leenhardt, Admiral Yves 86, 93
Leopard II tank 131
Lightning aircraft 136
Loi de Programmation Militaire *see* Programmation Militaire
Luxembourg 52
Lynx helicopter 129, 134, 135, 143-4, 157, 165

M-1 Abrams tank 131
M-4 and M-5 missiles 21, 38, 40, 112, 113, 167, 185
MBT-70 tank 131, 132
McDonald, Admiral Wesley L. 49
MacMahon law 19, 20
Macmillan, Harold 3, 8, 9, 10, 158; government 11, 12; *see also* Nassau conference
McNamara, Robert 10, 13, 34-5, 59, 60
Manhattan programme 157
Mansfield Amendment 172
Martel air-to-surface missile 129, 144, 157
Martinique 76
Mayotte 75, 92
MBFR (Mutual and Balanced Force Reduction) negotiations 172, 175
Messmer, Pierre 60
Milan Anti-Tank Guided Missile (ATGM) 65, 129, 135, 144
military expenditure: Britain 52-3, 116-26; (arms 117-19; budgets 120-4, 141; nuclear weapons 117-18, 122, 124, 141; personnel 119; reappraisals 111, 124-6); France 52, 53, 95-113; (arms 98-103, 112; budgets 104-11, 141; nuclear weapons 108, 109, 110, 112, 141; personnel 96-8, 111); comparison between 106, 111, 112, 117, 120-1, 124, 141
Mirage 111E aircraft 50
Mirage 2000 aircraft 137
Mitterand, François 23, 95, 150-1, 160, 162
MLF (multilateral force) 10, 12, 13, 157, 158
MLRS (multiple launch rocket system) 129, 160
Mururoa atoll 69, 76-7, 86

Namibia 75, 88
Nassau conference 10, 12, 19, 20-1,

59, 156, 158
National Service *see* conscription
Netherlands: and Britain 152, 174, 176, 178; collaborative arms development 132; multi-lateral co-operation 176, 177
New Caldedonia 47, 76, 86
New Hebrides 85
NFR-90 frigate 129, 132-3
NH-90 helicopter 129
Nimrod AEW (Airborne Early Warning) system 118, 138
Nott, John 21, 125
Noumea 77
NPG (Nuclear Planning Group) 13
nuclear co-operation: Franco-British 18-23, 47, 157-61 *passim*, 166-7, 184-6; multilateral 171-80, 181, 182
nuclear disarmament *see* arms control negotiations
Nunn, Senator Sam 173

Oman 92
Ottawa Declaration of 1974 158
'out-of-area' deployment 67-94; Franco-British 26, 73-83, 84-94 *passim*, 168, 180, 187; (institutional solutions 77-80, and a united Europe, 81-2)
Owen, Dr David 150, 161

Pakistan 74
Pershing II missiles 3, 39, 150
Phantom F-4 aircraft 136
Pierre, Andrew 5
Pitcairn Island 77
Pluton missiles 50, 60, 62
Poirier, General Lucien 24
Poland 49
Polaris missiles 14, 40, 41, 43, 178; acquisition 10, 11, 12, 78, 158; Labour Party policy 3, 13, 40; replacement 35-6; *see also* Chevaline system
Polynesia, French 47, 69, 76-7, 86
Pompidou, Georges 31, 158-9; and Heath 155, 158, 159, 164
Poniatowski, Michel 22
Programmation Militaire 1987-91 (France) 17, 107, 110, 112, 182-3
Ptarmigan military communications system 133, 137
Public Expenditure Survey Committee (Britain) 124
Public Sector Borrowing Requirement (Britain) 121
Puma helicopter 129, 134, 135, 143-4, 157
Pym, Francis 22-3, 160

Quebec agreement of 1943 19

RAF (Royal Air Force) (Britain) 8, 22, 175
RDJTF (Rapid Deployment Joint Task Force) 93
Reagan, Ronald 15, 23, 78, 185; and Thatcher 24, 25, 162; *see also* Reykjavik summit; SDI
Red Sea 87, 92; mine-clearing operation 47, 74, 91, 168
Réunion, La 47, 75, 92
Reykjavik summit 23, 154, 162, 164, 169-70
Rheinmetall 120mm gun 131
RITA military communications system 133, 137, 166
Rogers, General W. 52, 63
Roland missile 135
Rolls-Royce 135-6, 143
Roosevelt, Franklin D. 5
Royal College of Defence Studies (Britain) 169, 186
Royal Netherlands Air Force 175
Royal Ordnance Factories (Britain) 131

SA-10 missile 37
SALT I (Strategic Arms Limitation Treaty) 39
Sandys, Duncan, 1957 defence review 7, 8, 20, 120, 125
Saudi Arabia 74
Schmidt, Helmut 13, 172
SDI (Strategic Defense Initiative) 15, 23-5, 31, 38-9, 113, 162,

163; projects emerging from 65; Soviet attempts to match 37
Secrétariat Général de la Défense Nationale (France) 104
Senegal 47
Senegambia 92
Sikorsky helicopter company 138, 139
SIPRI (Stockholm International Peace Research Institute) 105
Skybolt stand-off weapons 8, 9; cancellation 10, 34, 158; Labour opposition 3
SLBMs (submarine-launched ballistic missiles) *see* SSBN forces
Slessor, Sir John 8
South Africa 75
South Yemen 168
Soviet Union: conventional superiority 49-50; defensive capabilities 38, 41, 166-7; military expenditure 105; overseas interests 74, 75, 77; and SDI 37
SP-70 self-propelled howitzer 131, 132
SS-4 missiles 39-40
SS-5 missiles 39-40
SS-20 missiles 39, 41
SSBN (submarine missile) forces 35, 36, 38, 39, 41, 42, 112; *see also* M4 and M5; Polaris; Trident
Standing Conservative Commission 38
START (Strategic Arms Reduction Talks) 41
Steel, David 150, 161
Straits of Hormuz 87, 91, 92
Strategic Studies Group (Franco-British) 160, 161
Suez crisis 47, 85
Super-Etendard 11F aircraft 50

tactical nuclear weapons 50-1, 62-4, 112, 153, 166
terrorism 69, 81
Thatcher, Margaret 22, 160, 162, 165; and Reagan 24, 25, 162; and Westland affair 130, 134
Third World 68; *see also* arms sales abroad; 'out-of-area' deployment
Thor rockets 20
Thorneycroft, Peter 10, 19
Tornado multi-role combat aircraft 22, 124, 129, 135, 136, 138, 175; export of 166
Torpedo programme 118
Trident missiles 15, 38, 40, 41, 43, 167, 185; cost 21, 36, 53, 117-18; Labour Party policy 3; Soviet Union's attitude 42
TRIGAT anti-tank weapons system 129, 144
Turbomeca 143

UK-Netherlands Amphibious Force 53, 173, 174
Ulster (United Kingdom) 123-4
United Nations 182, 185; and military expenditure 97, 98, 103, 106; peace-keeping forces 47, 74, 87
Upper Heyford (Britain) 20
USACDA (US Arms Control and Disarmament Agency) 101, 105

V-bombers 9, 11
Vanuatu 85

Watkinson, Harold 10
Westland helicopters affair 130, 134, 137-9
WEU (Western European Union) 6, 48, 156, 168-9, 170, 171, 172; revitalization of 55, 79; and United States 154
Williamsburg economic summit of 1983 79
Wilson, Harold 13, 159; government 12-14, 158
World Bank 105
world economic summits 78-9

Zaire 86, 88